Personalized Prayers and Confessions to Establish Your Heart and Mind in the Purposes of God

365 DAYS *of* INCREASE

RICK RENNER

ISBN: 978-0-9903247-4-4

Published by Harrison House Publishers
Shippensburg, PA 17257

Cover design by Eileen Rockwell

ISBN 13 TP: 978-1-6803-1725-1

ISBN 13 eBook: 978-1-6803-1726-8

ISBN 13 HC: 978-1-6803-1728-2

ISBN 13 LP: 978-1-6803-1727-5

For Worldwide Distribution, Printed in the U.S.A.

1 2 3 4 5 6 7 8 / 25 24 23 22 21

365
DAYS *of* INCREASE

Introduction

365 Days of Increase is a collection of powerful prayers and confessions designed to help you mature in your walk with God. Each devotional prayer and complementing confession is based on an empowering Scripture and an in-depth Greek word study taken from Rick Renner's 1,280-page devotional, *Sparkling Gems From the Greek, Volume 2.* This briefer version, containing all the original prayers and confessions, makes it easy for you to read and apply these godly gems of truth on a daily basis.

When you pray and confess the Word over your life every day, you will strengthen your spirit and grow in faith and confidence. Never underestimate the power of God's Word, the Bible—it is full of life and healing and strength for every area of your life!

Say Hello To the Future!

My Prayer for Today

Father, I repent for not doing what I should have done last year, and I receive Your forgiveness. I thank You for this new year and for the new opportunity it presents for me to make serious changes in my life. You are the God who makes all things new. I yield to Your power at work in me as I deliberately choose to do Your will and to walk in Your ways with diligent obedience. Holy Spirit, I ask for and receive Your help to fulfill the will of God for my life. My past is not a prophecy of my future! Today I make the decision to put aside memories of past failures, and by faith I reach out to the future You have planned for me. I pray this in Jesus' name!

Brethren, I count not myself to have apprehended: but this one thing I do, forgetting those things which are behind, and reaching forth unto those things which are before.

Philippians 3:13

My Confession for Today

I confess that I am not a failure and that my past is not a prophecy of my future! Even though I have not done as well as I should have in the past, God's Spirit in me will enable me to do better from this point forward. I am willing to make whatever changes I must make. I will alter my lifestyle. I will fix things in my life that are messed up. I will do whatever is required to move forward into the fabulous future God has waiting for me! From this moment on, I will run this race with my eyes fixed on the goal before me. I am committed, determined, and willing to pay any price to obtain full and complete victory in my life! I declare this by faith in Jesus' name!

JANUARY 2

Resolutions Take Determination!

Brethren, I count not myself to have apprehended: but this one thing I do, forgetting those things which are behind, and reaching forth unto those things which are before.

Philippians 3:13

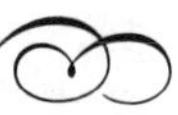

My Prayer for Today

Father, I am so grateful that You have gifted me with this new year and this new opportunity. I thank You for a fresh start to be more fruitful and to accomplish more for Your glory this year than I did last year. Help me set goals that are realistic and attainable so I can reach them by the power of the Holy Spirit assisting me. I ask You to strengthen me with might in my inner self to apply the determination and commitment to reach these goals. I praise You for the supernatural ability at my disposal according to the power that is already at work in me through Christ. I look to You to empower me as I press forward toward the finish line before me. I pray this in Jesus' name!

My Confession for Today

I confess that I can do all things through Christ who empowers me! I finish what I start, and I accomplish whatever I set my heart to do. I do not set goals based merely on my desire, but I listen to the direction of the Holy Spirit as He guides me in setting goals for this year. He knows me better than I know myself, and He knows what I should achieve this year and where I should apply my efforts. I run my race this year with commitment, determination, and diligence. At the end of this year, I will say with a satisfied heart: "With God's help, I have achieved each goal I set out to accomplish!" I declare this by faith in Jesus' name!

Time To Shed a Few Pounds?

My Prayer for Today

Father, today I repent for allowing food to control so much of my life. It really has affected me in so many ways—in my thinking, my self-image, my appearance, and even my self-respect. I have lived in condemnation for too long, and I'm ready for a real change in my life. Forgive me for tolerating gluttony and calling it everything else except sin. Today I confess that I have permitted sin to rule in my mortal flesh, and I ask You to forgive me and cleanse me from this unrighteousness. Holy Spirit, I am depending on You to help me walk free of this wrong habit and make Jesus the Lord of my appetite. I pray this in Jesus' name!

Let not sin therefore reign in your mortal body, that ye should obey it in the lusts thereof.

Romans 6:12

My Confession for Today

I boldly declare that Jesus is the Lord of my life and that nothing else may rule over me! My appetite for food does not lord itself over me any longer. Overeating is sin and a tool that Satan wants to use to hurt my health, my self-image, and my self-respect. I have lived in this mental prison long enough, and I refuse to live there any longer. From this day forward, I am giving Jesus the throne in every part of my life—and that includes my physical appetite and my eating habits! I declare this by faith in Jesus' name!

Time To Start Exercising?

Now no chastening for the present seemeth to be joyous, but grievous: nevertheless afterward it yieldeth the peaceable fruit of righteousness unto them which are exercised thereby.

Hebrews 12:11

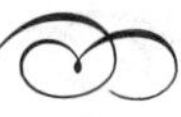

My Prayer for Today

Father, I made a commitment to begin an exercise program. It is my will to keep this promise that I made both to myself and to You. I have been convicted for a long time that I need to take better care of myself, to get into good physical shape, and to honor this body that is the temple of the Holy Spirit. I thank You for the indwelling power of the Holy Spirit who will help me take charge of my flesh in order to carry out this commitment. I receive Your grace and mercies that are new every morning to help me to exercise control over my flesh. I yield to Your quickening power that will help me maintain this position of victory. Thank You for strengthening me to remain steadfast in this area of my life, each day from this day forward. I pray this in Jesus' name!

My Confession for Today

I confess that I am in charge of my flesh and my flesh is not in charge of me. It has ruled and dominated me long enough! So starting today, with God's help, I am taking charge and submitting my fleshly desires to the sanctifying power of the Spirit of God. My body is His temple, and I will treat it with respect. I will care for it; I will discipline and exercise it. I will do everything I can to make sure it looks good, feels strong, and is equipped to live a long and healthy life. God has a lot for me to do in this world! Therefore, I will get my body in shape so I can run this race and have a long and blessed life with a physical body that is free from the adverse effects of physical inactivity and lack of discipline. I declare this by faith in Jesus' name!

Time To Shape Up Your Finances?

My Prayer for Today

Lord, I am so thankful that You have spoken to my heart today about my finances. The Holy Spirit has been speaking to my heart about getting my finances into better shape, and I now see how crucial it is that I pass this very important test. I want You to trust me with promotion to higher levels of responsibility, authority, and spiritual power. Therefore, I ask You to help me prove myself trustworthy by demonstrating my readiness for promotion by the way I handle my finances. Thank You for granting me divine wisdom, strategies, and strength to help me stay the course until I am finally debt free! I pray this in Jesus' name!

If therefore ye have not been faithful in the unrighteous mammon, who will commit to your trust the true riches?

Luke 16:11

My Confession for Today

I confess that I listen to the Spirit of God. I have the mind of Christ, and I walk in divine wisdom concerning finances in my life. I will exercise self-control, and I am disciplined in all things. I plan my purchases in advance and practice restraint so I can live a debt-free life. I am determined to remain free with the Holy Spirit's help. I make the decision to get my finances in order. Therefore, I diligently manage my money, and I spend it with prudence. As a result, I pass this test that is so important in the eyes of God. I declare this by faith in Jesus' name!

Time To Improve Your Relationships?

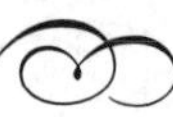

And the things that thou hast heard of me among many witnesses, the same commit thou to faithful men, who shall be able to teach others also.

2 Timothy 2:2

My Prayer for Today

Lord, I realize that I've made some mistakes in my relationships in the past. I know I was too busy at times and quit making deposits into the people I loved and needed. I expected them to perform for me, but I didn't put enough good back into them, and now I'm experiencing the consequences both of my actions and my inaction. Please forgive me for not showing appreciation to the people who are so precious to me. I repent for misplacing my priorities. I ask You to please help me restore the relationships that are restorable and to strengthen the relationships that remain in my life right now. Help me make solid investments into the people who are close to me so I can be a real blessing to them and so these relationships will stay strong and close till the very end of my life. I pray this in Jesus' name!

My Confession for Today

Today I shake off the spirit of despair that has tried to attach itself to me. I refuse to wallow in discouragement about things that are over and unfixable. I have repented and received forgiveness for my mistakes, so I will learn from them and let the Holy Spirit lead me into the wonderful future that lies directly ahead of me. Feelings of loneliness and isolation are lying emotions that must go in Jesus' name! The Lord surrounds me with people who stick with me through times of difficulty. These faithful people are worthy of my time, attention, and personal investments. Therefore, I forget the past and its pain, and by faith in God I allow myself to build new relationships and to trust again. I declare this by faith in Jesus' name!

The Power of Reading Your Bible Daily

My Prayer for Today

Lord, I am amazed at the power of Your Word and what it can do in the life of anyone who will read it, believe it, and apply it to his or her life. Every answer I need for life is in the Bible, whether it be for healing, deliverance, marriage, children, health, business, or success. Heavenly Father, thank You for giving us the Word of God. Please forgive me for the times I've let it sit on my shelf instead of reading it, meditating on it, and incorporating it into my life. This year I ask You to help me break the pattern of being on again, off again in reading my Bible. I thank You that by Your grace, I will become a consistent reader and applier of God's Word to every part of my life! I pray this in Jesus' name!

All scripture is given by inspiration of God, and is profitable for doctrine, for reproof, for correction, for instruction in righteousness.

2 Timothy 3:16

My Confession for Today

I confess that I read my Bible every day. I do not skip days, forgetting to read it. God's words are the very center of my existence, and I draw my strength from what I read in my Bible every day. It shines its glorious light into every dark part of my soul and renews my thinking to what God thinks. I receive the conviction God's Word brings to areas of my life that are wrong. It picks me up, sets me back up on my feet, and keeps me on level ground. The Word of God prepares and equips me with everything I need to live a successful and godly life in this world. I declare this by faith in Jesus' name!

JANUARY 8

Kick Back and Breathe Once in a While

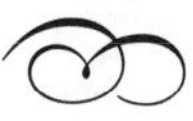

And to you who are troubled rest with us, when the Lord Jesus shall be revealed from heaven with his mighty angels.

2 Thessalonians 1:7

My Prayer for Today

Lord, I ask for wisdom to know how to balance my life and work with times of relaxation and recreation. I am tempted to work nonstop and never take a break, and as a result, I get tired and worn out. Forgive me for not taking better care of myself. I yield to Your peace, and I resist the feelings of guilt that try to overwhelm me when I am away from my work and responsibilities. I now know that You want me to take a break from this constant pace and learn to relax a little. Holy Spirit, I thank You for helping me make this change in my life. I pray this in Jesus' name!

My Confession for Today

I confess that I live my life in balance! I work hard, but I also set aside time for my mind and my body to be refreshed. God's Word declares that I need to take a breather from time to time, so I do it obediently and joyfully with no feelings of guilt or condemnation. God expects me to work hard, but He also expects me to be recharged and refilled! I am making a change in my life so I can include time to be revitalized and refreshed! I declare this by faith in Jesus' name!

The Life-Changing Impact of God's Power!

My Prayer for Today

Lord, I ask You to teach me when to step aside so that You can step in to do what I cannot do. Help me to speak the right words, to say those words with the right attitude, and to speak them under the anointing of the Holy Spirit. But also help me to know when words are not enough. Help me stay sensitive to You and to be bold to allow You to move through me in supernatural ways to confirm that the message is accurate and true. I pray this in Jesus' name!

That your faith should not stand in the wisdom of men, but in the power of God.

1 Corinthians 2:5

My Confession for Today

I confess that God is my Partner! It is His work to step in and do what I cannot do when I am presenting truth to people who are in darkness. The Holy Spirit's power is always available to confirm His truth, and it is the Father's desire to demonstrate His supernatural ability to people in order to bring them out of the darkness and into the light. So starting today, I will always ask the Holy Spirit to demonstrate His power as He desires through me. From this moment onward, I will look to Him as my Partner to flow through me with His power to fulfill His purpose in every situation and to meet the need of the moment in convincing unbelievers and doubters about the truth of God's Word. I declare this by faith in Jesus' name!

JANUARY 10

Do Your Best To Keep the Peace

If it be possible, as much as lieth in you, live peaceably with all men.

Romans 12:18

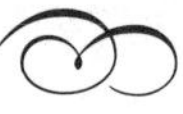

My Prayer for Today

Lord, I thank You for speaking to my heart today. I repent for my carnal response toward certain people in my life. I confess that I have allowed myself to become irritated with them, and at times I have even been judgmental of them. Today I release forgiveness toward them, and I choose from this point onward to see myself as a force for peace. I purpose in my heart to exercise the patience that is a quality of Your love within me. I ask You for wisdom to know what to say and do and what not to say and do when I am in the presence of these individuals. Thank You for leading and guiding me in each contact I make with them. I pray this in Jesus' name!

My Confession for Today

I let the peace of God act as umpire continually in my heart, deciding and settling with finality all questions or concerns that arise in my mind. I refuse to be ruled by my emotions, and I am not moved by what I see, feel, or hear. I have the mind of Christ, and I hold the thoughts, feelings, and purposes of His heart. The wisdom of God determines my responses and reactions to those I consider ill-mannered or badly behaved who are not within my realm of authority to correct. I boldly declare that I will not live my life upset or bothered by something I cannot fix. Whatever is necessary to be at peace and to remain at peace is what I will do, as I have been commanded in Romans 12:18. I declare this by faith in Jesus' name!

The Holy Spirit—The Great Revealer!

My Prayer for Today

Lord, I thank You for the presence and the ministry of the Holy Spirit in my life. Forgive me for the times I've ignored this precious Partner whom You have sent to instruct and lead me in all the affairs of life. I repent for trying to find my way in life without His counsel and assistance. I confess that I've often sought the advice of family, friends, counselors, pastors, books, and other sources more than I've sought the counsel of the Holy Spirit—yet He is the One who knows the end from the beginning. Father, I thank You for providing the greatest source of revelation inside my own heart through His presence within me. Starting today, I seek the guidance of the Holy Spirit for each and every decision I make in life. Father, since You have meticulously planned my life and have sent the Holy Spirit to reveal that plan to me, from this day onward I want to let the Holy Spirit provide the revelation I need to fulfill that plan! I pray this in Jesus' name!

But as it is written, Eye hath not seen, nor ear heard, neither have entered into the heart of man, the things which God hath prepared for them that love him. But God hath revealed them unto us by his Spirit: for the Spirit searcheth all things, yea, the deep things of God.

1 Corinthians 2:9-10

My Confession for Today

I declare that I am led by the Holy Spirit and that He reveals to me the will of God for my life. I am not ignorant, and I am not left to find my way on my own. God loves me so much that He sent the Holy Spirit to dwell within me and to provide me with all the details of God's awesome plan for my life. As I develop my spiritual sensitivity and listen to the Holy Spirit's voice, I am enlightened step by step to what He wants me to do with every part of my life. Because the Holy Spirit dwells in me, my eyes see, my ears hear, and my heart is able to comprehend the things God has planned for me! I declare this by faith in Jesus' name!

JANUARY 12

Abstain From All Appearance of Evil

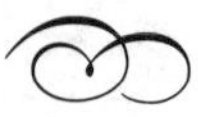

Abstain from all appearance of evil.

1 Thessalonians 5:22

My Prayer for Today

Lord, I understand that Your Word commands me to break off and desist from doing anything that would give the impression of evil to people who are looking at my life from the outside. Today I have a new and a fuller realization of the great impact my actions can have on my reputation and on other people. Please forgive me for doing things that could be misconstrued, misunderstood, or misinterpreted. I am truly sorry. Help me today to put safeguards in my life that will help me to abstain from all appearances of evil from this point forward. I pray this in Jesus' name!

My Confession for Today

I confess that I use common sense in the way that I conduct my life. I am thoughtful about my actions; I am careful to remember that people are watching me; and I am led by the Holy Spirit in how I conduct my life. Because I want to maintain a godly reputation, I care about what people think of me. I will not do anything that would cast a shadow on Jesus' name, my name, or my testimony as a child of God. With God's help, I will live a life that is free of accusation! I declare this by faith in Jesus' name!

Don't Give Up Your Seed

My Prayer for Today

Lord, I ask You to help me be patient as I wait for the seeds I've sown to grow and be multiplied back into my life. It seems like it has taken a long time, but I will not loosen my grip on the fixed, future harvest You have planned for me. You are the Lord of the harvest, so I fix my eyes on You and trust that You have set a season for my seeds and deeds to reach their full growth so I can enjoy the harvest of my endeavors. You are faithful; Your Word is true; and today I rest in those truths! I pray this in Jesus' name!

And let us not be weary in well doing: for in due season we shall reap, if we faint not.

Galatians 6:9

My Confession for Today

I boldly declare that I will continue to release my faith and believe for God to multiply the seeds and deeds I have sown in the past. At times, weariness has tried to attack me, injustice has been done to me, and other outside pressures have made me feel tempted to throw in the towel. But I will not surrender to any pressure to bend, break, or give up on God's promise that I will enter a season of reaping a harvest from the good seed I have sown. The Holy Spirit will empower me to hold tight, hang on, and remain steady and steadfast until I reap my harvest and enjoy the fruit of my faith and labor! I declare this by faith in Jesus' name!

God Hooked My Heart

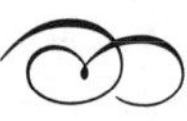

But when it pleased God, who separated me from my mother's womb, and called me by his grace, to reveal his Son in me, that I might preach him among the heathen; immediately I conferred not with flesh and blood.

Galatians 1:15-16

My Prayer for Today

Father, I thank You for the plan for my life that is already written by Your hand deep within me. Father, I realize that Your plan may be different from what I've previously assumed. So I choose now, as an act of my will, to lay aside my own preferences. I make a conscious decision right now that my will is to do Your will. Set my feet upon the path of Your perfect plan for me. Holy Spirit, help me not to frustrate the grace of God, but to be open-minded so I can hear You speak to me. And give me the courage to obey what I hear. I know that You have marked off my life and set boundaries around me, preparing me for a special purpose. Help me have open ears and an open heart so I can hear and understand and follow exactly what Your plan is for me. I pray this in Jesus' name!

My Confession for Today

I confess that according to Ephesians 2:10, Jesus Christ has a predetermined purpose for my life, and His grace is carrying me toward that divine destination. I will not follow the voice of a stranger, but I will follow the voice of my Shepherd as He leads and guides me on the path to the center of His will for my life. I am so thankful that God's grace is at work in me. I fully trust in this work of grace, and I declare that because of it, I will always be right on time and right where God wants me to be—doing precisely what He has asked me to do and thus fulfilling His will for my life. I declare this by faith in Jesus' name!

Don't Render Evil for Evil

My Prayer for Today

Father, I ask You to help me have a right attitude and heart toward people, including those who have hurt me and let me down. You know how deeply disappointed I have been in people that I expected to behave on a much higher level. Help me recall the many times I've let You down, yet You have never forsaken me, rejected me, or cast me aside. In spite of my personal failings, You continue to show Your love, mercy, and forgiveness to me—and Your blessings continue to abound in my life. Just as You have been steadfast in Your love for me, I ask You to help me have a steadfast heart filled with love, mercy, and goodwill for others. I pray this in Jesus' name!

See that none render evil for evil unto any man; but ever follow that which is good, both among yourselves, and to all men.

1 Thessalonians 5:15

My Confession for Today

I declare that I am filled with the love of God and never want to do harm to anyone. God wants me to be a blessing to everyone I know and meet. Therefore, I am determined that strife, vengeance, and retribution toward others are not, and will not be, part of my life. Jesus has called me to walk the high road, and I am committed to getting on the road of love and forgiveness. I will be a blessing to my Christian brothers and sisters and even to those who are without Christ. I will obey God's Word and always seek to do good to people I know and meet. Other people's lives will be more richly blessed as a result of being around me and knowing me. I declare this by faith in Jesus' name!

JANUARY 16

What Kind of Special Vessel Are You?

But in a great house there are not only vessels of gold and of silver, but also of wood and of earth…

2 Timothy 2:20

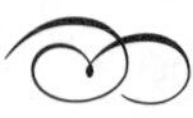

My Prayer for Today

Father, I thank You for speaking to me so strongly today about my role in Your House. I admit that in the past, there have been times when I was tempted to think that I was less important than others because my role wasn't as visible as theirs. But now I understand that my part in Your house is just as vital as those who are more public, for without my role, it would be much harder for them to do what You have called them to do. I ask You to give me grace to embrace, hold close, and take deep into my heart the position You have given me at this time in my life. Help me master it and fulfill my part in a way that is helpful to others and that honors and glorifies You. I pray this in Jesus' name!

My Confession for Today

I confess that I am thankful for the role I have in God's house. I am not a complainer or one who bemoans the task that has been given to me. I fulfill my role with a happy heart, as unto the Lord, knowing that I will answer to Him for the assignment He has given me. Because I do my part, others are able to do their part. We are a team, and each of us is very important to the proper functioning of God's household. I appreciate my role; I value those who have different roles than mine; and I am known as a person who expresses my gratitude to others for what they do in God's house. I declare this by faith in Jesus' name!

Stop Comparing Yourself To Others

My Prayer for Today

Father, I thank You for the ways in which You made ME unique and different from others. Forgive me for the times I've struggled with being different. Now I understand that my differences distinguish me from others. You specially made me to fulfill a role no one else can fulfill. I accept what You have made me to be, and, Holy Spirit, I surrender my life to You. I ask You to help me present all that I am to the Father, changing what needs to be changed, so that my life will bring glory to Jesus Christ. I pray this in Jesus' name!

For we dare not make ourselves of the number, or compare ourselves with some that commend themselves: but they measuring themselves by themselves, and comparing themselves among themselves, are not wise.

2 Corinthians 10:12

My Confession for Today

I declare that what I am, I am by the grace of God and that He didn't make any mistakes in the way He made me! He gifted me with talents, emotions, humor, insights, perspectives, and unique qualities that set me apart from others. My differences are some of the most positive attributes in my life, and I will not reject myself anymore simply because I am different. Being different puts me in a special category that I will no longer despise, but will use for the glory of God! I declare this by faith in Jesus' name!

JANUARY 18

Gold, Silver, Precious Stones...

Now if any man build upon this foundation gold, silver, precious stones, wood, hay, stubble.

1 Corinthians 3:12

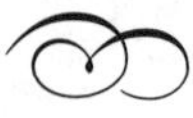

My Prayer for Today

Lord, as I start my day today, I ask You to help me seriously consider the way I've been building my life, my finances, my business, my ministry, my relationships, and my family. Forgive me for getting in a hurry and for doing things too hastily at times when I need to be concentrating on doing things right. Help me build my life in such a way that it will survive the test of time. Give me the insight I need to know when I am building correctly and when I am building too quickly. I know that my life is important and that You have trusted me as a steward over everything I have. So today I confess that I need Your help to build with the right materials and to build in such a way that what I do for You impacts future generations and passes the test of time. I pray this in Jesus' name!

My Confession for Today

I confess that with God's help, I am building my life wisely and with materials that will pass the test of time. My life is a gift from God, and I am a careful steward over this wonderful gift. Instead of being too hasty, I am carefully taking one step at a time, building my life, vision, business, and family so they will be strong for years to come. I would never be smart enough to build a life that lasts in my own strength, but with the assistance of the Holy Spirit, I am learning to build my life wisely, carefully, and for longevity! I declare this by faith in Jesus' name!

Could You Survive a Fire?

Every man's work shall be made manifest: for the day shall declare it, because it shall be revealed by fire; and the fire shall try every man's work of what sort it is.

1 Corinthians 3:13

My Prayer for Today

Father, help me take a good look at my life to see if I am building it correctly with the kind of materials that will last through any difficult time. I do not want to be irresponsible in the way I build my life, my family, my business, or my calling, so please help me be very attentive to what I am doing and how I am doing it. I realize that tests eventually come to everyone, and I know that if I am diligent with my life right now, I will stand up stronger and last longer when the storms of life try to assail me. So help me today, Holy Spirit, to start seriously pondering my life to see how I can be building better. I pray this in Jesus' name!

My Confession for Today

I confess that with the help of the Holy Spirit, I am building my life in such a way that I will be able to survive any attack! Because I am building wisely—with the right materials and the right methods—my life is becoming so strong that it will be capable of passing every test. I forsake hasty, irresponsible living, and I press forward with purpose to make a difference in this world. Therefore, I am giving my best efforts to build something that is excellent, respectable, and will bring glory to Jesus. I declare this by faith in Jesus' name!

January 20

Do You Follow the Rules?

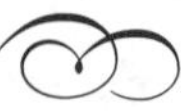

Moreover it is required in stewards, that a man be found faithful.

1 Corinthians 4:2

My Prayer for Today

Father, I thank You for making me Your child—and today I am renewing my commitment to live according to the rules of Your house. It is a great honor to be Your child. I want to honor You by being obedient to You. I want to understand Your rules—what they mean, why You require them, and how to apply them to every situation in my life. When You look at me, I want You to see me as a child of God who is ardently doing all I can to honor Your rules, to live by Your rules, and to help others honor and obey them too. In my own flesh, it is impossible to do it all, but with the help of Your Spirit who dwells inside me, I can do what You expect and live in a way that brings glory to Your name. Holy Spirit, today I am turning to You for help as I endeavor to honor God in the way that I live under His roof. I pray this in Jesus' name!

My Confession for Today

I confess that I am Christ-honoring and Word-keeping in the way I live and conduct my life. The Holy Spirit empowers me to think right, to do right, and to order my life according to the law of God. I am not a law-breaker—I am a law-abiding child of God. When God sees me, He finds me to be faithful and honoring of the rules that are so very important to Him. I am thankful to be saved and honored to be called a child of God. Therefore, I will do everything in my power to honor God in the way I live in His house and under His roof. I declare this by faith in Jesus' name!

The Most Important Requirement!

My Prayer for Today

Moreover it is required in stewards, that a man be found faithful.

1 Corinthians 4:2

Father, I admit that I've often been slack in the way that I've carried out the assignments You have given to me. I haven't always been diligent in many things You have expected of me, and yet I've somehow thought that You would promote me anyway. Now I understand that You are watching and waiting for me to be found faithful. Only then will You be assured that I can be trusted with something bigger than what I am doing right now. Forgive me for my faulty thinking in the past. I ask You to make my thoughts agreeable to Your will, as You create in me both the desire and the ability to do what pleases You. I thank You, Lord, for helping me do Your will Your way. From this moment onward, I will do my best to be faithful at the tasks in my life right now. Even if I don't relish what I am being asked to do, I will do it with all of my heart until You and I both know that I can be trusted with something bigger and better. I pray this in Jesus' name!

My Confession for Today

I confess that I am committed to doing my present job with joy and excellence. I do not complain; I do not drag my feet; and I do not behave lazily or half-heartedly. I am completely committed to doing this job with excellence and in a manner that brings praise to the name of Jesus Christ. When God looks at me, He smiles because He sees me giving 100 percent of everything I am to the task of doing this the best that it can be done. With the help of the Holy Spirit, I am a faithful steward over all that God has entrusted to my care and oversight. Because I am completing my assignment with my whole heart and with the highest level of excellence I'm capable of, God finds me faithful and will promote me to a higher level and a bigger assignment. I declare this by faith in Jesus' name!

Be Specific When You Pray!

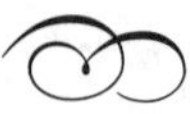

And if we know that he hear us, whatsoever we ask, we know that we have the petitions that we desired of him.

1 John 5:15

My Prayer for Today

Heavenly Father, today I come to You in Jesus' name, thanking You for the Holy Spirit who leads me and guides me into all truth. Your Word is filled with promises that meet every need in my life. Thank You for directing me to find Your promises that apply to the specific situations in my life right now. Holy Spirit, once You have enabled me to find those promises, I purpose in my heart to come to the Father in confidence and assurance as I submit specific, detailed requests to the concrete needs I am facing in my life. You have commanded me to ask that I might receive and that my joy would be made full. From this point onward, I commit myself to honor You with specific requests when I pray! And I will be faithful to glorify Your name when the answers are granted! I pray this in Jesus' name!

My Confession for Today

I confess that I am finished with praying only general, sweeping prayers for God's blessings. From this moment forward, I intend to be very specific when I pray. God's Word holds answers and promises that He wants to bring to pass in my life. With the help of the Holy Spirit, I will find those answers, discover those promises, and then be very concrete about the things for which I release my faith to receive from God. This is the confidence that I have in my heavenly Father: If I ask anything according to His will—and His Word is His will—He hears me. And according to First John 5:14, since I know that He hears me, I know that I have the petition I have desired from Him. Therefore, I am now stepping up to the next level of maturity in prayer, where I speak up, speak out, and pray with authority every time I make my requests known to God. I declare this by faith in Jesus' name!

Use What Influence You Have!

My Prayer for Today

Lord, I am deeply convicted that I need to be more open about sharing my faith with non-Christians I see and talk to every day. I know they feel empty and are searching for the real reason for life. I remember how lost I felt before You came into my life and gave me a new purpose. I thank You for giving me Your compassion for those who are without Christ. Let me speak words so filled with wisdom and grace that they will minister grace and clearly explain the hope I have in Christ—a hope that they, too, can share. Thank You for causing a burning passion to grow within me to see people saved. I don't ever want to be so busy in my own affairs that I forget people need to be saved. I don't want to be hardhearted or uncaring about people's eternal status. So I stir up a strong desire deep inside me to see people saved and delivered by Your power! I pray this in Jesus' name!

But sanctify the Lord God in your hearts: and be ready always to give an answer to every man that asketh you a reason of the hope that is in you with meekness and fear.

1 Peter 3:15

My Confession for Today

I confess that I am deeply concerned for unsaved people—especially those that I rub elbows with every day. I accept my God-given responsibility to share Jesus with those who are lost—especially to those who appeal to me for answers regarding the reason for the hope that is in me. When people ask me, I am not ashamed of the Gospel, for it is the power of God that leads to salvation; rather, I am bold, eager to answer, and ready to tell them the Good News about Jesus Christ. He has changed my life! Therefore, I am prepared at any moment to introduce others to the same saving and life-changing message that has revolutionized my life and given me a relationship with God Almighty. I declare this by faith in Jesus' name!

JANUARY 24

An Overflowing and Thankful Heart

We give thanks to God always for you all, making mention of you in our prayers.

1 Thessalonians 1:2

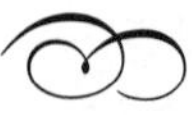

My Prayer for Today

Lord, I thank You for the people You have placed in my life who are a special blessing to me. In this world today, where disappointments and letdowns are so common, it is rare to find good friends and coworkers in Your Kingdom who are faithful, consistent, and truly genuine in their commitment to me. I am so sorry that I haven't previously made enough of an effort to let them know how grateful I am for them. Starting right now, I ask You to help me learn how to better communicate to these special people how thankful I am to God for them! I pray this in Jesus' name!

My Confession for Today

I confess that I am careful to let people know how grateful I am for them and for all they do. I am not negligent to say thank you, I don't take people and their kindness for granted. I express my heartfelt thanks to people who mean a lot to my life. I am blessed to have such friends, and the Holy Spirit is teaching me to convey my gratitude for all they do and for the valuable place they hold in my life. Every day I will spend a few minutes thanking God for them, and every day I will go out of my way to let someone know how thankful I am for the blessing he or she is in my life! I declare this by faith in Jesus' name!

Newness In My New Year!

My Prayer for Today

Father, I thank You for Your predetermined plan for my life—and that You want to launch me into it as soon as I'm ready. I ask You to help me prove myself faithful where I am, so I will be prepared for the call that lies ahead of me. Help me not to be stuck in my thinking—assuming that where I am is the ultimate end of what I am called to do. I ask You to open my eyes to see that great and wonderful things lie ahead of me if I will fully surrender to You! I pray this in Jesus' name!

As they ministered to the Lord, and fasted, the Holy Ghost said, Separate me Barnabas and Saul for the work whereunto I have called them.

Acts 13:2

My Confession for Today

I confess that God knows the good plans He has for me. He is ordering my steps along His ordained path, and I am following the Holy Spirit's direction to do all He is leading me to do in preparation for God's next phase of my life. I recognize now that all I have done thus far has been preparation for the next part of His call on my life. Jesus, You said if someone is faithful in little, You will put them over much. So I declare that I will be faithful in every assignment You've given to me now, and I believe that You will promote me to the next phase when You have found me proven and ready. I declare this by faith in Jesus' name!

JANUARY 26

Time To Stop Wrestling and Start Resting!

There remaineth therefore a rest to the people of God. For he that is entered into his rest, he also hath ceased from his own works, as God did from his.

Hebrews 4:9-10

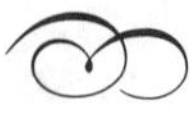

My Prayer for Today

Lord, I thank You that You died on the Cross for me and purchased my salvation. Thank You for saving me from sin and its penalty. Thank You that there is nothing I can do to add to Your work on the Cross. Today I am making the decision to quit struggling about my salvation and to simply rest in the salvation You have provided for me. I asked You to save me, and You saved me. I asked You to forgive me, and You forgave me. From this day forward, I will rest in the complete work of redemption that You purchased for me with Your precious blood. Thank You, Jesus, for saving me! I pray this in Jesus' name!

My Confession for Today

I confess that I am saved, forgiven, and born again by the Spirit of God. I asked Jesus to save me, and He saved me. I asked Jesus to forgive me, and He forgave me. I asked Jesus to come into my life, and now He lives in me by His Spirit. In Him I have redemption, deliverance, and salvation through His blood. In Christ I have the complete removal and forgiveness of sin in accordance with the generosity of God's great goodness and favor toward me (see Ephesians 1:7). I am as saved as a person can be! I refuse to let the devil torment me, steal my joy, or make me think that I haven't done enough to be saved. There is nothing I can add to the work of the Cross, so I am simply going to rest in what Jesus has already done for me! I declare this by faith in Jesus' name!

Golden Candlesticks

My Prayer for Today

Lord, I am so thankful that You saved me and made me part of Your Church. I now realize that even with all of our imperfections and weaknesses, You see us as golden and precious. Help me to treasure Your Church and Your people just as You do. Help me to truly love the Church, to serve Your people from my heart, and to give my time, talents, and gifts for the benefit of my brothers and sisters in Christ. From this moment forward, help me refrain my tongue when I am tempted to criticize the Church. And help me to become more and more aware that there is nothing in the world more precious to You, Father, than the Body of Christ! You died on Calvary for the Church, and I know I can't grasp how deeply You love those whom You have redeemed with Your own precious blood. But I ask You to help me see Your Church through Your eyes and to love Your people with Your love more and more in the days to come. I pray this in Jesus' name!

And I turned to see the voice that spake with me. And being turned, I saw seven golden candlesticks; and in the midst of the seven candlesticks one like unto the Son of man…

Revelation 1:12-13

My Confession for Today

I confess that I love and cherish the Church of Jesus Christ with all of my heart! Jesus died for her; He sent His Spirit to indwell her; and there is nothing in the world more precious to Jesus than the Church. Rather than criticize or judge others, I will seek to undergird and strengthen those who may be weakened from attacks by the enemy. Instead of judging others, I will inspect my own heart to see how I may become a purer example of Jesus Christ. I will no longer dwell on the imperfections that I see; instead, I choose to focus on the unchanging truth that the Church of Jesus Christ is golden to God and therefore golden to me! I declare this by faith in Jesus' name!

I Am a Life Ablaze

And I turned to see the voice that spake with me. And being turned, I saw seven golden candlesticks.

Revelation 1:12

My Prayer for Today

Father, I thank You for sending Jesus to give His life and His blood to purchase the Church! You have graciously filled me with the oil of the Holy Spirit so I can bring the saving light of the Gospel to those who sit in darkness. Set me ablaze with the fire of the Holy Spirit so those who are blinded by Satan can also come to know the boundless love and power of Jesus Christ! I pray this in Jesus' name!

My Confession for Today

I confess that as a believer, I am permanently placed in the Body of Christ, which is the Church. God's plan for me is to be saturated with the Holy Spirit, just as a wick would soak up oil, so that I can be set ablaze to shed light into the darkness of a lost and dying world. Even though I may seem fragile or imperfect, God has chosen to deposit the power and preciousness of His Holy Spirit within my earthen vessel so I can shine brightly to the glory of God! Therefore, I walk with confidence in life, knowing that the devil is terrified and Jesus Christ is glorified as I shine bright with the power and the presence of the Holy Spirit within me! I declare this by faith in Jesus' name!

Out-of-the-Ordinary Miracles!

My Prayer for Today

Lord, I make myself available for You to unleash Your power through me! You show no favoritism, so I know that if You did it through Paul, You can do it through me. Forgive me for thinking that some of the people in my life are too difficult to reach with the Gospel. Help me remember that You are acquainted with those I'm trying to reach and You know exactly what needs to be done to reach them and to keep them. I open my heart to You today with confident expectation that out-of-the-ordinary power will begin to flow through me for the glory of God and the benefit and blessing of others. So today I make myself available to You, Father, in a fresh way. Be glorified through my body as You stretch forth Your hand. I am Yours. I pray this in Jesus' name!

God wrought special miracles by the hands of Paul.

Acts 19:11

My Confession for Today

I confess that God wants to manifest Himself through me! From this day forward, I choose to live conscious of God's mighty power that is already at work within me. The same Spirit who raised Christ from the dead dwells in me. Therefore, I know that God wants to reveal Himself. The eyes of the Lord are searching throughout the earth, looking for someone through whom He can work and show Himself strong. That someone might as well be me! Starting today, I am opening my heart and mind to the possibility that God will reveal His amazing power through me! I believe it; I expect it; and I now anticipate the moment when this divine power starts operating in me! I declare this by faith in Jesus' name!

Ministry To the Sick, Diseased, and Those With Evil Spirits

So that from his body were brought unto the sick handkerchiefs or aprons, and the diseases departed from them, and the evil spirits went out of them.

Acts 19:12

My Prayer for Today

Father, I thank You for opening the eyes of my understanding today as I've read about the various types of sicknesses and diseases that were healed during Paul's ministry in Ephesus. I think I've made the mistake of thinking everything could be treated with medicine, but it is clear that some afflictions are spirit-induced and therefore can only be cured with the power of God. I ask You to teach me more about the gifts of the Holy Spirit—particularly the gift of healing. I ask also that You make me an instrument through which Your supernatural power flows to heal those who will never be healed in any other way. I pray this in Jesus' name!

My Confession for Today

I boldly confess that God uses me as an instrument of healing, deliverance, and freedom for the sick whom medical science has been unable to help. The Holy Spirit resides in me—and with Him are all of His gifts, including the gift of healing and the working of miracles. Father, I embrace the truth that You want Your power to operate in me and through me—and that I should be an extension of Jesus' ministry to bring healing and freedom to those who need relief. Therefore, I declare that I will yield to You and lay my hands on the sick, expecting You to cause them to recover. I will use my voice to release Your authority and command spirit-inflicted illnesses to go. In Jesus' name, I will see results and people will be made free, for the glory of God the Father! I declare this by faith in Jesus' name!

The Great Refiner

My Prayer for Today

Father, instead of resisting the changes You are trying to make in my life, I choose to willfully surrender to Your holy fire that exposes my flaws and brings correction. It is clear that Your refining fire is for my good. I know that You would never send a test that is abusive or hurtful. Your work in me produces strength, even as You guide me through situations designed to reveal and remove the flaws that need to be purged from my life. Therefore, Holy Spirit, I ask You to help me understand what You are teaching me. I choose to cooperate with the process so I can get out of the kiln and be placed in Your service! I pray this prayer in Jesus' name!

But as we were allowed of God to be put in trust with the gospel, even so we speak; not as pleasing men, but God, which trieth our hearts.

1 Thessalonians 2:4

My Confession for Today

I confess that the Lord is the Potter, and I am the clay. Jesus is molding me into the vessel that He wants me to be. He has every right to expose and remold what needs to be corrected and then put me in the kiln and turn up the heat. And when He brings me out, I know I will be freer than I've ever been before because the flaws that once hindered my walk with Him will be removed! I declare this by faith in Jesus' name!

FEBRUARY 1

When You Are Deliberately Maligned

Being defamed, we intreat: we are made as the filth of the world, and are the offscouring of all things unto this day.

1 Corinthians 4:13

My Prayer for Today

Father, I receive Your grace to help me mature to the point where I trust You to protect my name and vindicate who I really am when people say things about me that are untrue or unjust. I refuse to react emotionally with retaliation because of my hurt. Instead, I choose to obey Your Word by keeping myself in the love of God so my faith will not fail. You've promised me that no weapon formed against me shall prosper, and every tongue that rises against me in judgment or false accusation, I will prove or demonstrate to be in the wrong (Isaiah 54:17). Lord, You have assured me that if my ways are pleasing to You, Lord, You will cause my enemies to be at peace with me (Proverbs 16:7). So, I thank You, Father, for helping me to remember that this is warfare with Satan's unseen forces. I will never forget that You are ultimately in control and that if I respond in a Christlike manner when facing an attack, it will smother the fires and give You the freedom to bring about the outcome You desire in my life. I pray this in Jesus' name!

My Confession for Today

I confess that when the devil uses people to falsely accuse me, malign my name, or to do injury to my integrity, character, or name, I will respond as Jesus did and pray: Father, forgive them for they don't know what they are doing. Just because others act like the devil doesn't give me the right to react like the devil. I choose to yield to the Spirit of life in Christ Jesus that keeps me free from sin. Therefore, I make up my mind that I will walk in love and forgiveness, regardless of what people do to me or say about me. I will be a faithful soldier, and I will stay in the fight regardless of any attack that comes to assault who I am. Jesus is in me, and He is greater than anything that could ever come against me! I declare this by faith in Jesus' name!

When Your Spirit Is Disturbed

My Prayer for Today

Father, I thank You for Your Spirit, who is so faithful to alert me when things are not right. Please forgive me for the many times You tried to warn and help me, but I ignored Your voice and found myself in a mess I could have avoided. From this day forward, I am asking You to help me become more sensitive to my spirit. Help me pay attention to the peace or the lack of peace I inwardly sense so I can respond appropriately when You are trying to warn me that something isn't the way it should be. I pray this in Jesus' name!

I had no rest in my spirit, because I found not Titus my brother: but taking my leave of them, I went from thence into Macedonia.

2 Corinthians 2:13

My Confession for Today

I confess that I am sensitive to the Spirit of God. When He speaks to my heart, I quickly respond to Him and obey His instructions. I hear His voice indicating when I have God's green light to move ahead; therefore, I step out in faith. When I sense God's yellow light to move slowly and with caution, I am careful and cautious. When my spirit is inwardly disturbed and I have no peace, I know that this is God's red light—one of the ways He alerts me that something is not right. Because I am sensitive to what God is telling me in my spirit, I am able to move forward with confidence that I am not going to make a mistake! I declare this by faith in Jesus' name!

FEBRUARY 3

What Is Godly Sorrow and Its Purpose?

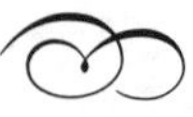

For godly sorrow worketh repentance to salvation not to be repented of: but the sorrow of the world worketh death.

2 Corinthians 7:10

My Prayer for Today

Father, I ask You to please forgive me for the things I've done or tolerated that are offensive to You. I know that when I willfully sin or tolerate attitudes that are wrong, it grieves the Holy Spirit. I ask You to help me feel the pain of my sin so deeply that I will never want to cross that line again. I never want to be hardhearted or stubborn toward You when Your Spirit speaks to me, so please help me keep my heart soft and pliable and remain tenderhearted to the dealings of the Spirit. I pray this in Jesus' name!

My Confession for Today

I confess that my heart is soft and pliable in the hands of God. I want to please the Lord, and I never want to grieve the Holy Spirit. I receive the empowerment of the Holy Spirit to strengthen me with His might and to guide me in life, because He is the last Person I would ever want to offend! The Lord creates in me the desire and the ability to do His will and good pleasure, as He conforms my thoughts to be in agreement with His will. When the Father's heart is grieved, my heart is grieved too. From this day forward, I will be quick to hear and to obey the Lord's voice, and as a result, I expect it to go well with me in all the affairs of life. I declare this by faith in Jesus' name!

Flee Fornication!

My Prayer for Today

Lord, I thank You for speaking to my heart today about making a break with my past and with the places that tend to pull me down. I admit that I've allowed my flesh to lead me, and I have been wrong for not making better choices for my life. I've tried to blame the devil and others for my failure, but today I am taking personal responsibility for the control and direction of my life—and I am walking away from those places, people, and deeds that negatively affect me. Holy Spirit, I tap into Your mighty power already at work within me to strengthen me with might in my inward man as I make these right choices. With Your help and by Your grace, I can and I will walk free and stay free! I pray this in Jesus' name!

Flee fornication...

1 Corinthians 6:18

My Confession for Today

I confess that I do not linger in compromising situations where I am tempted to think wrong, speak wrong, and do wrong with my mind, mouth, or body. I am the temple of the Holy Spirit, and I honor the Holy Spirit's presence in me. I never want to grieve the Spirit by slipping back into those sins from which I've been delivered. Therefore, I am making every effort to stay away from people, places, and deeds that have a negative impact on me! I declare this by faith in Jesus' name!

What Does Patience Look Like?

For ye have need of patience, that, after ye have done the will of God, ye might receive the promise.

Hebrews 10:36

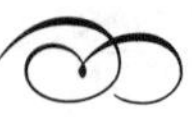

My Prayer for Today

Father, I repent for each time I have fallen short of Your promises simply because I gave up before my faith had time to fully work. I neglected to feed my faith on the Word of God. As a result, I began to give place to the fleshly tendency to become impatient when what I really needed to do was to persevere in faith and be strong. I receive Your forgiveness and cleansing, and I ask You to strengthen me with might in my inner self so I can let patience have its perfect work in me. I pray this in Jesus' name!

My Confession for Today

I let patience have its perfect work in me (James 1:4). Through faith and patience, I inherit the promises of God for my life. Having done all to stand, I stand with bulldog faith and tenacity, committed to seeing the will of God for my life fulfilled! I declare this by faith in Jesus' name!

Do You Know Your Role?

My Prayer for Today

Lord, I sincerely want to take just a moment to say thank You for the people who have played such an important role in my spiritual development. So many people have helped me, corrected me, assisted me, and taught me. When I think of how many people have made investments into my life, I am amazed and grateful that You would love me so much. Holy Spirit, help me express my gratitude to these people whom You have used to develop me. Most of all, I want to thank You for providing all the other ingredients that no one else could provide. Even though others invested so much in me, I know that You are the One who is responsible for the growth, increase, and success I am experiencing in my life. Without You, none of this would be happening today, so I want to say thank You! I pray this in Jesus' name!

I have planted, Apollos watered; but God gave the increase. So then neither is he that planteth any thing, neither he that watereth; but God that giveth the increase.

1 Corinthians 3:6-7

My Confession for Today

I confess that God is using me to play a significant role in other people's lives. Just as others loved me and invested in my spiritual development, God is now using me to help others. I consider it a privilege to plant spiritual seed into other people's lives. It is an honor to tend that seed with love and care and to nourish it with the water of the Word of God. All around me are people with great potential who need someone to help them. Because the Holy Spirit is working in my life and making me more like Jesus Christ, I am willing, ready, and desirous to be a blessing, just as key people have been to me. God has given me a role to play in the spiritual development of others, and I will faithfully do exactly what He has asked me to do. I declare this by faith in Jesus' name!

Faithfulness Is Key

Moreover it is required in stewards, that a man be found faithful.

1 Corinthians 4:2

My Prayer for Today

Father, help me to keep my eyes fixed on the task You have assigned to me. Help me to not complain that my beginning is so small, and teach me how to use this opportunity to learn everything I can before my venture grows larger. I know that You are with me—and You are watching to see what kind of steward I will be. So Holy Spirit, I draw upon Your mighty strength within me to rise up and help me be the best I can be. Most of all, I want to be found pleasing to the Lord and be one whom He can trust with much! I pray this in Jesus' name!

My Confession for Today

I confess that I am committed to be utterly reliable in every task that Heaven entrusts to my care. I will be-faithful to use what I have to the best of my ability and to demonstrate to the Father that I do not despise the day of small beginnings. I take this beginning time as an opportunity to learn, to excel, and to prove to God that I am a man or woman He can trust! I declare this by faith in Jesus' name!

God's Spirit Dwells in You!

My Prayer for Today

Lord, I thank You for coming to live permanently in my heart. What a miracle it is that You would want to live in someone like me. I am amazed and dumbfounded by this great act of grace—and my heart is overwhelmed with thankfulness that You have chosen to make my heart Your home. I know that I have a lot of areas in my life that need attention, and I'm asking You to give me the grace and power to deal with each of these areas one step at a time. Without Your help, I can't change myself. But with Your grace working inside me, I can be conformed to think with the mind of Christ, and my behavior can be transformed to reflect the character of Christ. I thank You in advance for helping me get rid of all the crooked and mismatched places in my soul so I can become a dwelling place where You are comfortable to abide. I pray this in Jesus' name!

Know ye not that ye are the temple of God, and that the Spirit of God dwelleth in you?

1 Corinthians 3:16

My Confession for Today

I confess that I obey the instructions of the Holy Spirit as He guides me to correct all the crooked and mismatched places in my mind, my soul, and my character. God's Spirit lives in me, and He is giving me the insight, wisdom, and strength to peel flawed areas away from my life so I can become a shining example of what Jesus desires His people to be. By myself I cannot change. But thank God, the Holy Spirit who lives within gives me the power to confront every area of my life that needs to be brought into alignment with His perfect will. His strength is MY strength to make wrong things right. I can do all things through Christ who strengthens me, as He continually helps me become all that He wants me to be! I declare this by faith in Jesus' name!

FEBRUARY 9

God's Payback System for Those Who Trouble You

Seeing it is a righteous thing with God to recompense tribulation to them that trouble you.

2 Thessalonians 1:6

My Prayer for Today

Father, I want to make sure that my own heart is right with You and others. I know I haven't always done right, so if there is anyone to whom I need to go and make it right, please bring it to my memory so I can take care of it today. I want to stay on the good side of the law of sowing and reaping. If I've ever sown bad seed, I want to rip it up through the act of repentance. And when I am tempted to be upset with others who have done wrong to me, please help me remember that my focus must be to keep my heart free, and it is Your responsibility to give people what is due them. Help me, Lord, to stay out of the vengeance business and to focus on keeping my own heart pure and clean! I pray this in Jesus' name!

My Confession for Today

I confess that I keep my heart free of judgment and I do not venture into the realm of revenge. God sees what is happening to me, and I can silently trust that He will be faithful to take care of me and to deal with those who have tried to harm or hinder me. That is His business, not mine, and I refuse to allow my emotions or anyone else to drag me into the ring to fight it out. I will focus on my own heart to make sure that I am inwardly clean. As the Holy Spirit reveals people I've hurt or wronged in the past, I will quickly go to them to ask forgiveness because I want to stay on the good side of the law of sowing and reaping! I declare this by faith in Jesus' name!

Continue in Watchful Prayer

My Prayer for Today

Lord, I am making the decision to turn up my fervency in prayer! You are telling me to pray consistently and persistently and to press in harder than ever before, so that is what I am going to do. If there are issues in my life that are blocking the answers to my prayers, please reveal them to me, and I will surrender them to You. With the help of Your Spirit, I will stay in faith with a watchful eye for the answer I have sought from You. Right now by faith, I thank You in advance for the answer I am seeking. I pray this in Jesus' name!

Continue in prayer, and watch in the same with thanksgiving.

Colossians 4:2

My Confession for Today

I confess that I press forward in the Spirit, persisting in prayer until I get a breakthrough from the Lord. As God's Word instructs me, I will be committed and unrelenting in prayer until every blockage is removed and the answer manifests in my life. By faith I keep a watchful eye for the answer I have requested from the Lord. Right now I lift my voice in faith and begin to consistently thank Him in advance for those things I have asked of Him. I declare this by faith in Jesus' name!

What Does It Mean To Be Blameless?

A bishop then must be blameless…

1 Timothy 3:2

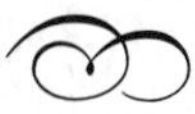

My Prayer for Today

Lord, I thank You for speaking to my heart today. I ask You to help me make a thorough inventory of my life to see if I have truly repented for past wrongs. If there is any area in me that requires attention, please show me so I can bring it to Your Cross and allow Your Spirit's sanctifying power to purify my life and conscience. I want to be used by You, so I ask You to delve into the deepest parts of my being and expose anything in me that would discredit me from being used. If you show me something that still needs to be changed, please give me the courage to do what is needed to bring correction to that area of my life. I pray this in Jesus' name!

My Confession for Today

I declare that I am not a prisoner to my past and that God has a good plan for me, regardless of my former mistakes. I confess those things as sin, and I do everything within my power to clear the slate. I declare that the blood of Jesus has left me blameless of the things that others once held against me. I pursue a life that is blameless; I seek to be an example of Christ; I endeavor to serve with a pure heart; and I know that Jesus Christ wants to use me more than ever before. Therefore, I am a candidate to be used by God in a powerful way to effect change in my generation! I declare this by faith in Jesus' name!

Presenting Everyone Perfect in Christ

My Prayer for Today

Father, I have long sought a purpose statement for my life. Today I align myself with the purpose that the apostle Paul wrote of in Colossians 1:28. I ask You to help me know with whom to share the Gospel, how to warn other believers who need to be warned, what ways I should teach believers, and how to let the power of the Holy Spirit flow through me. Shape me into an instrument to help bring other Christians to a place of spiritual maturity to do the will of God. I can do this consistently only if Your power is released consistently in me, so today I yield to the power of the Holy Spirit and commit myself to this great endeavor. I pray this in Jesus' name!

Whom we preach, warning every man, and teaching every man in all wisdom; that we may present every man perfect in Christ Jesus.

Colossians 1:28

My Confession for Today

I confess that God uses me to preach Christ to the lost, to warn and teach believers the truths of God's Word, and to help bring others into spiritual adulthood where they are no longer tossed to and fro as young spiritual infants. God wants all believers to reach spiritual maturity—including me—and He desires to use me to help others attain it as well. Although this is a huge task, I yield to the power of the Holy Spirit in me according to Colossians 1:28, and the Spirit works with me and through me to fulfill this God-given purpose. I declare this by faith in Jesus' name!

FEBRUARY 13

Coming into Compliance with God's Will

And he took with him Peter and the two sons of Zebedee, and began to be sorrowful and very heavy. Then saith he unto them, My soul is exceeding sorrowful, even unto death: tarry ye here, and watch with me. And he went a little farther, and fell on his face, and prayed, saying, O my Father, if it be possible, let this cup pass from me: nevertheless not as I will, but as thou wilt.

Matthew 26:37-39

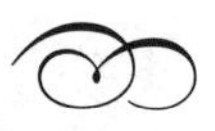

My Prayer for Today

Father, I ask You to help me push beyond my inward struggles concerning what You are asking me to do. Your requests have exposed my need to come up higher in my level of trust. This has revealed an area where I need to grow spiritually. Learning where I need to improve is good for me, so I thank You for leading me to this place where You can show me where I need to change and grow. Just as Jesus surrendered to Your will, I place my trust in You, and I will comply with Your plan regardless of how difficult it may be for me to understand in the moment. With the help of Your Spirit, I will trust and obey. I pray this prayer in Jesus' name!

My Confession for Today

I confess that God is faithful. If He is asking me to do something I don't completely understand, I can trust Him to have my best interest at heart. I don't need to be fearful of what He is telling me to do. I refuse to let my emotions get the best of me, and I choose to follow God's will for my life. I declare that I will not shrink back from the assignment God has given me, and I am determined that I will comply with His plan for my life! I declare this by faith in Jesus' name!

Escorted Into the Love of God

My Prayer for Today

And the Lord direct your hearts into the love of God, and into the patient waiting for Christ.

2 Thessalonians 3:5

I prayerfully admit that so often I have tried to figure out my route in life on my own, even though God has desired to lead me each step of the way. My heart moves out of peace when I struggle to figure out what steps to take, which way to go, or what to do. Since the Holy Spirit wants to be my Guide to personally escort me into His perfect plan for my life, I surrender to His leadership today and yield to Him as my Escort. Father, thank You for meeting me where I am and leading my heart on the most direct route into Your plan and Your love. I pray this prayer in Jesus' name!

My Confession for Today

Today I declare that I am sensitive to the leadership of the Lord in my life; therefore, I no longer wander aimlessly about as I attempt to fulfill God's will for my life. I want to do God's will, and He wants to lead me so I can get into the center of His plan more quickly, less expensively, and without wasting needless energy. Instead of trying to figure it all out by myself, I will heed God's Word; I will carefully listen to the voice of the Holy Spirit; and I will let the Lord be my personal Guide to escort me along the path of His love and into His plan for my life. I declare this by faith in Jesus' name!

A Demonstration of God's Power

My speech and my preaching was not with enticing words of man's wisdom, but in demonstration of the Spirit and of power: that your faith should not stand in the wisdom of men, but in the power of God.

1 Corinthians 2:4-5

My Prayer for Today

Lord, I ask You to help me surrender myself to the power and working of the Holy Spirit as I present the Gospel to people in darkness. Yes, I need to speak the right words and to speak it in a way that is relevant to those who are listening to me, but I also need to come with a demonstration of the power of God. Holy Spirit, I am looking to You to help me find the right words, to empower me and flow through me, and to do Your mighty work as I share Christ with people who are lost and in darkness. Today I ask You to release Your great power through me and to help me surrender when it's time to allow that power to operate! I pray this in Jesus' name!

My Confession for Today

I confess that I am an instrument through which the power of the Holy Spirit can flow to touch other people. I am not afraid of the power of God, nor do I hinder the operation of the gifts of the Holy Spirit. When it is time for God to show up in all of His marvelous supernatural ability, I move out of the way and make room so that God can do exactly what He wants to do. Rather than hinder or thwart the power of God, I am a facilitator that creates environments and provides time for God to show up and show off so that people will see and know His mighty strength! I declare this by faith in Jesus' name!

Does Someone's Name Cause a Smile?

My Prayer for Today

Lord, I want to say thank You for the people who are so faithful, kind, and encouraging that the mere mention of their names makes me want to smile. I am grateful for such people. Forgive me for focusing on the negative experiences I've had with people when the actual list of people who have been a blessing to me is so large. I ask You to help me remember those who put a smile on my face when I am attacked, hurt, or offended by others. Help me quickly remember that bad experiences with people are in the minor category, and that most people have been a blessing to me. As I make a list of those who have been true blessings in my life, show me how to express my gratitude to You and to them for the blessing they have been in my life. I pray this in Jesus' name!

But we are bound to give thanks alway to God for you...

2 Thessalonians 2:13

My Confession for Today

I boldly and easily declare that my life has been blessed with people who have loved me, cared for me, and have been a blessing to me. When I am tempted to drag up the names and memories of those who have hurt me in some way, I will refuse to dwell on those memories but will put on the brakes and act in reverse, compiling a list of the people who have been a blessing. The truth is, there are more who have been for me than those who have been against me. When I think of all the longstanding relationships with people who have loved and forgiven me in spite of myself and are still being kind to me even today, it would be ungrateful for me to dwell on negative people. So with the help of the Holy Spirit, I am reversing my mental focus! I'm going to thank God for the people He has used to put a smile on my face. I declare this by faith in Jesus' name!

FEBRUARY 17

Should You Ever Ask God for an Explanation?

If any of you lack wisdom, let him ask of God, that giveth to all men liberally, and upbraideth not; and it shall be given him.

James 1:5

My Prayer for Today

Father, You said if anyone lacks wisdom, we are to ask of You, and wisdom will be granted liberally. I thank You for Your willingness to give me answers, understanding, and clarification about my life and the situations I am facing right now. If I don't enjoy the answer or have the maturity to completely understand, I ask You for the grace to obey You regardless, as I know that You only have the best in mind for me and my family. I pray this in Jesus' name!

My Confession for Today

I confess that God is not offended by my questions for explanation and clarification. He invites Me—and even encourages me—to seek Him for answers. Whenever I am in need of understanding about what He is asking me to do. I declare that I know the Voice of the Holy Spirit and that He will not lead me astray or misguide me. I can trust what He tells me, even if I don't fully understand it. God has the best in mind for me; so regardless of how He answers, I will accept it and trust Him to be Lord and God of my life. I declare this by faith in Jesus' name!

Ask for Wisdom and Guidance

My Prayer for Today

According to James 1:5, I should ask God for the answers I need for my life. So in agreement with this verse, today I ask for Your wisdom and guidance in every area of my life. Father, in Jesus' name, I specifically ask You for answers to my questions involving ______________ (fill in the blank). I receive Your grace to understand what You're saying to me and to accept and apply Your wisdom to my life! I pray this in Jesus' name!

If any of you lack wisdom, let him ask of God, that giveth to all men liberally, and upbraideth not; and it shall be given him.

James 1:5

My Confession for Today

I declare that God has thrown open the doors and has invited me to come boldly to ask Him for the wisdom and answers I need for my life. There is no need for me to be embarrassed or to fear that God will get upset with me for asking. He wants me to be informed, and He asks me to ask! So today I ask in faith and I declare that I receive answers to the questions I have posed to the Lord! I declare this by faith in Jesus' name!

Fight the Good Fight of Faith!

Fight the good fight of faith....

1 Timothy 6:12

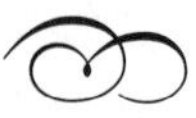

My Prayer for Today

Father, I admit that I'm in a fight. I need grace and strength to stay in this match and finish it to completion. I didn't realize how much would be required of me. But I am determined and committed to keep up the good fight of faith until I can say the fight is finished and victory is accomplished. Holy Spirit, I ask You to fill me with a fresh supply of Your power, strength, and resolve—a supernatural level of commitment—so I will stay in the fight till my assignment is fulfilled. I pray this in Jesus' name!

My Confession for Today

I boldly declare that God knows exactly what I am facing. I am not fighting this good fight of faith by myself! The Holy Spirit lives in me and fills me with His power—enough power to resist any opponent that would try to stop me from fulfilling God's plan. Today I yield to the Holy Spirit and allow Him to fill me to the brim with His power that resists every opposing force and endures strong to the end so I can stay in this fight until it is over and I've won the victory. I declare this by faith in Jesus' name!

Set Your Affection on Things Above

My Prayer for Today

Father, I thank You for the many blessings laid up for me in Christ to partake of here on this earth. And many more blessings and rewards are waiting for me when I reach Heaven. Please forgive me for getting stuck in low-level thinking about all the things it seems I lack right now. Instead of focusing on what I don't have right now here on earth, please help me reset my thoughts and begin focusing on things above. I pray this in Jesus' name!

Set your affection on things above, not on things on the earth.

Colossians 3:2

My Confession for Today

I confess that Heaven is loaded with spiritual blessings and treasures that are waiting for me! Only what pertains to eternal life awaits me! There will be no more tears, sickness, pain, or death. So I choose to refocus my thoughts and I declare that I will not dwell on low-level thinking about the earthly possessions I do not have. And I will receive by faith and enjoy all the blessings God has for me here on earth as well. These are all just a taste of the treasure trove of blessings that are waiting for me! I declare this by faith in Jesus' name!

FEBRUARY 21

Possessing a Trouble-Free Heart

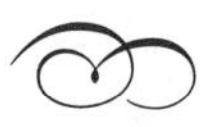

...Let not your heart be troubled, neither let it be afraid.

John 14:27

My Prayer for Today

Father, I acknowledge that I've allowed myself to get into a troubled state of heart and soul. Circumstances have left me feeling shaken and upset, and I haven't dealt with those feelings according to the Word. As a result, a door was opened to a spirit of fear that is now trying to call the shots in my life. I repent, because it is sin for me not to trust You, and I ask You to please forgive me for allowing these negative emotions to find a place to take up residence in my life. So now I open my heart for the Holy Spirit to infuse me with the power I need to take authority over the spirit of fear and tell it to leave me once and for all. I pray this in Jesus' name!

My Confession for Today

I confess that my heart, mind, and emotions are not made to be a refuge for fear and intimidation to take up residence in me and torment me. I refuse to nurse these negative emotions any longer or to let them operate inside my soul! I have tolerated fear too long! I refuse to retreat into a toxic state of isolation and self-preservation. God has too many things for me to do in this life to waste a moment in torment and fear, so I'm moving forward by faith to defeat the enemy's strategy against me today. I do it in the power of the Holy Spirit and with the name of Jesus! I declare this by faith in Jesus' name!

Praying With Boldness and Confidence!

My Prayer for Today

Father, thank You for inviting me to come boldly and confidently to You in prayer. I'm so thankful I don't need to feel embarrassed or sheepish when I come to You with vital needs in my life. As I stand on the promises of Your Word, I will lift my voice in humility and confidence, believing that You hear me and knowing that if I ask anything according to Your will, I will receive it. I pray this in Jesus' name!

In whom we have boldness and access with confidence by the faith of him.

Ephesians 3:12

My Confession for Today

I declare that I have no need to be embarrassed or ashamed when I come to God in prayer. The blood of Jesus has purchased me, cleansed me, and given me right standing with God. On that principle, I come before Him convinced to the core that His promises are alive, active, and at work in my life. When I pray, I pray like God really hears me, because I am absolutely convinced that He does! It's not arrogance; it's divinely inspired confidence. And when I pray like this, Heaven and earth move out of the way for God to activate His power and manifest His blessings on my behalf! I declare this by faith in Jesus' name!

Corrupt Communication

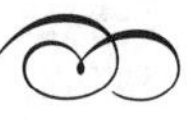

Let no corrupt communication proceed out of your mouth, but that which is good to the use of edifying, that it may minister grace unto the hearers.

Ephesians 4:29

My Prayer for Today

Father, I ask You to forgive me for allowing myself to get involved in conversations that were unfruitful and hurtful to those who were listening. Out of the abundance of the heart, the mouth speaks. Gossip is a form of putrid communication that defiles both the speaker and the hearer. I realize that I have been guilty of gossiping and discussing things that are none of my business, and I sincerely repent for these actions. I ask You to set a guard over my mouth so I no longer do this. I want to be only a river of life to others who are near me. Let my words be of benefit to others to build them up so that after I leave them, they are in better shape than they were before they talked to me. I pray this in Jesus' name!

My Confession for Today

I confess that my mouth speaks good things about others. I do not gossip about others, nor do I tear others down with my words. The Holy Spirit is inside me, and I do not grieve Him by foul talk. I yield to the Spirit, and as a result, I speak words that minister grace to those who hear me. After spending time conversing with people, I leave a sweet taste in their mouths and they are blessed by the fellowship they shared with me. I declare this by faith in Jesus' name!

Run!

...and let us run with patience the race that is set before us.

Hebrews 12:1

My Prayer for Today

Father, I thank You for the Person of the Holy Spirit, who positioned me in this race and who now empowers me to stay in the race until I reach completion. You are fair, Father, and You wouldn't give me a goal I couldn't reach. So when my mind and emotions argue with me, telling me that the finish line is too difficult to reach, I thank You that You've given me the mind of Christ that enables me to rule over my emotions. For the joy set before Him, Jesus endured in His race, and I thank You that I can do the same thing! I receive Your precious gift of divine strength that empowers me so that nothing moves me. I set my focus on Jesus and strive for the mastery, running according to Your ways so I can reach my goal. I can achieve whatever You have told me to do, Father, because Jesus has gone before me and prepared the way! I pray this in Jesus' name!

My Confession for Today

I confess that God's plan for my life holds only victory. He has made total provision for me to fulfill what He has called me to do through Jesus Christ. God has not called me to quit; therefore, I will not quit this race that I am running right now. He has already prepared me for this task. I will run my race; I will stay in the fight; and I will reach the finish line that Jesus has prearranged for me. I take the path He prepared ahead of time, and I will live the life He has made ready for me to live. Quitting is not an option. Therefore, I will say no to my flesh. I say no to the devil's attempts to insert thoughts of doubt that defy the word of the Lord for my life. I can and I will do what God has asked me to do. I will run this race to completion and finish my course with joy! I declare this by faith in Jesus' name!

The Unseen Power Behind the Throne

...take ye no thought how or what thing ye shall answer, or what ye shall say: For the Holy Ghost shall teach you in the same hour what ye ought to say.

Luke 12:11-12

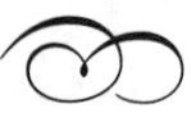

My Prayer for Today

Father, I thank You for the wonderful ministry of the Holy Spirit. I repent for the times I've allowed myself to become fretful and upset because I didn't know what to do or say. Holy Spirit, I receive and give place to Your ministry as my personal, private, invisible Advisor. I allow You to take this position in my life, and I purpose in my heart to learn to hear and trust Your voice. Thank You for giving me answers to questions and situations that I would be unable to answer or to solve on my own. I pray this in Jesus' name!

My Confession for Today

I confess that the Holy Spirit is my personal Counselor. In every situation of life, I listen to the voice of the Spirit. He speaks to my heart and mind, and He tells me precisely what I am to say and what I am to do. I am not helpless, confused, or caught off-guard because the Holy Spirit lives within me as my ever-present Helper. With Him inside me to guide me, I am never at a loss for wisdom in critical moments. He is my Helper, my Teacher, my Comforter, and my Advisor! I declare this by faith in Jesus' name!

The Past Is Past – Forever Free!

My Prayer for Today

Lord Jesus, words fail to express the depth of my gratitude for Your precious blood and for the price You willingly and completely paid to cancel all the debt from my past sin and actions. Your grace toward me is more than I can comprehend, but today I must stop to say THANK YOU for displaying Your amazing grace toward me! I pray this in Jesus' name!

In whom we have redemption through his blood, the forgiveness of sins, according to the riches of his grace.

Ephesians 1:7

My Confession for Today

I confess that I am completely forgiven. God has liberated me completely, discharged, sent away, and released me from all of my sin, which He has forgiven. By the blood of Jesus, my debt has been cancelled and I have been released from it. Neither the devil, others, nor I have the right to hold me captive to a previous wrong. I am totally and completely forgiven! I declare this by faith in Jesus' name!

Dead To Sin – Alive To God!

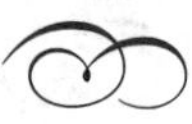

Likewise reckon ye also yourselves to be dead indeed unto sin, but alive unto God through Jesus Christ our Lord.

Romans 6:11

My Prayer for Today

Father, I sincerely ask You to help me embrace the truth that I've been set free from the past and from past behaviors. I am so thankful that Jesus has become the Lord of my life and that He has rendered my old personality, my old character, my old life, to be terminated. I likewise thank You that Christ didn't just slay my old self, but He has given me a new identity in Christ! Today I declare that I will step forward to embrace who Christ has made me to be and that I am free! I pray this in Jesus' name!

My Confession for Today

I declare that the past has no power over me. In Christ, I have been made free from the power of sin and its impulses to do wrong. The law of the Spirit of life in Christ Jesus has set me free from the law of sin and death; therefore, sin shall not have any dominion over me. I reckon the fleshly nature dead. Therefore, I refuse to allow its impulses to find expression through my body. If the past tries to raise its voice and speak to me, calling out to beckon me to let it assert itself, I will silence it forcefully and vocally by declaring my allegiance to obey Romans 6:11. Christ has set me free, and I declare that I am free indeed! My freedom is not a feeling—it is a reality! I embrace and enforce the truth of the liberty Jesus died to provide for me! I declare this by faith in Jesus' name!

Hoodwinked in the Last Days!

My Prayer for Today

And Jesus answered and said unto them, Take heed that no man deceive you.

Matthew 24:4

Father, I see that the world is slipping into falsehood and delusion on so many fronts, just as You said it would in Matthew 24:4-5. Long-held moral truths are being reconsidered and changed; truths of the Bible are being discounted and laid aside; and it seems that this process is occurring at a faster and faster pace as we come to the close of this age. I ask You to give me the inner courage to stand fast on the Word of God — to embrace it, dig my heels into it, and not sway from the unalterable truths of Scripture, even if the world around me is slipping away from it. Help me to embrace the Bible tighter than ever before and to keep my thoughts in agreement with Your will, regardless of what is happening in the world around me. I pray this in Jesus' name!

My Confession for Today

I declare that I am committed to the eternal, unchangeable truths of God's Word, regardless of what is happening in society all around me. The world may change what it believes and endorses, but not one word of God's truth ever changes. I declare that I will wrap my arms around the Word of God, embrace it, and dig my heels into it. I will never surrender my conviction to the truths of the Bible. Holy Spirit, I need Your power and inner fortitude to do this, so I am asking You to reinforce me, along with my other close Christian friends, so we stand by the truth and refuse to be bullied into lowering our standards of believing the deception that is at work in the world in these last days! I declare this by faith in Jesus' name!

Be Thou Faithful Unto Death

Fear none of those things which thou shalt suffer: behold, the devil shall cast some of you into prison, that ye may be tried; and ye shall have tribulation ten days: be thou faithful unto death, and I will give thee a crown of life.

Revelation 2:10

My Prayer for Today

Father, You are asking every believer for a higher level of commitment than we've ever made before. Today I understand that You are asking me personally for commitment of the highest magnitude—just as Jesus displayed a commitment of the highest magnitude to You, Father, in my behalf. Through that great sacrifice of Himself, I am now more than a conqueror through Him who loved me and washed me from sin in His own blood. Therefore, I do not fear death, but I joyfully commit my life unto You, Lord, knowing that I will not be able to be defeated because resurrection and exaltation await those who are faithful even unto death. So today I ask You to help me rise to a higher place of commitment so I can be faithful to the very end. I pray this in Jesus' name!

My Confession for Today

I confess that I am committed to do what God has called me to do. Regardless of the forces that are arrayed against me, I will endure to the end and receive an eternal reward—a crown of life presented to the faithful who stand before the Lord on that day when we give an account of what we've done. I will not only be rewarded in Heaven so I can have a crown to lay at Christ's feet on that day, but also I will taste victory here on earth. My best days are not behind me—they are before me! I declare that I am committed to the very end. Therefore, I reach a glorious conclusion because faith, confidence, and boldness arise in me! I fear no evil because the love of God in me and toward me drives out all fear! I declare this by faith in Jesus' name!

No Other Foundation!

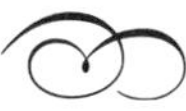

My Prayer for Today

Lord, I want to thank You for loving me so much that You placed people in my life to help build a solid foundation underneath me. Because of what they invested in me, my life is set on a firm foundation. I am so thankful for everything that was graciously done on my behalf! Please help me fortify my own foundation in every area that might need shoring up or strengthening. And I ask that You open my eyes to people around me who need the same kindness and care shown to them. Your Word says "freely ye have received, freely give," so I know I have a responsibility to give of myself as others gave to me. I want to be a positive influence in someone else's life, so I ask You, Holy Spirit, to show me how to be the same kind of blessing that others have been to me. I pray this in Jesus' name!

For other foundation can no man lay than that is laid, which is Jesus Christ.

1 Corinthians 3:11

My Confession for Today

I confess that I have a strong foundation in God, firmly based on the truth of His Word. And I allow Him to use me to positively influence other people's lives. I have gifts, talents, abilities, and experience that will help put others on a firm foundation for life. Rather than keep those gifts, talents, abilities and life experiences to myself, I allow God to use these to help other people get started on a firm foundation. Because I allow the Holy Spirit to use me, I am a great blessing to people who are around me. God works through me, and other people's lives are benefited because I am willing to invest myself in them and in their future. I declare this by faith in Jesus' name!

MARCH 2

On What Basis Will You Be Rewarded?

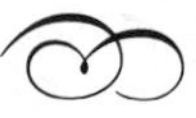

If any man's work abide which he hath built thereupon, he shall receive a reward.

1 Corinthians 3:14 NIV

My Prayer for Today

Father, I thank You for speaking to me today through what I just read. Now I understand that You are looking for excellence, permanence, and durability in my life. Forgive me for thinking that You would reward me only for being active and busy. Now I understand that You want quality from my life, not just quantity. You are looking for more than a lot of works—You are looking for works that remain! From this moment onward, I ask You to help me constantly take an honest appraisal of what I am doing and what I am building to make sure that I am investing myself wisely into works that will endure the tests of life. I want You to be pleased the day I look into Your eyes, so I am asking You to help me carefully measure my works and to make sure that I am living and building my life in a way that will merit a reward. I pray this in Jesus' name!

My Confession for Today

I confess that the Holy Spirit is helping me to build my life and works so strong that they will resist any test that comes in life. I am living by the Word of God, listening to the voice of the Holy Spirit and obeying God's commands. As I walk in obedience to the Word of God and build my life on this solid foundation, I can rest assured that what I am building will pass the test of time. I am committed to living a life of excellence, to building my life for permanence, and to bringing glory to the name of Jesus Christ in all that I do. I declare this by faith in Jesus' name!

The Smell of Smoke!

My Prayer for Today

Lord, I thank You for speaking to my heart today about what I am building with my life. I must admit that a lot of what I've done has already gone up in smoke. Yes, I know that I'm saved and headed to Heaven one day when I die, but when I see You face to face, I want to have something to show for my life. I don't want to have only the smell of smoke to show for the years You have given me here on planet earth. I repent and ask You to please forgive me for what I've built too hastily and wrongly in the past. Holy Spirit, I ask You to help me build my works correctly this time! I pray this in Jesus' name!

If any man's work shall be burned, he shall suffer loss: but he himself shall be saved; yet so as by fire.

1 Corinthians 3:15

My Confession for Today

I declare by faith that I am cautious in the way that I build my life, my works, my relationships, my business, my ministry, and my family. One day I will stand before Jesus, and on that day I will give account for my life. Because I am aware of that day, I live my life circumspectly and am very thoughtful and careful in the way I construct my life. Because the Holy Spirit guides me and I listen to Him, I build works that abide! I declare this by faith in Jesus' name!

MARCH 4

There's No Excuse for a Spiritual Superiority Attitude

For who maketh thee to differ from another? and what hast thou that thou didst not receive? now if thou didst receive it, why dost thou glory, as if thou hadst not received it?

1 Corinthians 4:7

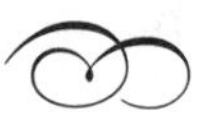

My Prayer for Today

Father, spiritual snobbery is a big turn-off. I ask You to help me look inward to discern if I have even the smallest hint of this in me. Lord, if anything like that exists in me, please show me, and begin the process to remove it from me! You resist the proud but give grace to the humble. Right now I humble my heart before You and I thank You for doing a work in my heart to remove any thought or attitude that does not please You or reflect Your holy ways. I pray this in Jesus' name!

My Confession for Today

I confess that I am thankful for every spiritual experience I've had with the Lord. I am grateful for the knowledge God has blessed me to attain. But I realize that I have so much further to go and so much more to learn. I don't think I've arrived, and I know there is so much more to reach for in God. Therefore, I choose to put my eyes on the adjustments I need to make, and I embrace God's grace to change me. And if I've carried bad attitudes about spiritually snobbish people, today I release those attitudes and those people from my judgment. They belong to the Lord, and they are not mine to judge! I declare this by faith in Jesus' name!

You Are Salt!

My Prayer for Today

Ye are the salt of the earth...

Matthew 5:13

Lord, I am so thankful that You called me to be "the salt of the earth." Today I want to step forward and surrender to be the salt of the earth that You intended me to be. Help me guard my mouth so that I speak words that bring preservation; words that make life better; words that bring healing to the sick; words that disinfect and free people who were once contaminated by evil; words that are filled with protection, safety, and deliverance; and words so faith-filled they create a blessed environment everywhere I go. Jesus has called me to be the salt of the earth, and that is exactly what I am going to be! I pray this in Jesus' name!

My Confession for Today

I declare that I am what God's Word says I am—and Jesus called me the salt of the earth, so that is exactly what I am. Because of who He is in me, I am a preserving, healing, delivering, life-enhancing force that positively affects every person every place I go. It isn't me, but it's the Greater One who lives in me that makes such a powerful difference in my environment. Because He lives in me, I am able to positively influence everyone my life touches. I am the salt of the earth! I declare this by faith in Jesus' name!

With God It's Possible!

He [Abraham] staggered not at the promise of God through unbelief; but was strong in faith, giving glory to God.

Romans 4:20

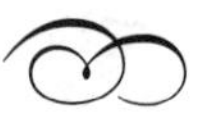

My Prayer for Today

Father, I thank You for revealing Your plan for my life. When I first understood the greatness of what You wanted to do through me, it boggled my mind. But now I understand that all things are possible to those who believe. Like Abraham and others who have seen You do the impossible in their lives, I believe that I will see my seemingly impossible dream come to pass in my life. You will always do exactly what You have promised to do. Ignite faith in my heart to believe, and help me stand firm, stable, and unwavering in my faith. Help me stay focused until I receive the manifestation of what You have revealed to me about my life! I pray this in Jesus' name!

My Confession for Today

I boldly confess that I will see the manifestation of what God has revealed to me about my life. Naturally speaking, it seems grandiose and far-fetched, but God delights in doing what seems impossible for those who believe, and I am among those who believe. I declare that my faith is confident and solid—that I do not waver or wobble in my faith! And I do not doubt the vision that God has shown me concerning my life. It's not a question of "if" it will happen, but merely a question of "when" it will come to pass. Until then, I will remain spiritually strong and stable, not staggering at the promise of God! I declare this by faith in Jesus' name!

I Choose Connection

My Prayer for Today

Father, I thank You for my church family and for the encouragement I receive from other church members. You have called us to be a body. I don't want to allow myself to be disconnected when discouragement tries to wage war against my mind and emotions. Help me run to fellowship in times like that instead of letting the devil talk me into staying away. The devil knows that fellowship will strengthen me and others. That is why he tries to keep us apart from each other during the times when we need each other the most. So today I take a firm stand against this diabolical strategy and declare that I will stay connected to my church family and other believers—and I will do all I can to keep others connected as well because we are stronger together! I pray this in Jesus' name!

And let us consider one another to provoke unto love and to good works: Not forsaking the assembling of ourselves together, as the manner of some is; but exhorting one another: and so much the more, as ye see the day approaching.

Hebrews 10:24-25

My Confession for Today

I confess that the enemy's plan to separate me from others will not work! God's Word plainly says that I am not to forsake the assembling of myself with other believers, and I will obey what the Word tells me to do. Even if I am under assault emotionally, assembling to fellowship with others is one thing I simply will not negotiate. Nothing will keep me from gathering with other believers to receive and to give supernatural strength. Furthermore, I choose to be a voice that speaks encouragement to others who are feeling outside, let down, or left behind. Rather than focus on myself and my own needs, I will focus on how to become a source of strength to others who are around me! I declare this by faith in Jesus' name!

MARCH 8

Indicators of Nicolaitanism in the Church Today

But this thou hast, that thou hatest the deeds of the Nicolaitanes, which I also hate. So hast thou also them that hold the doctrine of the Nicolaitanes, which thing I hate.

Revelation 2:6,15

My Prayer for Today

Father, I know that we are living in the last times, and during these days, false teachers will arise that will lure many people into compromise with the world. I ask You to heighten my spiritual discernment, make me sensitive to what I see and hear, and keep my spirit alert so that I will not consume strange doctrines that can only produce powerlessness and weaken my spiritual life. Help me love what You love and loathe what You loathe. As You do, I choose to have a loving attitude toward every person, and I draw on Your love in me to love people even if I loathe what they represent and teach. I pray this in Jesus' name!

My Confession for Today

I confess that I have nothing to do with teachings that will lure people into a powerless, weakened version of Christianity where sin is tolerated, separation is ignored, and the need for ongoing repentance is disregarded. I love everyone, but like Jesus, I do not appreciate or tolerate teachings that suggest there is no need for repentance or that we never need to change or be transformed. Holy Spirit, I know that You are calling us to be different from the world, and I declare my intention to You to cooperate with Your sanctifying work of holiness inside me. My deepest desire is to be like Jesus and not to tolerate the things of the world in my life. I declare this by faith in Jesus' name!

Keep the Fire Burning!

My Prayer for Today

Lord, I confess that I need to stir up the gift of God that is in me. There was a time when it seemed the fires burned much brighter, but for one reason or another, I've allowed the flame in my spirit to grow colder. I take responsibility for this, as it is my heart, and I ask You to forgive me for letting my condition go this far. Today I am accepting responsibility, and I will look at my heart and determine the truth. And with the help of the Holy Spirit, I will begin to actively and vigorously rekindle that glorious spiritual fire that You intended to burn inside me. Help me, Holy Spirit, to do this not just once, but to continually put spiritual fuel into my heart and stoke the embers. I pray this in Jesus' name!

Wherefore I put thee in remembrance that thou stir up the gift of God, which is in thee by the putting on of my hands.

2 Timothy 1:6

My Confession for Today

I confess that my heart is a hearth for the fire of the Holy Spirit. It is God's will for my heart to be spiritually ablaze, and today I will begin to do what I must do to rekindle the flame to burn as it once did and to blaze even brighter. I will not allow distractions—whether they come from my own busy schedule, from others, or even from myself—to take my attention off my spiritual condition ever again. I recognize my failure to tend to the fire has affected me, and I declare that from this moment onward, I will dutifully stoke the fire and the gifts of God that have been placed inside me. I will find fuel for the fire and I will take responsibility to make certain it is placed on the hearth of my heart regularly so that the fire burns bright continuously. I declare this by faith in Jesus' name!

First Things First!

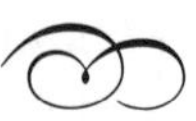

Now he which stablisheth us with you in Christ, and hath anointed us, is God.

2 Corinthians 1:21

My Prayer for Today

Father, I ask You to work deeply in my life to make me the kind of person I need to be. You know how I desire for You to use me. Your Spirit has filled my heart with dreams of greatness, and I long for the day when You trust me enough to give me a bigger assignment in life. For now, I ask You to delve deep into my life—into my character, my level of integrity, my faithfulness, and my personal purity—to show me any areas that are weak and deficient. Rather than complain that it's taking too long to get started at fulfilling my dream, help me realize that this is a God-given time to strengthen my foundation and to make sure I am ready for the big assignment when it finally comes along! I pray this in Jesus' name!

My Confession for Today

I confess that I am allowing God's Spirit to examine my heart in order to find any areas that could potentially discredit me, weaken me, or spoil my God-given dream. It is good that God has given me this time to look at my heart and to prepare myself. It is an opportunity to strengthen my foundation so that in the future, my life can support the great work that God will entrust to me. I don't complain that it is taking too long or grumble that this time of waiting is difficult. Instead, I embrace this season of preparation as a gift from God to make sure that I am right, that my foundation is right, and that I am ready for the long-awaited assignments that He will give to me. I declare this by faith in Jesus' name!

Time To Rise and Shine!

My Prayer for Today

Lord, I am thankful that You believe I can be a light in someone else's life! So often I am overly aware of my weaknesses and shortcomings, and I forget what a great work You have already done in me. Forgive me for not expressing my gratitude to You more frequently for the precious changes You have already brought about in my life. Many people sit in darkness and struggle to find their way in life, and today I hear Your Spirit beckoning me to let my light shine before people that they may glorify You and so that I might have a godly influence on someone else's life. I accept the call of the Spirit, and I will do my best to let Your light in me shine forth to those who are seeking direction for their lives! I pray this in Jesus' name!

Ye are the light of the world. A city that is set on an hill cannot be hid.

Matthew 5:14

My Confession for Today

I confess that God has done a great work in my life and that I have something I can share and impart to others who are seeking direction for their lives. I am finished with berating myself about what I've done wrong. God has done such a precious work in my life. From this moment onward, I will throw back my shoulders, hold my head high, acknowledge the good work that God has done in my life, and let His light in my life shine before all people! I declare this by faith in Jesus' name!

March 12

You Have What It Takes!

Neither do men light a candle, and put it under a bushel, but on a candlestick; and it giveth light unto all that are in the house.

Matthew 5:15

My Prayer for Today

Father, my heart is filled with gratitude today for Your Spirit inside me. What a miracle it is that You would place Your richest treasure in me! Today I want to surrender to You anew, and I ask You to refill me with a full supply of the Holy Spirit's oil so I may burn long and bright in this life. You have called me, equipped me, and anointed me to do great things in this life. I know I have been guilty of putting my light under a bushel, but I'll do it no more! I'm making the decision to step out of the shadows and allow God to release my gifts and talents when and how He desires. I choose to shine my light where it will be a benefit to someone else. Jesus, I thank You for helping me realize that it's time for me to step up and step out so that I can be the godly influence You want me to be in someone else's life. I pray this in Jesus' name!

My Confession for Today

I confess that I am stepping out of the shadows. I am releasing my gifts, and I am making the decision to let my light shine so I can be the blessing to others God intends me to be. I am finished badgering myself and putting myself down. I will no longer hide my light and life under a bushel. I am filled to the brim with the Holy Spirit's oil. His fire is burning brightly in me, and very soon it will be evident for all to see! I declare this by faith in Jesus' name!

Guts and Gumption!

My Prayer for Today

Father, I know it's time for me to quit thinking about what I'm going to do and to start doing it. I've prayed, dreamed, talked, and thought about stepping out in faith—and now You are telling me that it's my time to step up and get started. Your Spirit has been tugging at my heart, trying to get me to come out of hiding and into the light, but I've been afraid of what would happen if I took a step of faith. It's time for me to put my fear aside, put my trust in You, and begin to let my light shine. Holy Spirit, help me have the guts and gumption I need to bring my light out from under the bushel so I can begin to shine brighter and further for You! I pray this in Jesus' name!

Neither do men light a candle, and put it under a bushel, but on a candlestick; and it giveth light unto all that are in the house.

Matthew 5:15

My Confession for Today

I confess that I will no longer hide in the shadows and conceal the gifts, talents, and abilities that God has given to me. I've hidden them for too long—and now I am willingly making the decision to step out of the shadows and put my light in a place where it will be the blessing God intended it to be. God has gifted me and anointed me, and the Holy Spirit is now telling me that it is my time to rise up and shine. The day of timidity and complacency has passed! I now have the guts, gumption, and boldness needed to use my gifts and abilities to God's glory and to let them illuminate and influence the largest audience possible! I declare this by faith in Jesus' name!

MARCH 14

The Shortest Verse in the Bible

Jesus wept.

John 11:35

My Prayer for Today

Father, today I give You my emotions. I confess that at times they have tried to dominate me and steal my joy. I've allowed others to affect me, and I've permitted bad situations to impact me. I'm tired of living the way I've lived, Father. You have called me to live above defeat, and today I am making the choice to let the power of the Holy Spirit within lift me to a new place of victory I've never known before. Rather than just throw in the towel and quit in defeat, I will lift my voice and speak to the need, and I will see the power of God work on my behalf! I pray this in Jesus' name!

My Confession for Today

I confess that I'm not conquered by my emotions or by the situations I am facing in life right now. Jesus is Lord of all in my life! He is Lord over me, my family, my health, my business, my money, my relationships—absolutely everything. I refuse to allow my emotions to dominate my faith and my responses to life. With the Holy Spirit reigning in my spirit, I rise to the moment by the power of God! I speak powerful words of victory that turn potentially bad situations into glorious moments. I declare this by faith in Jesus' name!

Slow-Moving Judgment

My Prayer for Today

Father, I am deeply moved by Your Word, and I know that it is the truth. I know that You deal with those whom You love. Today I pray for my Christian friends who are living wrong and just assume that You don't notice. Now I understand that in Your mercy, You are giving them time to self-correct. Please speak to their hearts and bring them to a place of self-correction and repentance before they must be dealt with in another way. I pray this for myself as well today. I pray this in Jesus' name!

And his feet like unto fine brass [bronze]...

Revelation 1:15

My Confession for Today

I confess that I am quick to respond when the Holy Spirit corrects me. I serve God faithfully. I do those things that please Him. When I am inwardly made to know that I am doing something wrong—or if I have intentionally or unintentionally done something that requires correction—I am quick to admit it and to repent. If I must repent to someone else for something I have done wrong to them, I am also quick to do that. The Holy Spirit makes me sensitive to sin and gives me the desire to live a life of holiness. I declare this by faith in Jesus' name!

Convicted!

And when he is come, he will reprove the world of sin...

John 16:8

My Prayer for Today

Lord, I am thankful for the work of the Holy Spirit to produce conviction and change in our hearts and lives. I remember when I first became convicted of my own sin, and it eventually led me to salvation. Now I know that You want to use me to shine the Light of Your Word to others who are in darkness as I used to be in darkness. Forgive me for hesitating and being fearful to take this bold step of faith to act on the love of God in my heart for those who need You. Today I am rejecting that spirit of fear, and I am asking You to release Your power in me so I can help lead others to a place of repentance and lasting change. Help me do this for others just as others once helped me! I pray this in Jesus' name!

My Confession for Today

I confess that I am a bold witness for Jesus Christ. There are people I know—friends, relatives, acquaintances, and coworkers—who need to know Jesus Christ. I declare by faith that I am not selfishly holding back what I know to be life-giving truth. I will lovingly tell others the Good News that Jesus can save them and change their lives. I am a mighty vessel that the Holy Spirit can work through. Because I am available for His use, people in my life who need Jesus are coming to know Him and the freedom He brings! I declare this by faith in Jesus' name!

The Right Kind of Pain

My Prayer for Today

Lord, I ask You to help me be bold when I speak the truth to people who desperately need Your gift of salvation. I know I shouldn't be embarrassed about my faith. You said whoever is ashamed of You and Your words, You will be ashamed of them before the Father (see Mark 8:38; Luke 9:26). Many people are lost and headed for hell, and they need to know You in order to be saved. Father, I ask You to give me a heart of love for the lost and the boldness of the Spirit so I may unashamedly proclaim the truth to them and give them the opportunity to escape future judgment and to secure a home in Heaven. Teach me to understand that there is nothing in this world more precious than a soul, and help me reach out to souls in love with the saving message of Jesus Christ. I pray this in Jesus' name!

Now when they heard this, they were pricked in their heart, and said unto Peter and to the rest of the apostles, Men and brethren, what shall we do? Then Peter said unto them, Repent…

Acts 2:37-38

My Confession for Today

I confess that I make myself available for God to use me to share the truth with people who are lost and who are headed to an eternity in hell. Hell is a very unpleasant thought. However, the Bible teaches that it is a very real place of suffering and that those who die without Christ will inevitably go there. Starting right now, I make the decision to let God's Spirit put a new love for the lost in my heart. I repent for being calloused and insensitive to the spiritual needs of the lost, and from this moment forward, I will allow the Holy Spirit to release His love for them through me. I am yielding my life to God so He can use me as a vessel to reach into the fires of judgment to pull people out before it is too late. Christ died for the unsaved, and I confess that I will be His vessel to proclaim the Good News that Jesus saves! I declare this by faith in Jesus' name .

Repentance–God's Requirement

Then Peter said unto them, Repent...

Acts 2:38

My Prayer for Today

Father, I am deeply convicted by Your Spirit about areas of my life that need to change. I admit that I've been tolerating things that are unacceptable for a child of God. I have been living far below what You expect of me. I see areas where I have fallen short of Your glory in my thoughts and attitudes, and it has negatively affected my life, my relationships, and my conduct. But starting today, I am choosing to repent. I make up my mind that my life is going to change. I've been wrong to think the way I have thought, and I've been wrong in the way I've behaved. I am no longer ignorant because You have spoken to my heart about these things. Since I am accountable for my attitudes and my actions, I am making the choice to repent and to change--and it starts today! I pray this in Jesus' name!

My Confession for Today

I confess that I am unwilling to tolerate sin in any area of my life. I submit myself to the Holy Spirit and allow the Word of God to cause my thoughts and desires to become conformed to the mind of Christ and agreeable to His will. I align my thoughts and imaginations with the Lord so I can stay in step with His Spirit and in sync with His Word. I am obedient to the Lord, and I live a life that brings glory to His name. I do not just talk about making changes in my life—I prove my repentance is genuine by demonstrating the fruit of a transformed heart. I declare this by faith in Jesus' name!

The Day of Deliverance

Then Judas, which had betrayed him, when he saw that he was condemned, repented himself, and brought again the thirty pieces of silver to the chief priests and elders, saying, I have sinned in that I have betrayed the innocent blood. And they said, What is that to us? see thou to that. And he cast down the pieces of silver in the temple, and departed, and went and hanged himself.

Matthew 27:3-5

My Prayer for Today

Heavenly Father, I thank You that You have given me the power to choose life. Today I make the decision to turn away from those actions and thought processes that are negative, detrimental, and destructive to my life. I don't want to grieve Your heart in any way. What a joy to know I don't have to wait for emotions to repent! I made the mistake of thinking I had to "feel" something in order to repent, but now I realize that feelings and tears are not requirements for repentance. Therefore, I am responding to the Word of God and to the voice of the Spirit who is speaking to me about making concrete changes in certain areas of my life. Right now I choose to repent of those things that I know are wrong. I make the decision to walk free of them and to stay free of them for the rest of my life. This is my point of no return. I pray this in Jesus' name!

My Confession for Today

I joyfully declare that I walk free of things that have long bound me. God is on my side! He sent His Son to die for my freedom and deliverance; He sent His Spirit to empower me; and I do not have to sit in a spiritual prison any longer. I proclaim that today is the day of deliverance for me! I permanently walk free of those things that have been a hindrance to me. Jesus died so I can be free, and I am free! Today is the day that I begin walking in my victory! I declare this by faith in Jesus' name!

MARCH 20

Repentance–An Elementary Principle

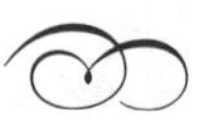

Therefore, leaving the principles of the doctrine of Christ, let us go on unto perfection; not laying again the foundation of repentance from dead works, and of faith toward God, of the doctrine of baptisms, and of laying on of hands, and of resurrection of the dead, and of eternal judgment.

Hebrews 6:1-2

My Prayer for Today

Lord, I want to thank You for helping me understand the importance of repentance and the need to establish this truth as a strong foundation in my life. Please help me meticulously examine my life to see if there are any areas in which I have never fully surrendered to your lordship. I make the decision now to turn those areas over to You, starting today. I have made my choice that I will no longer live for myself. I purpose to live the remainder of my life to please and serve You with all of my heart. By the help of the Holy Spirit, I move onward and upward in my spiritual growth and press on toward spiritual maturity! I pray this in Jesus' name!

My Confession for Today

I confess that Christ set me free and I have turned from the past sins, habits, and bondages that once held me captive. Those chains may no longer lord themselves over my life. Since I came to Jesus, I have renounced my past ways of thinking and living. Now I live to please Jesus. To serve Him with all of my heart and strength is my highest priority. Jesus is Lord of my life! I live to satisfy Him, and I am being carried onward and upward by the Holy Spirit to new levels of spiritual growth and maturity! I declare this by faith in Jesus' name!

Unlocking Hearts

My Prayer for Today

Lord, please help me remember that there are people in my sphere of influence who need to be washed in the blood of the Lamb. I ask You to help me love them enough to tell them the truth. I know that You have the key to every person's heart, so please give me the key to unlock people's hearts with Your words of truth so Jesus can come into their lives. I am so thankful that someone was loving and bold enough to tell me the truth so I could repent. Now it is my turn to do it for someone else. I ask You to help me get started reaching people today. I pray this in Jesus' name!

And the times of this ignorance God winked at; but now commandeth all men every where to repent.

Acts 17:30

My Confession for Today

I confess that the power of the Holy Spirit is working mightily in me and that I am a bold witness for Jesus Christ. I walk in His wisdom, and I am not afraid to open my mouth to proclaim the truth because it has the power to set men free from the darkness that binds their souls. When I speak the truth in love, people open their hearts and listen to me. Because they see Jesus in me, they readily want to know how to come to God and commit their lives to the lordship of Jesus Christ. I declare this by faith in Jesus' name!

Jesus Understands Your Struggles

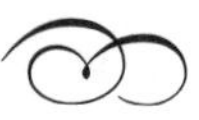

For we have not an high priest which cannot be touched with the feeling of our infirmities; but was in all points tempted like as we are, yet without sin.

Hebrews 4:15

My Prayer for Today

Father, I am so thankful that Jesus is my Great High Priest and that He understands everything that I face and feel in life. I can come confidently before You in His name to obtain mercy and find grace to help in time of need. The next time I feel tempted to get upset or frustrated with someone, Father, I make the decision now that I will walk in love and forgiveness just as Jesus did. I am so thankful that as my faithful High Priest, Jesus invites me to come boldly to Him to receive the grace I need to yield to His love and wisdom in me and to resist any temptation that comes against me! I pray this in Jesus' name!

My Confession for Today

I declare that Jesus understands precisely what I'm going through because He experienced that same temptation when He walked on this earth. He knows how to help me walk in love and forgiveness. Jesus has been where I am. He has felt what I feel. He has overcome the temptations arrayed against me. Therefore, I hold fast to my victory in Him. Because of Jesus' experiences as He walked on this earth, He understands the emotions, frustrations, and temptations that I face in life. There is no need for me to feel embarrassed to go to the Savior. If anyone can understand what I am going through right now, it's Jesus. And because of His blood and by the power of His name, I am more than a conqueror through Him! I declare this by faith in Jesus' name!

Blind To the Truth

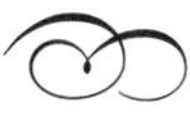

My Prayer for Today

Father, I pray for my family, friends, loved ones, and even my enemies as You told me to do. I ask in the name of Jesus that You would open the eyes of their understanding to Your truth and to the reality of what is taking place in the world around them. Holy Spirit, I ask You to help them turn from darkness to light so that they would abandon what's worthless and come to know and serve You, the Living God. Holy Spirit, I also ask You to help me recognize and respond to the opportunities you bring across my path for me to be a witness for Your glory. I am not ashamed of the Gospel, and I receive Your wisdom to win souls with the right words at the right time. I pray this in Jesus' name!

In whom the god of this world hath blinded the minds of them which believe not, lest the light of the glorious gospel of Christ, who is the image of God, should shine unto them.

2 Corinthians 4:4

My Confession for Today

I confess that I am aware I'm living in the last of the last days. Prophecy is unfolding before my eyes. The world has entered into the final chapter of history as we know it. I exalt You, Father God, and I thank You that Your Holy Word equips me with the strength and wisdom I need for the time and the age I'm living in. I choose to live soberly with eternity constantly in my view. I make the most of every opportunity to let my light shine for Christ brightly and without compromise. My lifelong desire is that others who sit in darkness will be drawn to a saving knowledge of the Lord Jesus Christ through the light they see in me! I declare this by faith in Jesus' name!

Opportunities and Adversaries!

For a great door and effectual is opened unto me, and there are many adversaries.

1 Corinthians 16:9

My Prayer for Today

Heavenly Father, You have set before me a rare opportunity for the sake of the Gospel. You have not opened this door for me to fail or to fall short. You opened this opportunity specifically for me; therefore, I know that You have equipped me precisely with all I need to succeed. Your plan for my life and for this opportunity is one of victory. Thank You for the supernatural weapons You have given me through Christ. I ask for and gratefully receive Your wisdom to know what to do and how to do it. By the wisdom and the power of the Holy Spirit, I put on Your mighty strength to exercise the courage and perseverance I need to obey You and to force hell to move out of the way! I pray this in Jesus' name!

My Confession for Today

I confess that I do not draw back, but I move forward in the power of the Spirit to walk through the open door the Lord has set before me! I acknowledge that through Christ, I have wisdom for this task. Dressed in the whole armor of God and in the power of God's Word, I can run through a troop and leap over a wall! (See Psalm 18:29.) I will not be deterred, distracted, frightened, or intimidated. Greater is He who is within me than any adversary that seeks to oppose me. The Lord has gone before me to prepare the way; therefore, I follow Him confidently through this new door so I can carve a path for the Gospel and prepare the way for others to enter and follow afterward. I declare this by faith in Jesus' name!

Your Life Is Your Pulpit!

My Prayer for Today

Lord, I ask You to help me be more aware of the unbelievers who are watching my life. Forgive me for the times I've been preoccupied and forgotten that my life is my pulpit and the strongest message I will ever preach. Holy Spirit, help me to stay mindful that non-Christians watch how I live, what I do, and how I treat others. Help me to constantly be aware that my life may be the only sermon some people will ever hear. Help me live my life wisely and in such a godly manner that others will see a contrast between me and the dark world around them. Help me take advantage of every opportunity to shine the light of God's love and His Word to those who sit in darkness. I pray this in Jesus' name!

Walk in wisdom toward them that are without, redeeming the time.

Colossians 4:5

My Confession for Today

I confess that I am a good witness for Jesus Christ! When people see me—how I live, how I talk, how I act, and how I treat others—they are left with a good impression of Jesus Christ. The Holy Spirit is teaching me how to shine like a light in darkness to those without Christ who are around me. Because of my Christlike example, many people without Jesus will come into the Kingdom of God. Since my life is the only sermon some people will ever hear, I will live my life each day in a way that accurately reflects the Person of Jesus Christ! I declare this by faith in Jesus' name!

Time To Swallow Your Pride?

Walk in wisdom toward them that are without, redeeming the time.

Colossians 4:5

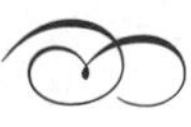

My Prayer for Today

Lord, I ask You to help me make up for time and opportunities I lost or wasted along the way in my life. You have been so good to give me many possibilities for success, to witness, and to advance in life, but I have not taken advantage of everything You have tried to give me. Please forgive me for not being more serious or thoughtful in the past. I ask You for wisdom to know what I need to do to regain the things I've lost. Without You, I know that lost opportunities are gone forever; but with Your grace helping me, I can regain the things I lost and buy back the time I squandered. Thank You for helping me as I set my heart to do the things that will enable me to recoup what I lost earlier in my life. I pray this in Jesus' name!

My Confession for Today

I confess that God can miraculously help me regain time and opportunities that I lost or squandered in the past. Because I am repentant and willing to do whatever I must to make it happen, God is helping me recapture moments, open doors, possibilities, and relationships that seemed forever lost. Time is spent and the clock cannot be turned back, but God's grace is so powerful that it will give me a new opportunity to do what is right. This time, I'll not fail, for I am determined to please Jesus Christ with my life! I declare this by faith in Jesus' name!

How Will You Respond To Negative Situations?

My Prayer for Today

Father, I thank You for the truth of Your Word. I allow it to transform me into a new person by changing the way I think. Anytime I feel seized and squeezed by eternal or internal forces designed to take me down, help me remember that there is no temptation that is not common to humankind. With every temptation that presents itself, You also present the way of escape from it. I pray this in Jesus' name!

There hath no temptation taken you but such as is common to man...

1 Corinthians 10:13 NIV

My Confession for Today

I declare that I make the decision to leave temptation in the dust. I choose to magnify the Lord and minimize every attempt to lure and appeal to my flesh through temptation in any form. I am not powerless or without authority and strength. I stand strong in the boldness, authority, and strength of God by the power of His Spirit within me. Because I am born of God, I am an overcomer in this life! Knowing that Jesus Christ Himself and countless others have resisted and defeated the very same temptation, I choose to walk away from these silly temptations and the emotions that surround them! The Holy Spirit in me is bigger than any temptation that tries to come against me—I can simply walk away from it! I declare this by faith in Jesus' name!

Building Your Life Correctly Is Important

Know ye not that ye are the temple of God, and that the Spirit of God dwelleth in you?

1 Corinthians 3:16

My Prayer for Today

Father, I want to thank You for speaking to my heart today about the things I am building both correctly and incorrectly in my life. In retrospect, I realize that I have built many things in my life that I now wish I had done differently. I no longer want to live my life in regret for making wrong decisions. I confess that much of what I have built, I have built hastily and with no regard for the wisdom of long-term thinking. As a result, I am reaping the consequences of my past decisions. I ask You to forgive me for not thinking more soundly in the past, and by faith I receive Your forgiveness. Now as I look to the future, I ask You to speak to my heart and show me how to bring correction to what I have done so that I will not repeat the same mistakes. Holy Spirit, I look to You for counsel and direction. I thank You in advance for Your help as I begin to build a life that will bring honor to You and that will gloriously survive all the tests that come in life. I pray this in Jesus' name!

My Confession for Today

I declare by faith that I build my life according to the wisdom of God, with forethought and sound planning. God lives in me—and because I respect His presence in my life, I build my life in a way that brings honor and glory to Him. I give place to the counsel of the Holy Spirit who helps and directs me in such a way that I build orderly, not hastily. I am the temple of the Holy Spirit. Therefore, I carefully build my life in a way that honors His presence in me. I repent for my carelessness in the past. Today I choose to be careful, thoughtful, and prayerful about building my life and my future. I ask for wisdom from above and God answers me—providing me with all the answers I need to build a life that lasts and a life that brings glory to His name. I declare this by faith in Jesus' name!

Heaven Rejoices Over One Sinner Who Repents!

My Prayer for Today

Lord, I repent for my own apathy concerning the miracle that takes place when a lost person is saved. I was one of those who has yawned and said, "Oh, that's nice." But in truth, there is no greater miracle than a person whose nature is changed. Nothing is more wondrous than the moment a sinner's heart is changed and that person is adopted as a child of God! Please forgive me for being so lackadaisical about this marvelous miracle that only You can perform in the heart of a human being. Help me never forget the price that You paid for my salvation—and to never forget how my life has changed since the day I repented. Even more, I ask for Your fire to burn in my heart in a fresh way for those who are still unrepentant. I ask You for open doors for me to tell others about the love of Jesus Christ so their hearts can be changed and they can be spiritually awakened by the Spirit of God. I pray this in Jesus' name!

I say unto you, that likewise joy shall be in heaven over one sinner that repenteth, more than over ninety and nine just persons, which need no repentance.

Luke 15:7

My Confession for Today

I confess that I will never take my salvation for granted. It is the greatest gift of God in my life, and my salvation is so precious to God that He gave His own Son that I might know Him today. I am thankful and so grateful for the privilege of being a child of God—a child of the Light. I recommit myself to serve Jesus with a passionate heart and a single mind all of my days. Just as Jesus' blood saved and changed me, it is still saving and changing people's lives all over the world. When people come to Christ in repentance, I join the throng of the heavenly host to celebrate this great victory. It is a commemoration of a human nature supernaturally changed, a spot in hell that has been vacated, and a place in the Father's house that will now be filled! This is worthy of my greatest joy and exultation. I declare this by faith in Jesus' name!

A Rescue Operation!

For the Son of man is come to seek and to save that which was lost.

Luke 19:10 NIV

My Prayer for Today

Father, I thank You that Jesus initiated a rescue operation in my life. He isn't merely salvaging me; He has put forth His best efforts to restore the ruined places of my life to a new splendor that brings glory to His name. Holy Spirit, today I surrender my life into Your power. Please take me and carry out the instructions of Jesus to rescue and restore me as He sees fit. I promise that I will not look at myself as a second-rate version of something that used to be better. Release Your power in me, let it transform me, and I will praise You for what You make me to be for Your glory! I pray this in Jesus' name!

My Confession for Today

I confess that in Christ, I am filled with the potential of the Holy Spirit, and I am not a weak, substandard version of God's original intent for my life. Because Jesus has released the Holy Spirit in me, I am stronger, better, and an improved version that far exceeds anything I used to be. I refuse to believe the devil's lies suggesting that I am less than who God made me to be in Jesus Christ. Because I am a partaker of the divine nature, the ideal image of Christ is being reproduced in me by His Spirit! I declare this by faith in Jesus' name!

Sword Power!

My Prayer for Today

And take the helmet of salvation, and the sword of the Spirit, which is the word of God.

Ephesians 6:17

Father, I am thankful for the ministry of the Holy Spirit. When I need sword power to stand against the enemy, the Holy Spirit quickens Scripture to my heart. When those verses are supernaturally revealed to me, please help me recognize and not forget or underestimate what is happening. Help me realize that the Spirit of God is placing a supernatural sword in my heart and that my job is to put it in my mouth and to wield it against the enemy. And, Father, just as the devil eventually "departed" from Jesus, at least for a season, I know that the devil will depart from me too. Thank You so much for the sword power that You give to me by the Spirit, quickening those verses to me at just the right time! I pray this in Jesus' name!

My Confession for Today

I confess that I have sword power to stand against the devil's attacks because the Holy Spirit quickens Scripture to my heart. When those verses are supernaturally quickened to me, the Spirit places a supernatural sword in my heart. As I release those words like a sword from my mouth, I wield a debilitating blow against the enemy. As I submit myself to God, I resist the devil and he must flee from me (James 4:7). I am thankful for the sword power that the Spirit gives to me and for quickening verses to me just in the right time! I declare this by faith in Jesus' name!

APRIL 1

Copy Every Stroke of the Master

For even hereunto were ye called: because Christ also suffered for us, leaving us an example, that ye should follow his steps.

1 Peter 2:21

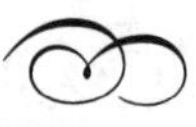

My Prayer for Today

Father, I've been struggling with a difficult situation. I have prayed for wisdom; I sought the advice and counsel of others. But now I know that I need to seek the example of Jesus as it is revealed in the four Gospels. Jesus is my Example and the One I am called to imitate. So, Holy Spirit, I am asking You to help me as I open my Bible to seek answers from the life of Jesus. Once I see what Jesus did and how He responded to situations that are similar to mine, I ask You to help me copy every stroke of His life. I know that if I will do what Jesus did, it will not only help me, but also it will positively affect those whom the devil has used to mistreat me. I pray this in Jesus' name!

My Confession for Today

I confess that I am a serious disciple of the Lord Jesus. He is my Example, my Teacher, my Master, and my Lord. As a serious disciple, I study His life and endeavor to imitate His every response in my thinking, in my actions, and in my relationships. I regularly read my Bible to learn from the life of the Master. As I seek answers from God's Word, the Holy Spirit enlightens my eyes and gives me the answers I need to successfully navigate through the difficult situations and relationships I encounter in life. By myself I could never know how to effectively maneuver through all these minefields, but the Holy Spirit sees what I do not see, He knows what I do not know, and He is helping me walk unharmed through life with the actions and attitude of Jesus! I declare this by faith in Jesus Christ!

Following in Jesus' Footsteps

My Prayer for Today

Lord, I thank You for setting the supreme example for me! Although You were abused, misused, and falsely accused, it never affected Your love or Your steadfast commitment to minister to the world. Today I make the choice to follow in Your steps as they are outlined in the Word of God. I refuse to allow my emotions to dominate me or to permit my feelings to be hurt. I make the decision to ardently follow the example that You left for me. With the help of the Holy Spirit, I will give my best efforts to walk in the footprints You left for me in the Word of God. I pray this in Jesus' name!

For even hereunto were ye called: because Christ also suffered for us, leaving us an example, that ye should follow his steps.

1 Peter 2:21

My Confession for Today

I confess that I will move out of the place of hurt feelings and step forward to walk in the same steps that Jesus took. His steps are clearly outlined in the Word of God, so I will read the Word, study Jesus' life, and learn how Jesus responded to people and situations. With His example before me, I will do what He did, say what He said, and walk how He walked. Following in His footprints makes it much easier for me to deal with the circumstances at hand! I declare this by faith in Jesus' name!

APRIL 3

When Perplexed, Entrust Yourself To God's Care

Looking unto Jesus the author and finisher of our faith; who for the joy that was set before him endured the cross, despising the shame, and is set down at the right hand of the throne of God.

Hebrews 12:2

My Prayer for Today

Lord, thank You for sending Jesus to die for me on Calvary. What a terrible price He paid to purchase my freedom from sin. When He hung on that tree, it was for me, and for this I want to say thank You from the depths of my heart. Today I ask You for grace to forgive those who have sinned against me, just as Jesus forgave those who sinned against Him. The devil has tried to make me bitter, but I know Your grace can make me better. Rather than focus on the injustice I have experienced, I am fixing my eyes on You and entrusting myself completely into Your loving care. I pray this in Jesus' name!

My Confession for Today

I joyfully declare that God is my judge and He is watching everything that is taking place in my life right now. I do not have to worry or fret that God doesn't know what is happening, because I have entrusted myself into His care and He is lovingly watching over me. I will not fight those who have wronged me and I will not retaliate with ugly words. I have made the decision to follow the example of Jesus. So today, I confess that I am not abandoned, I am not alone, but I am resting safely in the arms of my heavenly Father who deeply cares about me and all that I am going through in my life right now. I declare this by faith in Jesus' name!

Jesus Endured the Cross

My Prayer for Today

Father, I look to Jesus in all things as my Example of how to live and to walk in a manner that is pleasing to You. Jesus endured the Cross for me and remained committed to His task without weakening beneath the weight of all that opposed Him. Because Jesus refused to abandon Your plan, even when it cost Him greatly, I will not run from my responsibility to obey Your plan for me, despite the difficulty of what I am facing. I draw upon the power of His might to declare that although I may feel weak, I am strong in Him. Just as Jesus endured His Cross, knowing that it was crucial to His obedience to and fulfillment of God's divine plan, I take up my cross and follow Him—knowing that as I endure to the end, I will see the salvation of the Lord on my behalf. I pray this in Jesus' name!

Looking unto Jesus the author and finisher of our faith; who for the joy that was set before him endured the cross, despising the shame, and is set down at the right hand of the throne of God.

Hebrews 12:2

My Confession for Today

I confess that no temptation is beyond my ability to resist it and no trial can come to me that is not common to man or beyond what I can endure. But God is faithful to His Word and to His own compassionate nature. He is at work in me, creating both the desire and the ability to do what pleases Him. I know and trust that He will not allow me to be pressed beyond the measure of my ability and my power to endure so that I can bear up under it patiently. I let patience have its perfect work in me so I can come out on the other side of this situation strong in character and in spirit, lacking nothing. I declare this by faith in Jesus' name!

Jesus Took Our Shame

Looking unto Jesus the author and finisher of our faith; who for the joy that was set before him endured the cross, despising the shame, and is set down at the right hand of the throne of God.

Hebrews 12:2

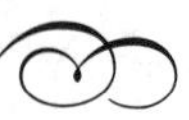

My Prayer for Today

Heavenly Father, how can I ever begin to thank You for Your great plan of Redemption? Jesus not only became sin for me, He also bore for me the humiliation and pain of it in ways far deeper than anything I could ever imagine. I am overcome with gratitude to know that Jesus endured such unspeakable horror so I could know Your perfect love and be set free from the torment of fear and shame. Holy Spirit, teach me how to walk in the reality of this freedom and love so that I will cause others to know the power made available through Christ's sacrifice on the Cross. I pray this in Jesus' name!

My Confession for Today

I confess that never again will I allow myself to wallow in self-pity because of the pain I feel, the loss I've endured, or the abuse I've experienced. Jesus knows exactly how it feels to be humiliated and shamefully treated in the most degrading ways. Because Jesus is personally acquainted with such pain and such mental and emotional anguish, He is able to fully sympathize with all my feelings. Therefore, with confidence I come boldly before His throne of grace to receive His help in just the way I need it most! I declare this by faith in Jesus' name!

The Joy Set Before Jesus!

My Prayer for Today

Father, I thank You for the example of faithful endurance Jesus displayed when He suffered the pain and the shame of the Cross for me. Jesus kept His eyes fixed on the joy set before Him, knowing He would occupy His seat at the right hand of the Father reserved for Him once His victory was complete. When You raised Jesus from the dead, Father, You raised me up also to be seated in Him. Lord Jesus, I worship You, and I fasten a steady gaze on You so that I will finish my course with joy to the glory of God! I pray this in Jesus' name!

Looking unto Jesus the author and finisher of our faith; who for the joy that was set before him endured the cross, despising the shame, and is set down at the right hand of the throne of God.

Hebrews 12:2

My Confession for Today

I confess that I am focused on the goal of completing God's plan for my life. I realize that I am not my own, but I belong to God. Therefore, I draw upon the mighty strength that is available to me in Christ—and by the help of His Spirit within me, I move daily with unwavering devotion in the direction toward the prize of fulfilling my divine purpose as God has revealed it to me. I declare this by faith in Jesus' name!

The Exceeding Greatness of His Power for Believers!

And what is the exceeding greatness of his power to us-ward who believe, according to the working of his mighty power, which he wrought in Christ, when he raised him from the dead…

Ephesians 1:19-20

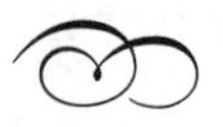

My Prayer for Today

Heavenly Father, You held nothing back when You exercised Your mighty power in raising Christ from the dead. I am in awe that You not only raised me from death unto life by that same power, but You have also breathed that mighty power into me by the same Spirit who raised Christ. Holy Spirit, I acknowledge the presence of Your power within me. And I ask You to conform me more and more unto the image of Christ as I let that irresistible power of God work in me and through me according to the counsel of Your will! I pray this in Jesus' name!

My Confession for Today

I confess that the mighty power of God that raised Christ from the dead dwells in me. That power, which is at work in me, is beyond measure. It is vast, boundless, immense, limitless, and measureless! The power that is in me now by the presence of the Holy Spirit eclipses all other power and cannot be resisted by any work of the enemy. Glory to God! Greater is He who is in me than he that is in the world! I declare this by faith in Jesus' name!

Financial Freedom!

My Prayer for Today

Father, I recognize that fiscal responsibility and financial freedom are essential for me to be effective in my service to You. I repent of the poor choices I've made financially due to fear, negligence, lack of self-control, or ignorance. Holy Spirit, I ask You to show me Your plan and wisdom for my finances so I can be the blessing I desire to be for the Kingdom of God. Please bring to me the knowledge I need, and then grant me the understanding and self-discipline I need to gain a heart of wisdom. I make a decision now to do what You reveal to me. I am willing to sacrifice what I want now in order to obtain what I need to possess later. Father, it glorifies You for me to be fully supplied so I can do the work You have given me to do without hindrance or delay. I receive Your help, and I commit my way to You. I pray this in Jesus' name!

But the fruit of the Spirit is love, joy, peace, longsuffering, gentleness, goodness, faith, meekness, temperance: against such there is no law.

Galatians 5:22-23

My Confession for Today

I confess that I honor the Lord with my tithes and offerings, and I seek first His ways in everything—including my finances. I declare that I am not wasteful of my time or my money. I acknowledge that wisdom is the principal thing in all the affairs of life. Therefore, I cultivate temperance by allowing this wisdom and patience to have its perfect work in me. I am diligent in business, obedient to the Word of God, and my finances steadily increase. I exercise wisdom in my sowing, saving, and spending. I am faithful in little, and God can trust me with much because I am proving that I am satisfied in Him and I no longer seek to gratify undisciplined impulses with my finances. I declare this by faith in Jesus' name!

APRIL 9

Human Body and Local Church Similarities

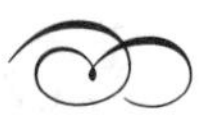

For as the body is one, and hath many members, and all the members of that one body, being many, are one body: so also is Christ.

1 Corinthians 12:12

My Prayer for Today

Father, I am amazed by the many similarities between the operation of the physical body and the local church body. I ask You to give my pastor and the spiritual leaders of my church the discernment to recognize when a spiritual infection has begun to fester inside the church, as well as the wisdom and insight to know how to deal with it before it becomes a bigger issue. Holy Spirit, You are the Spirit of wisdom, counsel, and might. Thank You for revealing not only to leadership but also to the local body how we are to deal with these issues so that we can walk in spiritual health and wholeness, free from spiritual contamination of any kind. I pray this in Jesus' name!

My Confession for Today

I confess that I am a contributor to wholeness in the Christian community. The Body of Christ is healthier because I am in it. I think with a sound mind; I appreciate sound doctrine; I respect spiritual authority; and I am a contributor to the overall health of the Church. When I see that something is amiss, I bring it to the attention of spiritual leadership, and they have the God-given wisdom to know what to do in every situation. The Holy Spirit is our Leader. He is the great Restorer, and I declare that He brings order and restoration to every place where spiritual infection has tried to take root. I declare this by faith in Jesus' name!

Making Time for Prayer

My Prayer for Today

Father, with all that I have to do today, I cannot afford to miss spending time alone with You. I repent for the days I have sought to serve You in my own strength. I was busy, but not always fruitful because I failed to maintain my vital connection with You. Lord Jesus, I deliberately look to You, and I look away from all that would distract my attention from You. Father, I diligently seek You, and I thank You for rewarding me with a greater revelation of Your wisdom and Your ways. Holy Spirit, teach me to order my days with the Lord occupying first place. Please refill me today with Your power and Your joy, which is my impenetrable strength! I pray this in Jesus' name!

And straightway he constrained his disciples to get into the ship, and to go to the other side before unto Bethsaida, while he sent away the people. And when he had sent them away, he departed into a mountain to pray.

Mark 6:45-46

My Confession for Today

I confess that I will daily spend time in the Father's presence. No matter how full my schedule may be, I will come to Him for direction and to be refreshed and renewed. I make God's Word my priority. I will not allow my flesh to lure me away from staying vitally united to the Vine because apart from Him, I know I can't do anything of eternal value. I set aside time to read the Word, pray, and fellowship with the Lord. I search my own heart on a regular basis and allow Him to change me so His anointing will flow pure and strong through my life. I declare this by faith in Jesus' name!

Faith Makes the Impossible Doable

Jesus said unto him, If thou canst believe, all things are possible to him that believeth.

Mark 9:23

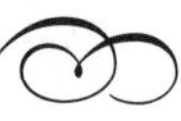

My Prayer for Today

Father, I believe Your Word! I will not listen to the naysayers who haven't accomplished anything. They want to halt and entangle me with their fear and unbelief. It doesn't matter how unqualified I may have been, Your explosive, supernatural power will energize me and make me capable. Faith comes when I hear Your Word, and I am determined to release my faith through obedient action. Regardless of the difficulty or impossibility before me, I know that when faith is present, anything is doable. Holy Spirit, I ask You to help me instantly discern when someone is not in agreement with You so I won't allow their polluting doubt to sink down into my heart. I am determined to push doubt and unbelief out of the way. I believe God, and it will be exactly as He spoke it to me. I believe God, and all things are possible to me. I pray this in Jesus' name!

My Confession for Today

I confess that my faith is not just past tense—I am a believer this very moment! My faith is actively reaching forward right now to grab hold of what God has promised. My faith is unwaveringly straining forward to take hold of that desired goal set before me! My faith ignites the impossible, causing it to become possible, and sets supernatural power in motion that enables me to do what others thought I would never be able to do. With confident expectation, I say it out loud repeatedly: I believe God, and all things are possible to me! I declare this by faith in Jesus' name!

Miracles Catch People's Attention!

And a great multitude followed him, because they saw his miracles which he did on them that were diseased.

John 6:2

My Prayer for Today

Heavenly Father, I am so thankful that Jesus came to earth to reveal Your will and to show us Your ways. Just as Jesus went about manifesting Your goodness by destroying the works of the devil, He is the same—yesterday, today, and forever. Father, it's Your goodness and lovingkindness that leads people to repentance. I make myself available to You as a vessel through whom Jesus can manifest Himself to others. Jesus was the best thing that ever happened to every person who ever came in contact with Him. Holy Spirit, bring people into contact with Jesus through me as You use my life. Demonstrate Your miracle power through my life to open hearts and change lives. Make me a vessel You can flow through to cause people's health to be restored and their hope to be renewed by a personal encounter with You. I pray this in Jesus' name!

My Confession for Today

I confess that I give place for Jesus Christ to perform His miracle-working, life-changing ministry through me. When Jesus walked the earth, He went about doing good, healing all, and destroying the works of the devil. I am anointed and commissioned by Him to lay my hands on the sick in His name and to see them recover. That is God's promise in Mark 16:18, and I boldly claim it by faith as I yield to His compassion and reach out to others with confident expectation to see His miracle-working power released to others through my life. I declare this by faith in Jesus' name!

I'm a New Creation!

Go ye therefore, and teach all nations, baptizing them in the name of the Father, and of the Son, and of the Holy Ghost.

Matthew 28:19

My Prayer for Today

Father, today I see more clearly than ever the significance of water baptism as a powerful demonstration of my spiritual transformation in Christ. Father, just as Jesus publicly obeyed You when He suffered and died to purchase my redemption, I obey the Lord's command to publicly proclaim through the waters of baptism that I have been washed in the soul-cleansing blood of the Lamb. I thank You that because Jesus died in my place and You raised Him to new life, I take every step to demonstrate that I am a disciple of the Lord Jesus Christ. Clothed in His righteousness alone, baptism symbolizes that I've been dipped and dyed in the crimson flood of Jesus' blood as I gratefully proclaim: I am a child of God! I pray this in Jesus' name!

My Confession for Today

I confess that I am a new creation in Christ Jesus. Old things have passed away and through Him, all things have become new. Crucified with Christ, I follow the Lord into baptism to bury my old self in a watery grave. And when I rise up, it is as a demonstration of how Jesus saves. I declare this by faith in Jesus' name!

Grace Abounds

My Prayer for Today

Father, although sin once dominated in my life, Your lavish, overflowing grace has abounded even more in me. Your grace far exceeds the work or influence of sin. Holy Spirit, I ask You to open the eyes of my understanding and help me begin to understand how to cooperate more fully with the grace of God that is at work in my life. I pray this in Jesus' name!

Moreover the law entered, that the offence might abound. But where sin abounded, grace did much more abound.

Romans 5:20

My Confession for Today

I confess that the grace of God abounds in my life, teaching me to say no to ungodliness and yes to living a morally upright life in this present age. The grace of God working in me is unsurpassed and unrivaled by any past rule of sin in my life. In the areas of my life and thoughts where fear and other sins once held control, the grace of God released to me now holds the superior position, and I allow that grace to reign supreme. I declare this by faith in Jesus' name!

Led by the Spirit of God

For as many as are led by the Spirit of God, they are the sons of God.

Romans 8:14

My Prayer for Today

Father, I now recognize that every time I have ever struggled to do what You asked me to do, the reason behind the struggle was that I had allowed fear and carnal reasoning to hinder me. Father, I repent for yielding to the pull of my own flesh instead of to the direction of Your Spirit. I want to live a fruitful life. Holy Spirit, right now I yield to Your strength, and I receive the courage I need to step out by faith and follow Your leading so I can obtain a heavenly outcome to the glory of God! I pray this in Jesus' name!

My Confession for Today

I confess that I obey God and I am led by His Spirit. I put to death all self-interest and every fleshly thought to make decisions based on self-preservation. I belong to God! My life is His, and His strength is mine! I refuse to allow my flesh to stop me from obtaining the supernatural results the Lord wants me to have. I choose to do the will of God. I declare right now that in those moments when the struggle to stay on track with His plan seems great because I'm tempted to let natural reasoning pull me off course, I will not fall short but will fulfill all the will of God without wavering! Greater is the courage of God within me than any fear that rants against my mind or any opposition that rises against me in this world! I declare this by faith in Jesus' name!

Becoming a Living Sacrifice

My Prayer for Today

Father, Jesus asked us why we call Him Lord, yet fail to do what He tells us to do. The one I obey is the one I truly serve. Today I see areas where I have allowed the voice of my flesh to call the shots. Instead of mastering and subduing my flesh into silence, I have silenced the voice of my spirit that calls for me to present my body as a living sacrifice in obedient surrender to You. Father, I humble myself beneath Your mighty hand, and I repent for the ways I have indulged the carnal mind, which is not subject to You. I judge that as rebellion and I refuse to give it place any longer. Father, I thank You for Your great mercy in opening the eyes of my understanding to see this as You see it. I choose to submit to You and to resist the devil's attempts to exploit my flesh to gain access to my life. You alone, Lord Jesus, have the right to lead me and conform my thoughts to Your will. I pray this in Jesus' name!

I beseech you therefore, brethren, by the mercies of God, that ye present your bodies a living sacrifice, holy, acceptable unto God, which is your reasonable service.

Romans 12:1

My Confession for Today

I confess that I make a decisive dedication of my body and my faculties to the Lord. I choose to follow the example of my Lord Jesus, who learned obedience through the things He suffered by walking in continual obedience to the will of the Father. I choose to make a continual commitment to refuse to live life according to fleshly dictates. Although this may be the biggest fight of my life, I decide and decree that this is a fight that will be won as I yield to the power of the Greater One inside me! I declare this by faith in Jesus' name!

APRIL 17

Making Wrongs Right

Therefore if thou bring thy gift to the altar, and there rememberest that thy brother hath ought against thee; leave there thy gift before the altar, and go thy way; first be reconciled to thy brother, and then come and offer thy gift.

Matthew 5:23-24

My Prayer for Today

Father, here in Your light, I see the light of Your truth shining on the reality of the nonsense I've allowed to become a dividing wall of offense. I acknowledge my part in this, and I repent of thinking and responding contrary to the love of God. I will not ignore the situation any longer or harden my heart in pride. In obedience to Your Word, I will humbly go to my brother or sister with the sincere desire to make this right. This may be difficult and somewhat embarrassing, but a clear conscience and unhindered fellowship with You means more to me than anything. As I seek to make peace, I entrust the outcome to You, Lord. I pray this in Jesus' name!

My Confession for Today

I confess that I keep a clear conscience toward God that is void of offense toward any man. I keep myself in the love of God as I continually seek peace and pursue it. I refuse to make mountains out of molehills and allow petty nonsense to escalate into an offense that will produce bitterness in me or in others. I am quick to repent and also quick to forgive. Holy Spirit, I ask You to quicken my heart any time I need to make things right with anyone for any reason. I commit to You that I will do what You tell me to do so I can live peaceably with everyone and enjoy unbroken fellowship with You at all times. I declare this by faith in Jesus' name!

Work While There Is Light

> *I must work the works of him that sent me, while it is day: the night cometh, when no man can work.*
>
> John 9:4

My Prayer for Today

Father, wherever I may reside, I am on a mission field. I was sent when Jesus said: *"Go into all the world and preach the Gospel."* You have given me many opportunities to make Christ known through my words, the works of my hands, or the associations You have brought across my path. Each window of opportunity You opened before me was time-sensitive. Some I seized in swift obedience; others I let close through procrastination, laziness, or plain disobedience. Father, I repent for wasting time and opportunities because souls were affected or neglected by my choices. Holy Spirit, I ask You to help me be sensitive to the spiritual needs of others and to obey You quickly when You prompt me to release Your love and truth into people's lives. I make a fresh commitment to worship You by working to reach, warn, and rescue as many lives as possible so they can have eternal life in Jesus Christ! I pray this in Jesus' name!

My Confession for Today

I confess that I will place first things first. I will reverence God and esteem what He values. People are precious to God; therefore, people are precious to me. Daily I will thank God for the gift of my salvation through Jesus Christ. I will also show Him my appreciation daily by doing all I can do to tell as many people as I can that there is a Heaven to gain and an eternal hell of never-ending torment to shun. I will not hesitate. I will not draw back. I am compelled to work while it is day, before the window of time closes and the hour comes when no one can work. I declare this by faith in Jesus' name!

Money's Power in the Spirit Realm

If therefore ye have not been faithful in the unrighteous mammon, who will commit to your trust the true riches?

Luke 16:11

My Prayer for Today

Father, I take a fresh look at how I handle my finances. It is not Your will for me to be in bondage to anything—including and especially to debt. I make the decision once and for all to be financially freer than I've ever been. Holy Spirit, I ask You to reveal to me the ways I can exercise more wisdom and restraint in financial matters, so that you can count me trustworthy with the true riches of Your Kingdom. I pray this in Jesus' name!

My Confession for Today

I declare that from this day forward, I will give more attention to listening to the Spirit of God, using common sense, exercising self-control, and planning my purchases in advance so I can live a life that is more debt-free than the way I'm living right now. I desire to be and to remain completely free from any financial hindrance so I can give and go without hindrance. In all my affairs, especially in the area of my finances, I commit to making choices that prove me to be a faithful steward of the natural power and influence God has entrusted to me so I can be trusted with true spiritual riches for the glory of God and the blessing of others! I declare this by faith in Jesus' name!

Does God Ever Resist Anyone?

But he giveth more grace. Wherefore he saith, God resisteth the proud, but giveth grace unto the humble.

James 4:6

My Prayer for Today

Father, I thank You for Your divine discipline. It is a safeguard to me and also proof of your great love. I ask You to help me see where my attitudes or actions are not in alignment with Your Word and Your ways. Father, I know that You resist the proud and I don't want to be resisted by You! I willingly choose to humble myself beneath Your mighty hand so that I won't be humiliated as a consequence of needing to change my ways. I pray this in Jesus' name!

My Confession for Today

I confess that I am quick to hear and quick to obey. I walk humbly before God and His grace abounds in my life. I am not rebellious or stiff-necked, but I yield to the promptings of the Holy Spirit and I remain pliable in the Lord's hand, as I deliberately, day-by-day, keep His words before my eyes and I continually ponder them in my heart. I choose to cultivate a sensitive and obedient heart, and the Holy Spirit helps me to judge myself so I won't need to be judged. I declare this by faith, in Jesus' name!

Choose To Let it Go

Forbearing one another, and forgiving one another, if any man have a quarrel against any: even as Christ forgave you, so also do ye.

Colossians 3:13

My Prayer for Today

Father, I repent for allowing myself to become angry, frustrated, and unforgiving. That is wrong and I refuse to yield to selfishness any longer. No matter what has been said or done, I have no right to harbor ill will—especially when You have commanded me to forgive others as You have forgiven me. Jesus, You paid a horrific price for my sins. Even as You hung dying on the Cross at Calvary, You prayed not only for me but also for the person I'm upset with now. Lord, I deeply apologize. If I had been focused on You instead of myself, I would not have become upset in the first place. Help me to see this person and this situation through Your eyes. I choose to get over this offense right now. I let this drop and I refuse to think on my feelings anymore. Instead, I will seek to honor You in this matter. Holy Spirit, teach me how to love as Jesus loved me. I pray this in Jesus' name!

My Confession for Today

I confess that I take heed to myself and I refuse to walk in unforgiveness, bitterness, or strife. I cannot control what others may say or do, but I am responsible for the condition of my own heart. I do not give place to the devil by indulging selfish thoughts or emotions. Neither do I attempt to justify my own negative behavior in response to what upset me. Instead, I choose to give place to the love of God, which is shed abroad in my heart by the Holy Spirit who indwells me. And I make a daily decision to love and to forgive others as God through Christ has loved and forgiven me. I declare this by faith, in Jesus' name!

A Guaranteed Investment

My Prayer for Today

Father, I believe it is Your will for my needs to be met, and, as a giver, I lay hold of Your promise to supply ALL my needs according to Your riches in glory by Christ Jesus. I admit that I have been anxious at times because I paid attention to financial markets as well as to my personal financial situation. But You, Lord, are my Source. You are ready to demonstrate that Your goodness and Your faithfulness to me are not affected by world economies. I will continue to give sacrificially to the Kingdom of God, knowing that as I give, I activate the law of seedtime and harvest, and You will pour out Heaven's resources to meet my needs. I receive Your provision today because You are faithful. I pray this in Jesus' name!

But my God shall supply all your need according to his riches in glory by Christ Jesus.

Philippians 4:19

My Confession for Today

I confess that I am a sacrificial giver and I have something to shout about because Philippians 4:19 is mine to claim! I qualify for God's promise to supply all of my needs according to His riches in glory by Christ Jesus. I lay hold to God's promise, and He faithfully meets my needs lavishly, abundantly, excessively, and richly! I declare this by faith in Jesus' name!

Discerning God's Plan for Your Life

But as it is written, Eye hath not seen, nor ear heard, neither have entered into the heart of man, the things which God hath prepared for them that love him. But God hath revealed them unto us by his Spirit…

1 Corinthians 2:9-10

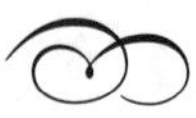

My Prayer for Today

Father, I thank You that the Holy Spirit is a Revealer of truth. He will lead and guide me into all truth and show me things to come. I thank You that I never need to worry or even wonder about what You want me to do in any area of my life. If I ask You for wisdom and open my heart to hear, the Holy Spirit will make Your will clear to me. I praise You for Your wonderful plan and for helping me fulfill my part in it for Your glory! I pray this in Jesus' name!

My Confession for Today

I confess that the Lord guides me continually by His Spirit within me. I trust in the Lord with all my heart and don't lean to my own understanding. In all my ways I acknowledge His wisdom and His presence, and He meticulously directs my steps to follow the good path He has prepared for me! I declare this by faith in Jesus' name!

Remembering Your First Love

My Prayer for Today

Father, as I evaluate my own heart, I realize that I have allowed distractions and the cares of life to dull my passion for You. Somewhere along the way, I became more focused on working for You than walking with You. I repent and turn away from the prayerlessness and hardness of heart that led me to this state. Renew a steadfast spirit within me. Restore to me the joy of Your salvation; lift me up from the place where I've fallen; and uphold me by Your generous Spirit. Teach me afresh to reverence You and to truly love You by being a doer of Your Word and not merely a hearer only. I pray this in Jesus' name!

Remember therefore from whence thou art fallen, and repent, and do the first works; or else I will come unto thee quickly, and will remove thy candlestick out of his place, except thou repent.

Revelation 2:5

My Confession for Today

I confess that I give to the Lord the glory due His name. I am His and my heart is wholly devoted and undivided in its affections. I choose the better part of being with Him above all else—that I may know Christ and become increasingly transformed into His likeness. I declare this by faith in Jesus' name!

Preaching Isn't Always Easy

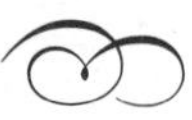

Now while Paul waited for them at Athens, his spirit was stirred in him, when he saw the city wholly given to idolatry.

Acts 17:16

My Prayer for Today

Father, I ask You to help me adjust my attitude about the difficult situation I am facing in life. I have been tempted to complain about how hard this assignment is. You have positioned me where I am for a reason. I repent for the times I have grumbled, complained, and entertained my feelings because I was relying upon my own strength instead of Your mighty power. Holy Spirit, You are my Helper and my Standby—I know that with Your power, I can do all things through Christ. From this moment onward, I ask You to help me focus my faith and confident expectation on You. Show me how to navigate my situation and my current station in life by the power of the Holy Spirit who will put me over the top every time! I pray this in Jesus' name!

My Confession for Today

I confess that I am an overcomer and can do all things through Jesus Christ. I can do whatever He calls me to do; I can go wherever He calls me to go; and I can fulfill whatever assignment He gives me because His Spirit lives within me and is empowering me! I look away from all that would distract or discourage me as I look to Jesus, the Author and Finisher of my faith! What You have called me to do, You have equipped and enabled me to do! I will not complain about the difficulties of life. Instead, I choose to take advantage of every opportunity God has given me and to make the most of every situation I encounter in life. With God's help, I can turn any difficult situation into an opportunity for advancement and victory! I declare this by faith in Jesus' name!

Never Insult Your Audience!

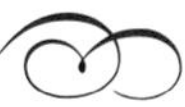

My Prayer for Today

Lord, I thank You for helping me rethink the way I am addressing people who are lost and living their lives without You. I ask You to forgive me for the times I have approached them in a condescending or a negative way, and I ask You to help me find a way to reach them that will build a permanent bridge between You and them. I pray for their hearts to be open as I share with them so I can shine the truth of Jesus into the dark recesses of their lives. You are the best at reaching all our hearts, Father, so I ask You to teach me to do this as You would do it. I pray this in Jesus' name!

Then Paul stood in the midst of Mars' hill, and said, Ye men of Athens, I perceive that in all things ye are too superstitious.

Acts 17:22

My Confession for Today

I confess that the Holy Spirit is teaching me how to reach people in a positive way with the message of Jesus Christ. I am kind, tender, sincere, and respectful in the way I speak to all people including people who are lost in sin. I declare that even though I walk by God's standards of what is right and wrong, I am not haughty or insulting to people who are different from me. With God's help, I am learning how to reach out to those who are lost and without God and to those who are sinking lower and lower into a sinful lifestyle. Because of the respect and love I show to them as humans created in the image of Almighty God, their hearts are wide open to hear the truth that God is asking me to speak into their lives. I declare this by faith in Jesus' name!

APRIL 27

Wisdom in Sharing Christ

For as I passed by, and beheld your devotions, I found an altar with this inscription, To The Unknown God. Whom therefore ye ignorantly worship, him declare I unto you.

Acts 17:23

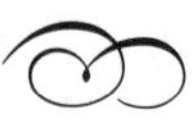

My Prayer for Today

Lord, I am so thankful that You teach me step by step how to be more effective in the way I witness and share Your love with people. You know the key to every person's heart, so I ask You to give me the key to reach into the hearts of those people You have laid on my heart. I know they are part of my assignment, and I will do whatever You ask me to do in order to reach them effectively. But I ask You to speak clearly to me. Help me understand the proper steps to take and the right things to do so their hearts will be open to receive the love You want to give them. I ask this in Jesus' name!

My Confession for Today

I confess that I am growing wiser in the ways I share Christ with unbelievers. Because I pray and seek the assistance of the Holy Spirit, He is helping me, showing me how to touch people's lives in a way that opens their hearts both to me and to the love of God that I am commissioned to bring to them. I declare by faith that God's Spirit is guiding me and teaching me how to be more effective in my methods of reaching both the unsaved and those who are in deep spiritual need. I declare this by faith in Jesus' name!

Make the Most of Every Opportunity

My Prayer for Today

Lord, I ask You to help me become more aware of special opportunities that arise for me to speak Your name and Your Word to people who have open hearts. Forgive me when I get so busy that I forget to tell others about Jesus. I realize that Jesus is the only real solution to life's problems and that I have a special responsibility to share Him with people who don't know Him yet. Holy Spirit, I can only do this if You empower me, so today I am asking You to strengthen me and grant me a new awareness when a door of opportunity stands before me. Give me the boldness to speak Jesus' name in a way that pierces the spiritual darkness and brings answers to those who are in need. I pray this in Jesus' name!

Therefore disputed he in the synagogue with the Jews, and with the devout persons, and in the market daily with them that met with him. Then certain philosophers of the Epicureans, and of the Stoicks, encountered him. And some said, What will this babbler say? other some, He seemeth to be a setter forth of strange gods: because he preached unto them Jesus, and the resurrection.

Acts 17:17-18

My Confession for Today

I declare by faith that I am bold to sow seeds of truth and love everywhere I go. I am sensitive to God-given opportunities to share the name of Jesus and the Word of God with people who are in need. Because the fruit of the Spirit is produced in my life, I think of others; I see their needs; and I look for ways to help them find the answers they need. The Holy Spirit is my Helper who is always present to assist me as I listen to Him and follow His leading. I am making the decision today to open my heart wider than ever before so God can depend on me to see and help meet the needs of others. Starting today, I am persistent and bold to walk through every open door and proclaim the name of Jesus and the Word of God to those who need to hear God's truth, just as others once did for me! I declare this by faith in Jesus' name!

APRIL 29

Strange Gods and New Ideas

Then certain philosophers of the Epicureans, and of the Stoicks, encountered him. And some said, What will this babbler say? other some, He seemeth to be a setter forth of strange gods: because he preached unto them Jesus, and the resurrection. And they took him, and brought him unto Areopagus...

Acts 17:18-19

My Prayer for Today

Lord, I am so thankful that the Holy Spirit is my Guide and Teacher. Because the Spirit of God is in my life, I am not an orphan who has to figure out everything on my own. I am willing to follow You—to do whatever You tell me to do and to go wherever You tell me to go—but I am depending completely on You to lead me, anoint me, and empower me as I take the steps of faith that are directly before me. Lord, I am willing to take the message to the people You have called me to reach. But I am asking You to show me how to most effectively package my message so they will receive the life-changing truth of the Gospel! I pray this in Jesus' name!

My Confession for Today

I confess that I am careful in what I do and what I say as I reach out to people who are lost. They don't know Jesus; therefore, I must learn to speak to them in a way that touches their hearts and souls. Holy Spirit, You are the One who knows everyone's heart, so today I declare that You are giving me the keys, the words, the methods, and the ways to reach the audience that God has put on my heart. I have the message that saves lives, and the Holy Spirit is teaching me how to package the message so it will be received and people's lives will be redeemed. I declare this by faith in Jesus' name!

Results of Paul's Preaching on Mars Hill

My Prayer for Today

Lord, I ask You to help me know exactly what I am to say, how I am to say it, and when I am to speak. Then once I have obeyed You, help me trust You with the results. I admit that I've been affected by people's reactions in the past and have allowed those reactions to influence my obedience in the present. Please forgive me for allowing people's opinions to affect me, even when I know I've done exactly what You told me to do. Help me keep my eyes on You when I step out in faith to obey the prompting of Your Spirit in my heart. I pray this in Jesus' name!

And when they heard of the resurrection of the dead, some mocked: and others said, We will hear thee again of this matter. So Paul departed from among them.

Acts 17:32-33

My Confession for Today

I confess that I am not negatively affected by people's mixed reactions when I speak the Word of God. People will always respond differently to truth; therefore, I put my trust in the Lord and keep my eyes on Him, not on the responses of people. I will do my best to speak His Word accurately, and I trust the Holy Spirit to assist me. He is my Helper, my Standby, my Assistant, and my Mentor, so I am depending on Him to teach me how to speak as I ought to speak. From this moment on, I will no longer worry or fret about the reactions of people when I do what I am instructed to do with a right heart. Instead, I will rest my case and then leave the results with the Lord. I declare this by faith in Jesus' name!

What God Thinks About You

Put on therefore, as the elect of God, holy and beloved...

Colossians 3:12

My Prayer for Today

Heavenly Father, I am in awe of Your great love toward me. Thank You that even before the foundations of the world, You looked into eternity and saw me personally. When You fastened Your gaze upon me, Your heart of love opened toward me and You deliberately chose me that I might know You. Holy Spirit, You are the treasure within my earthen vessel. Help me see myself as the Father sees me. Then empowered by the confidence of His love and favor, strengthen and guide me to walk as a continual demonstration of that love to others for the glory of Your name! I pray this in Jesus' name!

My Confession for Today

I confess that I am personally summoned by God to know Him intimately. When God sees me, His great "agape love" for me compels Him to behold me with an admiring gaze as when one beholds a treasure with awe and wonder. I am the chosen dwelling place of God's own Spirit. Therefore, I am valued greatly and esteemed highly by Him. I believe and receive God's great love for me, and today I walk in the reality of its irresistible strength and power. I am continually aware of His love for me, and for that reason, I remain secure and my faith in Him never fails! I declare this by faith in Jesus' name!

No One Is Higher!

My Prayer for Today

Lord, I acknowledge and declare that You are literally and utterly Lord over all! You reign supreme and powerful above everything and everyone that is or is to come. I worship and exalt You, Jesus. No one and nothing is equal to or greater than You! I reverence and submit to your lordship, and I resist any work of the flesh or the devil that would defy Your lordship in my life! I pray this in Jesus' name!

Far above all principality, and power, and might, and dominion, and every name that is named, not only in this world, but also in that which is to come.

Ephesians 1:21

My Confession for Today

I confess that Jesus is my Lord, and I exalt Him as Supreme Ruler over every area of my Life! Every title conferred upon Him establishes a specific victory in my life. Jesus rules as my Prince of Peace; therefore, anxiety, agitation, and fear may not dominate me. Jesus reigns as my Redeemer; therefore, sickness, poverty, oppression, or any work of the enemy may not establish any control or influence over me. I walk in truth that Jesus alone is my Lord, and this truth makes me free indeed! I declare this by faith in Jesus' name!

Under His Feet!

And hath put all things under his feet, and gave him to be the head over all things to the church.

Ephesians 1:22

My Prayer for Today

Father of glory, I thank You that when You raised Jesus from the dead, You raised me up and made me to sit down together with Him at Your own right hand. Father I honor You for the blood of Jesus Christ that purchased my salvation. Holy Spirit, teach me day by day to exalt the name of Jesus in every situation of my life, as I crush every strategy the enemy wages against me through the power of Christ's magnificent name! I pray this in Jesus' name!

My Confession for Today

I am seated together in heavenly places with Christ Jesus, far above all rule and authority and power and dominion. My life is hidden with Christ in God. I am in Christ, and by His Spirit, Jesus Christ dwells in me. He is the Head of the Church, which is His Body on the earth. Since I am a member of His Body, as He is, so am I in this earth. In every situation, I honor the Head by exercising His authority to enforce His will upon the earth. I declare this by faith in Jesus' name!

Church: His Precious Body

My Prayer for Today

Father, I thank You for saving me and calling me to be a member of Your precious Church. Help me see Your Church the way You see it—anointed, precious, and powerful. I ask You to help me be faithful in the church where You have planted me so that I will flourish as I use my gifts and talents there and do all I can to be a positive contributing member. In conjunction with everyone else in our church, I ask You to help us be an expression of Your voice that affects the city where I live. I pray this in Jesus' name!

But if I tarry long, that thou mayest know how thou oughtest to behave thyself in the house of God, which is the church of the living God, the pillar and ground of the truth.

1 Timothy 3:15

My Confession for Today

I confess that I love the church where God has called me. I use my gifts and talents to help in the various ministries and departments of the church. I give my tithes and offerings there, as God commands me to do in His Word. I pray for my pastor and listen carefully as he preaches what he believes God has to say to us each week. When he looks for someone on whom he can depend, my pastor knows that I am one he can turn to rely upon. I declare that our church is growing, is getting stronger and stronger, and that we are becoming a greater light to our city. I declare this by faith in Jesus' name!

The Ultimate Sign of Jesus' Return

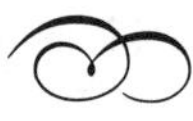

For nation shall rise against nation, and kingdom against kingdom: and there shall be famines, and pestilences, and earthquakes, in divers places. All these are the beginning of sorrows.

Matthew 24:7-8

My Prayer for Today

Father, I thank You for the privilege of contributing toward the spread of the Gospel across the earth. I ask You to help me always put first things first. Help me focus on Heaven's priorities—souls—so that I will not become distracted by the cares of this life or the pressures and anxieties of this age. Teach me how to prepare for the difficult times to come without slipping into self-preservation. I submit myself to You, Father, and I resist the spirit of fear. As I receive Your wisdom and grace, I follow the Holy Spirit's guidance to do my part in building the Kingdom of God and hastening Christ's return. I pray this in Jesus' name!

My Confession for Today

I consistently sow financial seed into the work of preaching Jesus Christ among the nations. I strengthen the work of missionary outreaches throughout the earth through my participation in prayer and offerings. As I do my part to spread the Gospel, I am helping to hasten His return. I remain focused without distraction—and bold without fear—to occupy until He comes. I declare this by faith in Jesus' name!

Looks Can Be Deceiving!

My Prayer for Today

Lord, I admit that I've judged others by what they look like externally, and today I am asking You to forgive me. I'm sure that others have thought they could figure me out by what they see, yet have missed it many times. Please help me do all I can to improve my outward appearance, but help me remember that I carry Your power and the revelation of Your Word inside me and that there is more to me than meets the eye! I pray this in Jesus' name!

Do ye look on things after the outward appearance?...

2 Corinthians 10:7

My Confession for Today

I confess that I am the temple of the Holy Spirit and that the power and the life of God live inside me. I carry within me the authority of the name of Jesus; my voice is an instrument that speaks life; and I am filled with divine treasures. Just as I do not want others to judge me by my external appearance, I will no longer judge others only by what my eyes see. From this moment forward, I will remember and live by the truth that there is more than meets the eye in me and in those whom I meet. I declare this by faith in Jesus' name!

What Does Diligence Look Like?

...he is a rewarder of them that diligently seek him.

Hebrews 11:6

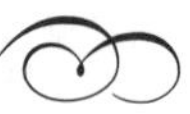

My Prayer for Today

Father, I realize that I can apply more concentrated effort in my pursuit of You and Your will for my life. Thank You, Lord, for revealing to me the areas where I need to make adjustments and how I need to make them. I ask You for clearer revelation of my life's assignment so I can walk with greater focus and commitment to fulfill that purpose—whatever may be required. Holy Spirit, I ask for and receive Your help to apply diligence and all that it entails. Strengthen me in my inner self to lay aside slothfulness in every area of my life so that I can experience the reward of those who devote themselves to seek Your will with all diligence. I receive fresh grace from you now, in Jesus' name!

My Confession for Today

I choose to live diligently, and I refuse to live like a slug! I am zealous and persistent in my pursuit of God's plan for my life. Instead of being fickle, flighty, or erratic, I am hardworking, attentive, busy, and constant! I give earnest attention to being a consistent doer of the Word of God. As a result, my mind is continually being renewed, and my thoughts are conformed to be in agreement with God's will. I inspect and evaluate my ways on a regular basis. As I do this, I am quick to make any adjustments necessary in order to persevere in the fulfillment of God's will for my life. I declare this by faith in Jesus' name!

Sin and Its Creeping Effect

My Prayer for Today

Father, I hear what You are saying to me, and I take this responsibility deep into my heart. You have called me to be the guardian and sentinel of my life and to retain this vigilant position until the end of my spiritual journey. Forgive me for times when I have been spiritually slack. I pray for the Holy Spirit to empower me to remain alert and wide awake and to stay on track—completely unresponsive to and unaffected by sin and its creeping effects that are in the world. Regardless of what the world and society may say or do, I thank You for Your continual supply of supernatural strength to draw upon, Father, to keep myself from sin and to live my life according to Your Word. I pray this in Jesus' name!

Little children, keep yourselves from idols. Amen.

1 John 5:21

My Confession for Today

I confess that I am dedicated to obeying the Word of God and that I do not allow society or the world around me to dictate what is right or wrong. Sin is looking for a way to creep back into my life—and into the lives of all believers—but I have determined that I will remain on guard, as a sentinel of my life. God expects this of me and will hold me responsible for keeping my life free from the contaminant of sin and its creeping effects. With the help of the Holy Spirit, I will walk with God in a manner that is pleasing to Him and that is free of the sinful influence of the world. I declare this by faith in Jesus' name!

MAY 9

The Right Place at the Right Time

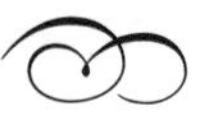

For as many as are led by the Spirit of God, they are the sons of God.

Romans 8:14

My Prayer for Today

Lord, as I reflect on my life, I can see how You have led me at times when I didn't understand that I was even being led. You put me exactly where I needed to be. You surrounded me with the people who were essential for my training and preparation. I am so thankful that I allowed You to show me what to do and that You gave me the courage to obey. I ask that You reignite that willingness and courage in me right now as I follow Your leading again and again. I receive Your wisdom and strength to do Heaven's work upon the earth. I believe that You are doing everything to develop the gifts and callings in my life so that I can fulfill my divine mandate. I pray this in Jesus' name!

My Confession for Today

I thankfully confess that God leads me even when I don't understand that I'm being led. He puts me exactly where I need to be and surrounds me with the people that are essential for my training and preparation. God's Spirit shows me what to do. He gives me courage to obey. And right now, He is reigniting that willingness and courage in me as I follow His leading again. He is doing everything to develop the gifts and callings in my life so I can fulfill my divine mandate! I declare this by faith in Jesus' name!

Perilous Times Shall Come

My Prayer for Today

Father, I thank You for choosing me to live in the last days when prophecies are being fulfilled before my very eyes. I ask You to help me keep a soft heart and not become hardened when others around me grow cold and hardened through the deceitfulness of this age. People everywhere need freedom, and deliverance from the torment of fear and pain. Instead of retreating into self-preservation mode, I will deliberately yield to Your heart for the hurting world that is all around me. Your love is shed abroad in my heart by the Holy Spirit who was given to me. Therefore, I give place to Your love within me to see them with Your eyes, to feel for them as You feel for them. I hear and respond to Your call that is beckoning me to step forward with the authority of Jesus to make a difference in the lives of everyone near to me. I pray this in Jesus' name!

This know also, that in the last days perilous times shall come.

2 Timothy 3:1

My Confession for Today

I declare by faith that I am anointed by God to live in this day and age! I am alive today for a purpose. God has chosen me to be part of this special generation so that I can shine His glory and power into the darkness that exists in so many places and in so many people's lives. I will not allow fear to paralyze or intimidate me. Instead, I will allow God's goodness, power, and love to operate in me for the freedom, deliverance, safety, and preservation of those who are near me. I am fully equipped by the Holy Spirit to glorify God without compromise in these difficult times. God is depending on me to do my part to bring His authority, His peace, His rule, and His reign into every place where Satan wants to create hurt, harm, hazard, and fear. Jesus commanded me to occupy until He comes. Therefore, I choose to establish His Kingdom and to enforce His will on the earth as it is in Heaven! I declare this by faith in Jesus' name!

MAY 11

Living in the Last Days

This know also, that in the last days perilous times shall come.

2 Timothy 3:1

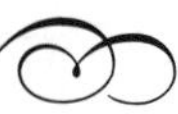

My Prayer for Today

Father, I recognize that I am living in the last of the last days. Your Word gives me a clear description of the end times and the characteristics that will be evident. Help me live more soberly than ever before with a constant awareness of eternity. Show me day by day how to fulfill my responsibility not only to pray for people to awaken to righteousness, but also to spread the Gospel to the uttermost parts of the earth, starting with those nearest to me now. I ask You, Father, to give me a spirit of boldness to speak and live without compromise. Jesus is coming, and soon everything will change forever. Help me to be prepared and to prepare others also. I pray this in Jesus' name!

My Confession for Today

I confess that I live soberly in this hour. I set my affections on things that are eternal as I seek first the Kingdom of God and pursue His ways. I do not allow myself to become entangled in low-level living or distracted by the cares of this life. I give myself to prayer, to the study of God's Word, and to a lifestyle that honors God and blesses people. I keep myself in the love of God so that I remain strong in faith to please God in all things. I declare this by faith in Jesus' name!

Signs of the Last Days—A Self-Absorbed, Self-Consumed Society

For men shall be lovers of their own selves, covetous, boasters, proud, blasphemers...

2 Timothy 3:2

My Prayer for Today

Father, I ask You to help me keep my heart free from materialism and to keep the Gospel as the greatest and highest priority in my life. I know that You want me to be blessed and to be financially and materially increased, but I don't want to set my heart on riches and fall into the trap of this lost world in these last days. Help me stay focused on souls—what You love most—and to do my part to help establish Your covenant in every part of the earth. With the help of the Holy Spirit, I know I can maintain the godly balance You desire for my life regarding possessions and finances. I pray this in Jesus' name!

My Confession for Today

I am sensitive to the Spirit of God in regard to money, materialism, and riches. God wants to massively bless me, but He also wants me to make Him and the preaching of the Gospel worldwide the greatest priority in my life. Jesus gave His life for souls—and I must give my all to help see that those souls hear the Good News. Therefore, I will walk in balance in regard to money and possessions. I will pursue the things I know the Lord wants me to have, but I will not overstep and become so self-absorbed that I ignore the souls that need to know about the saving knowledge of Jesus. I refuse to be self-consumed, so I make the willful decision to let the Holy Spirit rule this area of my life. I declare this by faith in Jesus' name!

More Signs of the Last Days–Situational Ethics, Disrespect for Parents

For men shall be lovers of their own selves, covetous, boasters, proud, blasphemers, disobedient to parents, unthankful, unholy.

2 Timothy 3:2

My Prayer for Today

Lord, I am deeply moved by the accuracy of Your Word and Your long-planned desire to prepare us in advance for the developments that are happening in the world around us today. Because Your Word is so clear, I know exactly what I need to do to protect my heart, safeguard my home, and keep Your law alive and fresh in my mind. Holy Spirit, I ask You to help me stay free from the distorted reasoning of the world and to stay on fire with the love of God. And I sincerely ask You to help me reach out to those who have been affected by the deceived thinking of the world those whose lives have been made shambles as a result of no moral law. So today I surrender my life to be Your helping hand to this hurting world around me. I pray this in Jesus' name!

My Confession for Today

I boldly declare that regardless of what the world or society says, I will live my life according to the law of God. The world does not dictate my moral code because I am a child of God. When the world around me mocks, laughs, or ridicules me for taking a stand that is contrary to theirs, I am empowered by the Spirit of God to stand strong and to remain true to my convictions. God's Word is unchanging—and just as the truth of His Word never changes, I will not change my behavior or my convictions to be like the world. Due to my conviction and godly life, I will be a beacon of hope and help to others who have been devastated by the lost immoral standards of the world. I declare this by faith in Jesus' name!

Even More Signs of the Last Days—Ungrateful, Unholy

For men shall be lovers of their own selves, covetous, boasters, proud, blasphemers, disobedient to parents, unthankful, unholy.

2 Timothy 3:2

My Prayer for Today

Father, I ask You to help me remember all the good things You have done for me! Forgive me for being so focused on what I don't have that I've overlooked what I do have. I refuse to be unthankful. Today I pause to rehearse all the good and wonderful things You have done in my life. I repent for allowing ingratitude and a lack of thankfulness to creep into my life when the list of things I have to be thankful for is so long that I don't know if I can even recall all of Your goodness. Thank You for being so good to me! I pray this in Jesus' name!

My Confession for Today

I confess that I have a grateful and thankful heart! My soul blesses the Lord, and I forget not all His benefits toward me! The world around me may forget God's goodness, but I will not be guilty of this neglect. He saved me from sin; He rescued me from myself; He delivered me from harm and destruction; He has kept me safely through all kinds of situations in life; and He has given me His Word as His promise and His Spirit to empower my life and to help keep me free from sin. He has done so much for me! I make the decision right now that my mouth is going to be filled with His praises, and thankfulness will spring forth from my heart. By recognizing Him and what He has done in my life, I will positively affect my attitude and super-charge my environment with the Spirit of God! I declare this by faith in Jesus' name!

Signs of the Last Days–Breakdown of Family Relationships

Without natural affection, trucebreakers, false accusers, incontinent, fierce, despisers of those that are good.

2 Timothy 3:3

My Prayer for Today

Lord, I am so glad that You saved me and delivered me from the destruction that is at work in the lost world today. When I read your Word and watch what is happening in the world around me, I see how carefully You tried to warn us of these things and to prepare us to live victoriously in them. How can I ever thank You enough for so carefully revealing the future and the truth to those of us who love You and Your Word? Now that I really see what a pivotal time this is, I ask You to help me live each day wisely and not to waste a minute. And please teach me to take advantage of each opportunity when I can tell the Good News of Jesus' saving grace to people who are lost and in need of Him. I pray this in Jesus' name!

My Confession for Today

I boldly confess that the Holy Spirit lives in me. Therefore, I am more than enough to face the challenges of living in these last days. It is no accident that I am alive right now. God chose me for this time; He needs me on the earth. I am anointed to break burdens, to destroy the yoke of bondage in people's lives, and to manifest the glory of God to all those who are around me. Thank You, Lord, for allowing me to see the end of the ages that the prophets saw by faith. I purpose to obey the Word of God, walk in obedience to the Holy Spirit, and see the glory of God manifested in my life. I declare this by faith in Jesus' name!

Signs of the Last Days—Confusion Between Right and Wrong

Without natural affection, trucebreakers, false accusers, incontinent, fierce, despisers of those that are good.

2 Timothy 3:3

My Prayer for Today

Father, I ask You to give me a heart for people who have been victimized by the floating moral standard that is trying to dictate what is right and wrong in the world today. Because they listened to the advice of the world, so many people have made decisions they later regretted—decisions that hurt their hearts and wounded their souls. Help me not to condemn them for past mistakes, but to assist them in receiving forgiveness, hope, and healing. I know that You stand with arms wide open to anyone who comes to You. I want to have the same heart and mind that You have, so help me be a beacon of help and hope to people who are looking for answers in these last days. I pray this in Jesus' name!

My Confession for Today

I confess that I will base my life on the Word of God, and I refuse to be led by the loose ethical standards that are in the world today. As a child of God and a member of God's Kingdom, I live by a superior law and higher standard. I have made the choice that God's Word will be a lamp to my feet and a light to my path that I may not sin against God. Because the Holy Spirit lives within me, He will help me to walk in the paths of righteousness even in the midst of a world that is headed in a wrong direction. With His help and power, I can always do what is right and make correct choices for my life. I declare this by faith in Jesus' name!

Signs of the Last Days—Widespread Violence

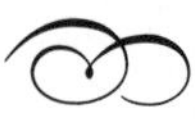

This know also, that in the last days perilous times shall come. For men shall be lovers of their own selves, covetous, boasters, proud, blasphemers, disobedient to parents, unthankful, unholy ...Traitors, heady, highminded, lovers of pleasures more than lovers of God.

2 Timothy 3:1-2,4

My Prayer for Today

Father, I am deeply convicted by what I have read today. I admit that I have allowed myself to watch movies and listen to messages that are detrimental to my relationship with You. I didn't mean to do wrong, but now I understand how damaging it is to permit wrong images to enter my soul. Holy Spirit, I am sure that I have grieved You by watching wrong images and listening to words and messages that You find foul, so today I repent. I ask You to please forgive me for grieving You, and I ask You to help restore my soul from any desensitizing effect that these things have had on me. I don't want to be like Lot who became desensitized by the things he saw and heard, so I am asking You to help me do what is right and to turn away from all contaminating influences that have the power to negatively affect my spirit and soul. I pray this in Jesus' name!

My Confession for Today

I confess that I acknowledge my responsibility to watch over my own soul, and I will not permit the filth of this world or the violence so accepted in society today to tarnish God's work in my life. God wants my spirit to be sensitive, tender, and compassionate, but the constant images of violence dulls that sensitivity. Therefore I make the decision to turn off and walk away from any bombardment of images and sounds that will affect the spiritual sensitivity I need to be effective in this world for Jesus Christ. With the help of the Holy Spirit, I will do everything I can to make sure that no vile thing enters my eyes or my ears! I declare this by faith in Jesus' name!

Signs of the Last Days—Lovers of Pleasure More Than Lovers of God

Traitors, heady, highminded, lovers of pleasures more than lovers of God.

2 Timothy 3:4

My Prayer for Today

Father, it is very clear that self-centered living does not produce happiness. As believers in Jesus Christ, we have been commanded to live according to the law of love—and love does not seek its own. Father, I repent right now for each time I have been more focused on doing what resulted in convenience for me rather than doing what produced obedience to You. Today I make a fresh commitment to deny myself, to pick up my cross, and to follow Jesus Christ as my Lord and example in all things. Holy Spirit, I ask You to open the eyes of my understanding and teach me to how to truly seek first Your Kingdom and not my comfort, to pursue Your holy ways instead of temporal pleasures. I pray this in Jesus' name!

My Confession for Today

I declare that nothing may surpass my devotion, respect, and service to God. I purpose in my heart that my thoughts and actions will reflect a sanctified heart that desires to please God rather than to gratify self-indulgent preferences for personal comfort or gain. I choose to be conformed to Jesus Christ and not to the culture of the world around me. I put first things first and establish my priorities based on what will honor God, build His Kingdom, strengthen His Church, and ransom lost souls for whom Christ died. I declare this by faith in Jesus' name!

MAY 19

Comfort and Edify One Another

Wherefore comfort yourselves together, and edify one another...

1 Thessalonians 5:11

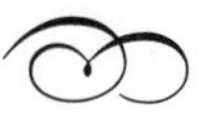

My Prayer for Today

Father, I thank You for the way You have often comforted me through encouragement from people you placed in my life at just the right time. Lord, You are the Father of mercies and the God of all comfort. I ask You to speak words of life and strength through me to the weary who come across my path. Holy Spirit, You are the Comforter. I yield to Your power and presence within me to bring deliberate and specific support to those who are in the middle of a battle or great trial. You know what they need—whether comforting words or silent support. I make myself available to You, Holy Spirit. Let my words be Your words—so full of wisdom and grace that they minister grace to people in their times of need. Make me an instrument of Your peace and comfort, that I may comfort others the way You faithfully comforted me when I needed it the most. I pray this in Jesus' name!

My Confession for Today

I declare that my actions and words encourage and build people up. What I say and the way I live will advance, enhance, and improve the lives of others in some way. I put deliberate, well- thought-out effort into making other people's lives richer, fuller, and better. I look for ways to cheer them up or give them some kind of boost. I appreciate when I can accidentally be a blessing, but I purpose to deliberately and consistently be a blessing to every life I have the privilege to reach to the glory of God. I declare this by faith in Jesus' name!

Impartation!

My Prayer for Today

Father, I ask You to flood me to overflowing with Your Spirit. When people are in my presence, I pray that they will become more deeply aware of You and Your nearness. Let Your life and kindness be expressed through me in such a way that people receive a supernatural impartation and spiritual blessing that will cover and penetrate their hearts and lives with Your wisdom, goodness, and love. I pray this in Jesus' name!

For I long to see you, that I may impart unto you some spiritual gift…

Romans 1:11

My Confession for Today

I confess that I walk in communion with the Holy Spirit daily. When people are in my presence, they are enveloped by the life of God that flows through me by His Spirit within me. The fragrance of Heaven overflows through my life so that when I am with others, the peace and love of God rests upon them and takes them to a higher place in Him. I declare this by faith!

May 21

When God Calls You, He Also Equips You

Being confident of this very thing, that he which hath begun a good work in you will perform it until the day of Jesus Christ.

Philippians 1:6

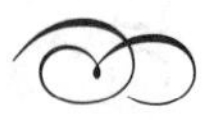

My Prayer for Today

Father, I am so thankful that since You have called me, You will also equip me for the task in front of me. You never call anyone that You do not also equip to do the job. Help me have an open heart so I'll know where and with whom I need to be in order to be in the environment that will prepare me for the next phase of my life. Help me see where I am right now with spiritual eyes and to hear with spiritual ears so I can receive the maximum preparation You want to provide for me. I know that Your hand is guiding me. And even if You lead me to places with unfamiliar faces, I know You are doing what is necessary to get me ready for the next God-ordained phase of my life. I pray this in Jesus' name!

My Confession for Today

I confess that I respond to God's call on my life and I cooperate with how He is equipping me for the task ahead of me. I know that God never calls anyone whom He does not also equip to do the job. My heart is open to follow the leading of the Holy Spirit. God's hand is guiding me, and He is doing what is necessary to get me ready for the path that lies ahead! Therefore, I will be at the right place, at the right time, with the right people, in an environment that will prepare me for the next phase of my life. My spiritual eyes and spiritual ears are attuned to the Spirit so I can receive the maximum preparation that God wants to provide for me. I declare this by faith in Jesus' name!

Take Off Your Old Clothes

My Prayer for Today

That ye put off concerning the former conversation the old man...

Ephesians 4:22

Father, as I conduct an inventory of my spiritual wardrobe, I realize that I've not always walked about clothed in Christ. I've worn mismatched attitudes that are too small because they have nothing to do with my identity in Christ and do not reflect Your greatness in any way. Lord, I repent for the times I've displayed myself haughtily in garments of self-righteousness, which are equal to filthy rags before You. Your work in my life has also exposed attitudes and beliefs that are out-of-date because You've opened my understanding. Reveal to me trait by trait what needs to stay and what needs to go. I open wide the door of my heart, and I ask You, Holy Spirit, to direct my attention to remove the attitudes or actions I've held on to that no longer fit who I have become in Jesus. I submit to Your work in my life, and I put on Christ so that every part of me is practically and effectively hidden in Christ in God. I pray this in Jesus' name!

My Confession for Today

I confess that I am a new creation in Christ Jesus. I have put off the old attributes of the flesh—anger, wrath, malice, blasphemy, filthy communication—and I put on the new attributes that are compatible with who I have become in Jesus Christ. Clothed in Christ, I wear peace, patience, kindness, faithfulness, and self-control as my garments. I regularly inspect my spiritual wardrobe to verify that I am no longer holding on to attitudes and actions that do not serve God's purposes in my life. I will not fall short of the grace of God by clinging to old patterns and mindsets that keep me dangling on the verge of victory but not moving into lasting change. I will strip off, lay aside, and discard anything that is a hindrance to my walking in all God has planned for me! I declare this by faith in Jesus' name!

A New Set of Clothes!

And that ye put on the new man...

Ephesians 4:24

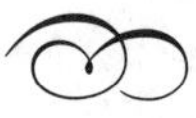

My Prayer for Today

Father, You are an amazing Designer! You have decorated and adorned all Your creation in stunning array! But nothing compares with the way You adorned Your children when You clothed us with Your own righteousness to showcase the beauty of Your holiness in a glorious display. I honor You, Father, by putting on the garments that Jesus died to provide for me. And I thank You that because of what Jesus has done, when I put on Christ, people will see and recognize Your goodness each time they look at me. I pray this in Jesus' name!

My Confession for Today

I confess that I am a new creation in Christ Jesus. I have laid aside the old clothes of my former way of thinking and acting, and I have put on the new wardrobe prepared for me as a partaker of God's own nature. For my permanent new set of clothing, I put on mercy, kindness, humility of mind, gentleness, patience, and forgiveness. This new wardrobe will never wear out, and it will always be in style with God's best. Thank You, Lord, for clothing me with dignity and strength, and for making my way perfect as I put on your character like a garment of glory. I declare this by faith in Jesus' name!

Diversity in the Church

My Prayer for Today

Dear heavenly Father, You are so wise. You have placed every member in the body as it pleases You. According to Your divine plan, our differences are designed to complement and complete each other. Thank You for the relationships you have given me that are like iron sharpening iron. Holy Spirit, I receive Your wisdom and counsel on how to interact with others who are completely unlike me—and how not to allow differences in people to divide and separate me from them. Instead, I choose to yield to Your work by the Holy Spirit to allow our differences to produce a sanctifying experience in my life to conform me into the image of Christ for Your glory. I ask this in Jesus' name!

And the eye cannot say unto the hand, I have no need of thee: nor again the head to the feet, I have no need of you.

1 Corinthians 12:21

My Confession for Today

I confess that I am positioned in the Body of Christ according to divine design. God is working through my unique gifts, talents, experiences, and personality to make me a blessing to people and to His Kingdom. I will not evaluate others for not thinking or acting in a way that I would prefer. The only standard of measure is the Word of God. Upon that common foundation, God Himself is building His Body with great diversity and distinction. Instead of comparing myself with others, which is not wise, I will develop the fruit of godly character and diligently apply my efforts to increasing in understanding and skillfulness in all I do so that I can be a valuable member in the Body of Christ. I declare this by faith in Jesus' name!

Your Heart, Christ's Home

That Christ may dwell in your hearts by faith; that ye, being rooted and grounded in love.

Ephesians 3:17

My Prayer for Today

Heavenly Father, I am so grateful that by Your great love and kindness, in Christ I am Your temple, Your sanctuary. Your Spirit has His permanent dwelling in me individually and in Your Church collectively. From this day forward, I will make it a practice to remind myself that Christ in me is my hope of Glory. As Your permanent dwelling place, I know I carry You into every situation I face, so I thank You that You empower me to walk honorably in all I do to the glory of Jesus Christ. I pray this in Jesus' name!

My Confession for Today

I confess that when the shifting tides of life threaten to unnerve me, I remain stable and unmoved because I am anchored in the solid Rock, the Lord Jesus Christ. He is my permanent stability and my true foundation; therefore, my steps do not slide. The name of the Lord is my strong tower and my shelter. My life is hidden in Christ in God. And not only do I abide in Him, but He also dwells in me! I am the living temple of the Most High God. He has chosen to make my heart HIS permanent dwelling place. Knowing that He will never leave me or forsake me, I boldly proclaim: Victory is mine because greater is He who is in me than he that is in this world! I declare this by faith in Jesus' name!

Faith Stands Still!

My Prayer for Today

Father, I repent for the times I have made a declaration of sincere faith, but then allowed myself to waver because of something I saw or felt. I acknowledge that such vacillating is to be double- minded, and the double-minded person will not receive anything from the Lord. I acknowledge that without faith it is impossible to please You. And I choose to please You, Father! Therefore, because I believe that You reward those who diligently seek You, I purpose in my heart to remain fixed and stable in my position of faith until Your reward is fully manifested in my life. I pray this in Jesus' name!

But let him ask in faith, nothing wavering. For he that wavereth is like a wave of the sea driven with the wind and tossed.

James 1:6

My Confession for Today

I confess that this is IT—today I focus, and I boldly REFUSE to move from my stance in faith! I let patience have its perfect work, and I do not vacillate! I am not tossed like a wave to and fro, but I stand firm in one spot—fixed, immovable, and determined. I am confident that I will see what I have believed because my faith is based upon God's Word, and His Word is His will. Therefore, this day I confess that the will of God shall be manifested in my life! I declare this by faith in Jesus' name!

The Importance of Honesty in Relationships

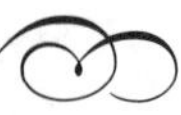

Wherefore putting away lying, speak every man truth with his neighbour: for we are members one of another.

Ephesians 4:25

My Prayer for Today

Father, I thank You for the Holy Spirit whom Jesus sent to help me in this life. He is the Spirit of Truth who alone can lead and guide me into all truth. I receive His counsel and help to open the eyes of my understanding and grant me revelation knowledge as I search my own heart in the light of Your Word. Help me discern the areas where I have become dishonest in my relationships in an attempt to deal with hurts and disappointments. I believe that I receive Your help today as I purpose to change! I pray this in Jesus' name!

My Confession for Today

Today I choose to yield to the love of God that is shed abroad in my heart so I can forgive and move forward with integrity and in truth. I recognize the importance of maintaining honesty in my relationships—and that it starts by first being honest with myself. I receive the help of the Holy Spirit, who teaches me how to speak the truth in love so that I may walk with integrity and that I may honor my Lord Jesus in all areas and relationships in my life. I declare this by faith in Jesus' name!

Don't Inflate the Truth About Yourself!

My Prayer for Today

Heavenly Father, I repent for the times I have sought to impress people by inflating the facts rather than seeking to please You by simply telling the truth. To exaggerate my abilities or accomplishments is utterly foolish since people usually see right through it! I realize now that if I engage in self-aggrandizement, not only am I deceiving myself, but I am also attempting to manipulate others by controlling their perception of me through a lie. That is not the way I want to live! I now see that to blow things out of proportion in order to exalt myself before others is actually a symptom of fear, not confidence—and fear brings a snare. Holy Spirit, I ask You to forgive me for the times I've grieved You by exalting myself instead of exalting Jesus. I ask You to set a watch over my lips as I commit to place my hand on my mouth and to give all glory to the Lord Jesus Christ alone! I pray this in Jesus' name!

If thou hast done foolishly in lifting up thyself...lay thine hand upon thy mouth.

Proverbs 30:32

My Confession for Today

I confess that I choose to resist the temptation to exaggerate the truth and embellish the facts in an attempt to make myself seem more important or accomplished than I am. To safeguard against foolish speaking, I will put my hand over my mouth. I am complete in Christ, and my sense of security in Him continually increases as my identity in Him becomes more and more established. I declare this by faith in Jesus' name!

A Supernatural Answer To Prayer!

Again I say unto you, That if two of you shall agree on earth as touching any thing that they shall ask, it shall be done for them of my Father which is in heaven.

Matthew 18:19

My Prayer for Today

Heavenly Father, I thank You for the tremendous power You have enabled us to tap into through unified prayer. When we come together in agreement with faith in Your Word, I am grateful that You not only hear us when we pray in accordance with Your will, but You also answer to perform Your will and purposes in our lives. It pleases and honors You when Your people take advantage of this powerful type of prayer that enables our spirits to harmonize in faith as we come before Your throne of grace (Hebrews 11:6; Matthew 18:19) with each one of us adding our parts. Father, You have instructed us to pray with all manner of prayer (Ephesians 6:18). I will, therefore, pay attention to engage this type of prayer with another believer when dilemmas arise so that Your power can be released. I pray this in Jesus' name!

My Confession for Today

I confess that I deeply touch the heart of my heavenly Father when I create a harmonious sound of faith by entering into faith-filled agreement with another believer in prayer. I do not fear when difficulties suddenly appear. Instead, I tap the power of agreement in prayer! As each of us add our part in a harmonious symphony of unified prayer, our agreement with God's Word and with one another releases the supernatural power of God in our behalf. I declare this by faith in Jesus' name!

Use Every Possibility To Escape!

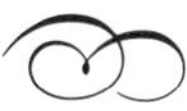

My Prayer for Today

Dear heavenly Father, I come before You right now and repent for having given place to the devil because of hurt and offense. I see now that the enemy set a trap for me to fall into temptation. I also ask You to forgive me for judging the faults and failings of others, when in fact my own impatience and carnality were on full display by the way I responded to their behavior. I ask You, Holy Spirit, to open the eyes of my understanding and reveal to me the ways I need to change so I am not susceptible to unhealthy attitudes that would keep me socially isolated or emotionally immobilized. I choose to walk away from the devil's traps, and I trust You to help me escape the net of temptation. I pray this in Jesus' name!

There hath no temptation taken you but such as is common to man: but God is faithful, who will not suffer you to be tempted above that ye are able; but will with the temptation also make a way to escape, that ye may be able to bear it.

1 Corinthians 10:13

My Confession for Today

I confess that I realize no one is perfect—and neither am I! I am not ignorant of the devil's devices to destroy my relationships. Therefore, I refuse to be held hostage by crippling attitudes of negativity and disappointment when others fall short of my expectations. When I am tempted to become offended by a deliberate act of betrayal, rejection, or wrongdoing, I will look to the Holy Spirit. He is my Helper, my Strengthener, my Comforter, my Counselor, my Teacher, and my Advocate! The Holy Spirit will show me how to escape this temptation and respond according to the wisdom and the will of God. He will help me keep myself in the love of God so my faith will not fail and the devil cannot overtake me through his wiles against both me and the person who sought to do me harm. I declare this by faith in Jesus' name!

Follow After Peace

Follow peace with all men, and holiness, without which no man shall see the Lord.

Hebrews 12:14

My Prayer for Today

Heavenly Father, Your Word is very clear on how I am to respond to people who have hurt or offended me. When I am dealing with difficulties in relationships, You expect me to take the responsibility of hunting down peace and pursuing it. I ask You to show me what path I am to take in this pursuit so that I can please You by walking in the high level of love You have already shed abroad in my heart by the Holy Spirit who was given to me. I will not allow hurt, bitterness, or resentment to separate me from Your immediate presence. I receive Your help, Holy Spirit, to maintain a pure heart so that not only can I see God, but also so that I can see others as He sees them. I pray this in Jesus' name!

My Confession for Today

I confess that because the Holy Spirit lives in me, I have the power I need to walk in forgiveness on a much higher level than the world. The Holy Spirit gives me the power to walk in freedom from the bondage of bitterness and strife. God requires me to follow after peace—to hunt it, seek it, and pursue it—with all people. Therefore, because I am required to do it, I am equipped to do it. I yield to the Holy Spirit, and I walk in holiness and in consecration to God and His ways. I deliberately separate myself from ungodly attitudes and actions because I refuse to be separated from the presence of God. I declare this by faith in Jesus' name!

Jesus and the Holy Spirit

My Prayer for Today

Father, my heart yearns to know the Person of the Holy Spirit more deeply and to experience His power personally. I ask You to reveal truths and grant me understanding so I can cooperate with and respond to the Holy Spirit's ministry in my life. Father, I desire to walk in the spiritual depth and fullness that Jesus made available to me when He prayed in John 14 that You would send the Helper, the Holy Spirit, to indwell me. I ask You to open the door for me to embark on a spiritual path that I've never been on before. I know that this is Your will for me, so today I come before Your throne boldly and confidently to receive this with gratitude and joy! I pray this prayer in Jesus' name!

He that believeth on me, as the scripture hath said, out of his belly shall flow rivers of living water. (But this spake he of the Spirit, which they that believe on him should receive: for the Holy Ghost was not yet given; because that Jesus was not yet glorified.)

John 7:38-39

My Confession for Today

I confess that it is God's will for me to know the Person, power, and work of the Holy Spirit. In John 14, 15, and 16, Jesus taught explicitly about the Holy Spirit so that every believer could learn about the Spirit of God and knowledgeably respond to and experience His power. I recognize that this is why Jesus taught so much about the Holy Spirit's ministry in those three chapters. Therefore, I boldly declare that I will act on the truths I learn in the days to come about the Holy Spirit and His work in my life. I choose to cooperate with God as I embark on a new, deeper, and higher walk with God's Spirit than I've ever known before in my life. I declare this by faith in Jesus' name!

JUNE 2

Jesus' Teaching in the Upper Room

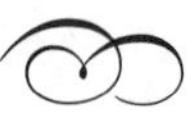

I will not leave you comfortless: I will come to you.

John 14:18

My Prayer for Today

Holy Spirit, I want to begin enjoying fellowship with You. Since Jesus depended on You, I know that I need to depend on You too. So right now, more than ever before, I express my inner yearning to begin a new and deeper journey in learning how to have fellowship with You. I want to know You; I want to know Your power; and I ask You to come alongside and help me as Jesus said You would do! I pray this in Jesus' name!

My Confession for Today

I acknowledge that because I am a child of God, the Holy Spirit lives inside me as a continual Resident. He longs to have fellowship with me and to reveal the depths of Jesus' love to my heart. I repent for the times that I have ignored Him and treated Him as an unrecognized Resident. From this moment onward, I confess that I will live with an awareness of His presence and that I will embrace the wonderful ministry that He has come to provide for my life. I declare this by faith in Jesus' name!

Jesus' Prayer

My Prayer for Today

Holy Spirit, I admit that I have often neglected to acknowledge Your presence in my life. I repent, and I ask You to please forgive me. It's not that I've tried to ignore You; I have just been ignorant of Your role in my life and how deeply I have needed Your fellowship. I confess that I've even had fears about opening my heart more deeply to You because of things I've seen and heard others do that seemed a little strange. Forgive me for being closed to You when, in fact, I cannot live the Christian life without Your power and Your help. Right now I take the next step to invite You to move powerfully in my life. I take down all the guards, and I decide to trust You to bring Jesus closer to me. I pray this in Jesus' name!

And I will pray the Father, and he shall give you another Comforter, that he may abide with you for ever.

John 14:16

My Confession for Today

I declare that the Holy Spirit works mightily in my life. I am not afraid to surrender to the Holy Spirit's power. I acknowledge that I cannot successfully live the Christian life without His involvement, so I open every part of my life to Him and to His powerful workings. As a result, I am filled with spiritual power; I am supernaturally led by the Spirit of God because I am a child of God; and I am being transformed into the image of Jesus Christ. As a result of my fellowship and obedience to the Holy Spirit, my Christian life is filled with victory and adventure! I declare this by faith in Jesus' name!

Another Comforter!

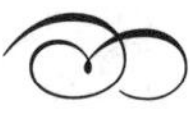

And I will pray the Father, and he shall give you another Comforter, that he may abide with you for ever.

John 14:16

My Prayer for Today

Father, I thank You for speaking to me about how the Holy Spirit perfectly represents Jesus in my life. In light of this, I ask You to help me gain more understanding regarding the four gospels and their account of the life of Jesus. I understand that if I know Jesus better from the New Testament, it will help me become more familiar with the way the Holy Spirit thinks and acts. Now I understand that Jesus and the Holy Spirit are similar in every way, so I desire to open my heart to the Holy Spirit in the same way I open my heart to Jesus. I pray this in Jesus' name!

My Confession for Today

I declare that reading the four gospels—and getting to know Jesus better through reading them—is a top priority in my life. According to what Jesus taught about the Holy Spirit, I now know that Jesus and the Holy Spirit are identical in how they think, act, and behave. Therefore, as I get to know Jesus better from the New Testament, it will prepare my heart and mind to better recognize and know the voice and promptings of the Holy Spirit in my life. I declare this by faith in Jesus' name!

The Comforter, Part 1

My Prayer for Today

Holy Spirit, I know You live inside me, but I never understood that You are also side by side with me as my Partner in life. I have treated you like an invisible Guest, when, in reality, You have been sent to me to be at my side as my Helper and Standby in times of need. Please forgive me for overlooking and ignoring You when You have been waiting so long to assist me in life. Today I throw open my arms and my heart, and I say "Welcome, Holy Spirit"—I receive You as my side-by-side Partner who has been called alongside my life! I pray this in Jesus' name!

And I will pray the Father, and he shall give you another Comforter, that he may abide with you for ever.

John 14:16

My Confession for Today

I confess that from this moment onward, I am wide open to the ministry of the Holy Spirit. Jesus sent the Spirit to be my Helper, and I certainly need His help. I will no longer ignore Him or disregard His presence in my life. I open my heart, mind, and soul to His ministry, and I will endeavor to recognize His voice, His leading, and His guidance, and I will strive to receive His supernatural help. I declare this by faith in Jesus' name!

JUNE 6

The Comforter, Part 2

And I will pray the Father, and he shall give you another Comforter, that he may abide with you for ever.

John 14:16

My Prayer for Today

Father, my eyes are being opened to the wonderful ministry of the Holy Spirit. I am shocked that I never really understood what profound help You sent to me in the Person of the Holy Spirit as my divine Partner. My heart is simply overflowing with thankfulness that You have sent the Holy Spirit into my life to assist me wherever I am and in whatever I am doing. Now I understand that He is called by YOU to be with me all the time. Please help me to be more cognizant of His presence and to honor His holiness as He comes to assist me in life! I pray this in Jesus' name!

My Confession for Today

I declare that I receive the Holy Spirit as my Partner. I choose to acknowledge Him and to cooperate with His counsel and direction. I listen to Him; I pay attention to Him; and I obediently follow when He leads or prompts me to take action. For a long time, I didn't understand the power of this gift God gave me. But now I understand, and I will honor the Holy Spirit and His role as senior Partner in my life. I declare this by faith in Jesus' name!

The Heavenly Coach

My Prayer for Today

Father, I thank You for sending the Holy Spirit to mentor, teach, advise, correct, instruct, train, tutor, guide, direct, and prepare me for my upcoming assignment. From this moment forward I am going to start thinking of the Holy Spirit as my personal Coach. I will open my spiritual ears to listen to His instruction, I will obey what He tells me to do, and I will carefully implement the instructions I hear Him speak to my heart and mind. You sent the Holy Spirit as a Coach to teach me, so I don't have to figure everything out on my own. So from this moment onward, I position myself as a pupil to the Holy Spirit, who is my divine Coach. I pray this in Jesus' name!

And I will pray the Father, and he shall give you another Comforter, that he may abide with you for ever.

John 14:16

My Confession for Today

I declare by faith that I am a willing, obedient, and teachable apprentice of the Holy Spirit! He speaks to my heart, tells me what to do or what actions to take, and I do exactly what I am told to do. My courage to obey is getting stronger by the day. As a result of listening to the Holy Spirit and taking my cues from Him, I am growing in my walk with the Lord, developing more confidence and experiencing greater victories day by day! I declare this by faith in Jesus' name!

The Spirit of Truth

And I will pray the Father, and he shall give you another Comforter, that he may abide with you for ever; even the Spirit of truth…

John 14:16-17

My Prayer for Today

Father, I confess that I have been fearful about following the leadership of the Holy Spirit. Today I admit it; I confess it; and I turn from it. I want to experience the coaching ministry of the Holy Spirit in my life. The Holy Spirit is the Spirit of truth. Therefore, I know He will never mislead me. Starting today, I choose to put aside my apprehensions and surrender to the leadership of the Holy Spirit. With Him helping me, I will begin to follow His leading and let Him guide me through life. I pray this in Jesus' name!

My Confession for Today

I confess that when the Holy Spirit inspires a thought in my mind to do something, it is right. When He nudges my spirit to do something, I can rest assured that He sees and knows something I don't know and is trying to guide and direct me according to truth. He is always the Spirit of truth and will never mislead me. I long for real, supernatural Christian living, so I confess by faith that I will surrender to the Holy Spirit. In this act of surrender, I give Him permission to be my heavenly Coach and Counselor. I declare this by faith in Jesus' name!

Learning To Follow the Leader

My Prayer for Today

Heavenly Father, I want to learn how to become a "tagalong" behind the leadership of the Holy Spirit. I know You sent the Holy Spirit to be my supernatural Coach—but that His Help is only a reality to me if I choose to obey His leading. I admit that I have often struggled with obedience, and I ask You to forgive me. I really want to obey. Today I ask You to give me the strength of will and the inward surrender of heart to trust and obey the Holy Spirit and do exactly what He is trying to lead me to do. I pray this in Jesus' name!

For as many as are led by the Spirit of God, they are the sons of God.

Romans 8:14

My Confession for Today

I declare that I am tuned in to the Spirit of God and that I boldly obey whatever He instructs me to do. Fear and lack of trust do not dictate my obedience to the Holy Spirit. He is the Spirit of truth. He will never mislead me or misguide me, and I am confident of His leadership over my life. Even when I do not understand the reasons why He is leading me in a certain way, I choose to obey Him. He is the Spirit of truth. Therefore, I am confident that He is directing me into the perfect will of God for every sphere of my life. I declare this by faith in Jesus' name!

A Different Kind of Leading

And when Jesus departed thence, two blind men followed him, crying, and saying, Thou son of David, have mercy on us. …Then touched he their eyes, saying, According to your faith be it unto you.

Matthew 9:27,29

My Prayer for Today

Father, I ask You to help me learn to be keenly sensitive to the leading of the Holy Spirit—paying attention not just to when I should take action, but also to when I should do nothing. I've never thought about the Holy Spirit leading me to do nothing, but I can see that sometimes it is not His will for me to take action because He wants to work in a different way, at a different time, or through someone else. I admit that I've often assumed I knew what the Holy Spirit wanted me to do and then acted presumptuously without even praying. Now I understand why my success rate has not been as high as I desire. Help me be like Jesus—taking action only when the Holy Spirit is leading. I pray this in Jesus' name!

My Confession for Today

I confess that I am led by the Holy Spirit and that I refuse to jump into action simply because I see something that needs to be done or because I am aware of a need that should be met. I put on the brakes; I listen; and I wait for the Holy Spirit to speak to my heart. Because I take action when He speaks to me and I do exactly what He tells me to do, I experience His supernatural power and supernatural results in my life. I confess that I will endeavor to do things the way Jesus did—doing only what He knew was being initiated by the Father and the Holy Spirit! I declare this by faith in Jesus' name!

Your Heart Is Not a Hotel!

My Prayer for Today

...for he dwelleth with you, and shall be in you.

John 14:17

Father, I thank You that the Holy Spirit is not a temporary Guest, but a permanent Resident inside my heart. Help me to remember this and to live my life in a way that honors His indwelling presence. Help me to live with the constant awareness that He is with me always. I am so thankful that He does not come and go and that He is not a fleeting relationship in my life. Help me to cultivate my fellowship with Him until I come to know Him deeply in my life on a practical level. I pray this in Jesus' name!

My Confession for Today

I acknowledge and declare that God's Spirit dwells permanently inside my heart. He will never waver or pack His bags to move to another location. My heart is not meant to be a hotel, but rather a permanent residence for the Holy Spirit. The Holy Spirit is not a temporary Guest—He has come to indwell my heart for the rest of my life! He has moved in, taken up residence, and is committed to staying with me until I am ultimately relocated to Heaven itself! I declare this by faith in Jesus' name!

JUNE 12

The Holy Spirit's Teaching Ministry

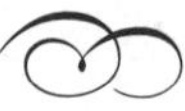

But the Comforter, which is the Holy Ghost, whom the Father will send in my name, he shall teach you all things…

John 14:26

My Prayer for Today

Lord Jesus, You said that when the Holy Spirit came, He would teach me all things I need to know. I am thankful for my pastor, my church, my books, and my various teaching materials—but there is nothing that could ever replace the teaching ministry of the Holy Spirit in my life. I admit that I've leaned on my own understanding on too many occasions, but starting today, I sincerely dedicate myself as a pupil and apprentice to the Spirit of God. I pray this in Jesus' name!

My Confession for Today

I confess that I am in need of the Holy Spirit's teaching in my life. I am thankful that I don't need to beg for it or work to earn this work of the Holy Spirit. Jesus knew I needed divine instruction, and that is one reason why He prayed for the Father to send the Holy Spirit into the world. He is my Teacher, and I am His pupil. He is the Instructor, and I am the apprentice. I am serious about learning, and I take it as my responsibility to internalize and put into practice what He teaches me through diligent study and by application of His words in my life experience. I declare this by faith in Jesus' name!

The Holy Spirit's Reminding Ministry

My Prayer for Today

Father, I am so thankful for the wonderful work of the Holy Spirit to put me in remembrance of the words and acts of Jesus Christ. I confess that there have been times when I found it difficult to remember Scripture verses, but now I understand that in times when my memory fails me, the Holy Spirit will step forward to help me remember exactly what needs to be brought to my attention. I will no longer claim a poor memory but will now embrace this special reminding ministry of the Holy Spirit! I pray this in Jesus' name!

But the Comforter, which is the Holy Ghost, whom the Father will send in my name, he shall teach you all things, and bring all things to your remembrance, whatsoever I have said unto you.

John 14:26

My Confession for Today

I confess that the Holy Spirit brings to my memory everything I need to recall about the life, words, and acts of Jesus Christ. I have the mind of Christ working in me because the Holy Spirit lives in me and is helping me. Part of His ministry is to remind me of everything that Jesus said or did, and I declare that because of the Holy Spirit's faithfulness to remind me, I recall everything I need to—on time and in every situation where it is needed. I declare this by faith in Jesus' name!

The Holy Spirit's Testifying Ministry

But when the Comforter is come, whom I will send unto you from the Father, even the Spirit of truth, which proceedeth from the Father, he shall testify of me.

John 15:26

My Prayer for Today

Lord, I admit that I am one of those who has been uneasy and fearful about witnessing in the past. I've felt so uncomfortable—afraid that I'll say the wrong thing or that someone will ask a question I can't answer. I've been controlled by fear and dread when it comes to sharing my faith with others. In fact, I've even tried to avoid it, even though I know that I am commanded to be a witness for Jesus. I realize now that all that fear, frustration, and anxiety was the result of my attempt to do Your will in my own strength without the enabling power of the Holy Spirit. Starting right now, I want to do my best to surrender to the Holy Spirit—and let Him release His testifying ability through me. Holy Spirit, You love to talk about Jesus, and You know precisely the words to speak because You hold the key to every person's heart, so speak through me to others and touch the part of their hearts that is ready to hear and receive the truth of the Gospel. I thank You, Holy Spirit, for making me an effective fisher of people! I pray this in Jesus' name!

My Confession for Today

I confess that I am NOT afraid to witness for Jesus Christ. My testimony is powerful. People want to hear it. Because the Holy Spirit is my Partner, He knows exactly how to start every conversation, how to touch each heart, and how to win each person to Jesus Christ. I do not do this on my own, but I do it in partnership with the Holy Spirit. The Holy Spirit is jubilant when it comes to the subject of Jesus, and He releases that joy-filled attitude victoriously through me as I open up and testify of Jesus to others! I receive the power of God that makes me an effective witness for Him! I declare this by faith in Jesus' name!

The Holy Spirit's Convicting Ministry

My Prayer for Today

Heavenly Father, I know Jesus Christ today because of the convicting work of the Holy Spirit. I remember when You first awakened me to my sin—a realization that had never gripped me before. But when I saw my spiritual condition, I really understood that I was lost and needed to be saved. Thank You for the convicting work of the Holy Spirit and for bringing me to a place where I could be saved. I could have never arrived there on my own, so today I want to say thank You! And I trust You to complete that work in the lives of those for whom I pray to come to a saving knowledge of You. I pray this in Jesus' name!

And when he is come, he will reprove the world of sin, and of righteousness, and of judgment.

John 16:8

My Confession for Today

I confess that the Holy Spirit is working in the lives of my family, friends, coworkers, and acquaintances to bring them to a place where they really see and understand their lost condition and need for salvation. Jesus Christ died for them, and He sent the Holy Spirit to draw them to Jesus. If the Holy Spirit prompts me to testify to them, I will do so, for the Holy Spirit knows how to touch each and every heart. I declare that they will finally hear, understand, and come to a saving knowledge of Jesus Christ because of the convicting and converting power of the Holy Spirit at work in their lives. I declare this by faith in Jesus' name!

June 16

The Holy Spirit's Convincing Ministry, Part 1

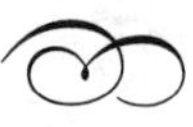

And when he is come, he will reprove the world of sin, and of righteousness, and of judgment.... Of righteousness, because I go to my Father, and ye see me no more.

John 16:8,10

My Prayer for Today

Father, I ask You to bring me to that place of realization where I really understand the righteousness that has been imparted to me through Jesus Christ. I don't want to struggle with guilt and condemnation anymore. Since Jesus was made sin for me that I could be made the righteousness of God in Him, help me to step into that place of awareness and remain there, forever free! I pray this in Jesus' name!

My Confession for Today

I declare by faith that I am the righteousness of God in Christ Jesus. I didn't earn it or deserve it, but by faith I repented, and I received righteousness as the gracious, free gift of God. I do not struggle with my past. It has no hold on me. I am, in fact, a new creature, totally new in Christ Jesus. The Holy Spirit has done His work to convince me of my right standing with God, and I am free from the past forever! I declare this by faith in Jesus' name!

The Holy Spirit's Convincing Ministry, Part 2

My Prayer for Today

Father, I thank You that Jesus conquered Satan through His death on the Cross and His resurrection and that Jesus is truly Lord over all! The ministry of the Holy Spirit in my life is a daily reminder to me of this glorious fact. Especially today, when it seems so many things are changing and it looks like evil is winning so many battles, I rely upon this special convincing ministry of the Holy Spirit that the prince of this world is judged—and from this condemnation he has no possibility of escape. Thank You, Holy Spirit, for keeping me in remembrance of the truth that Jesus is Lord now, that He is Lord tomorrow, and that He will always be Lord of all! I pray this in Jesus' name!

And when he [Holy Spirit] is come, he will reprove the world of sin, and of righteousness, and of judgment.... Of judgment, because the prince of this world is judged.

John 16:8,11

My Confession for Today

I confess that Jesus is Lord over everything in this world. When I am tempted to fear or to give sway to the bad news that is going out over the airwaves all the time, I will stand tall, throw my shoulders back, hold my head high, and boldly declare that Jesus is Lord and Satan is the loser! I declare that the decision has already been made, the court is closed, and Satan's doom is sealed. Jesus is coming back soon, and everything will change! I declare this by faith in Jesus' name!

JUNE 18

The Holy Spirit's Guiding Ministry

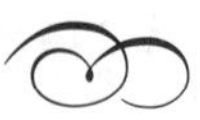

Howbeit when he, the Spirit of truth, is come, he will guide you into all truth...

John 16:13

My Prayer for Today

Holy Spirit, I open my heart to Your leading and guiding in life. I repent for foolishly having tried to lead myself through difficult decisions and questions, when you were always right there, wanting to lead me along the way. You know the plan of God for me down to the smallest detail, and from this time forward, I will do my best to consult You and to yield to Your guidance for my life. You know everything about me, my future, and which steps I need to take next. Rather than try to figure it all out on my own, I entrust myself to you as my official Guide to lead me each step of the way! I pray this in Jesus' name!

My Confession for Today

I declare by faith that I am led by the Holy Spirit. He was sent to lead and direct me, and I am learning to hear His voice, to recognize His leading, and to allow Him to be the Senior Guide in my life. I know that as a result of being guided by the Spirit, my life is going to be more adventuresome and filled with less mistakes, for the Holy Spirit is the Spirit of Truth, and He will never lead me down a wrong path. Holy Spirit, I'm ready—let's get started today! I declare this by faith in Jesus' name!

The Holy Spirit's Prophetic Ministry

My Prayer for Today

Holy Spirit, today I receive You as One who speaks into my life to show me things to come that I really need to know. I've tried hard to figure out things on my own. Forgive me for not developing my trust in You the way I should have in this area of my life. Starting right now, I ask You to fulfill the prophetic role of Your ministry in my life and to show me things to come. I know You want me to know how to plan my life, how to circumvent demonic attacks, and how to be prepared for every phase of my journey in You. Your Word promises that as I keep my spiritual ear tuned to You, You will show me exactly what I need to know about every step in front of me. I believe You and I gratefully receive Your ministry in my life day by day. I pray this in Jesus' name!

Howbeit when he, the Spirit of truth, is come, he will guide you into all truth: for he shall not speak of himself; but whatsoever he shall hear, that shall he speak: and he will shew you things to come.

John 16:13

My Confession for Today

I confess that my ears are open and that my spirit is attuned to the voice of the Holy Spirit. Jesus said that He would show me things to come, and by faith, I embrace the prophetic ministry of the Holy Spirit in my life to show me everything I need to know about my future. I am not left to figure anything out on my own. The Holy Spirit speaks to my heart about things to come. I listen to His directions, and I make plans to do what He shows me. This spares me wasted time, helps me avoid mistakes, and puts me on a solid path that leads to His highest will for my life. I declare this by faith in Jesus' name!

June 20

The Holy Spirit's Glorifying Ministry

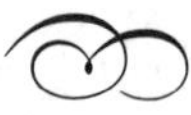

He shall glorify me: for he shall receive of mine, and shall shew it unto you.

John 16:14

My Prayer for Today

Father, I thank You that the Holy Spirit reveals Jesus—and I ask You to help me abandon my inhibitions and enter into the freedom of worship. I know that there are realms of worship that I have never experienced, but today I am opening myself to those realms and asking that the Holy Spirit unleash worship in me as never before. I surrender myself to be an instrument of worship and, Holy Spirit, I ask You to take me on an adventure as I learn to worship Jesus as You reveal Him to me on a level I've never experienced before. I pray this in Jesus' name!

My Confession for Today

I declare that my entire body—all that I am—is an instrument that the Holy Spirit uses to magnify and to exalt the name and Person of Jesus Christ. Inhibitions have no part in my worship. I am free to express my adoration and love for Jesus—the One who is higher than all others and whose name is more highly exalted than any other name. Inhibitions must go from me in Jesus' name, for I am liberated to worship Jesus in the power of the Holy Spirit! I declare this by faith in Jesus' name!

Spiritual Adultery!

My Prayer for Today

Holy Spirit, I repent and ask You to forgive me for all the times I've walked too close to the world and violated Your holy indwelling presence by allowing sinful actions and attitudes to persist in my life. I am truly sorry, and today I repent before You. I ask You to strengthen me with Your mighty power to walk with a higher discernment and with the spiritual awareness to know when I am doing something that is grievous to You. I want to honor Your presence and honor You by the way I treat You with my life. I pray this in Jesus' name!

Ye adulterers and adulteresses, know ye not that the friendship of the world is enmity with God? whosoever therefore will be a friend of the world is the enemy of God.

James 4:4

My Confession for Today

I confess that I live a life that is pleasing to the Holy Spirit. When I do something that hints of displeasure to Him, I quickly recognize it and repent of it. I do not permit wrong attitudes and actions to rule me. Instead, I surrender to the fruit of the Holy Spirit, and it produces the life and character of Christ in my own life. Day by day, I am becoming more sensitive and spiritually aware of the things that displease the Lord, and I am learning to walk a higher walk in Him. I declare this by faith in Jesus' name!

Friendship With the World

Ye adulterers and adulteresses, know ye not that the friendship of the world is enmity with God?

James 4:4

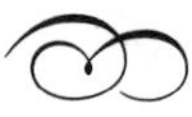

My Prayer for Today

Father, I want to burn brightly and live on fire for You. I ask You to search my heart. If worldliness has found a place in my heart and soul, today I repent of it. I turn toward You to walk in holiness and sanctification unto You. I can see how worldliness can slowly creep up on me, and I ask You to forgive me for allowing the lure of the world to affect me. It wasn't intentional. I repent for allowing myself to become distracted and for not keeping first things first. I got busy and involved, and before I knew it, I had sunk to a spiritual low that I detest. I ask You to refire me and help me return to my first love and to keep You in that position for the rest of my life. I pray this in Jesus' name!

My Confession for Today

I declare by faith that I am on fire and burning brightly for the Lord. I live in the world, but I am not a part of it. It has no lure on my heart and soul. Every day I am growing more passionate to know Christ practically, through experience for myself, and to become more fully committed to Him. Jesus Christ is the Object of my heart's desire—and I refuse to ever live the kind of life that would make Him want to say I am guilty of spiritual adultery. I declare this by faith, in Jesus' name!

Grieve Not the Holy Spirit

My Prayer for Today

Holy Spirit, I repent for the times that I have subjected You to ugliness and ungodliness that I have tolerated in my life. I am truly sorry. It is my heart's desire to honor You and Your holy presence in all I do and say. After all the wonderful things You have done in me to change me, to restore me, and to make my life better, I am so sorry that I have ever done anything that would bring pain or sorrow to You. I repent—and that means I am changing my behavior, and I am going to start right now. I pray this in Jesus' name!

And grieve not the holy Spirit of God, whereby ye are sealed unto the day of redemption.

Ephesians 4:30

My Confession for Today

I confess that I live continually aware of the Holy Spirit's indwelling presence in my life. I am very aware that He lives inside me—so much so that this realization impacts how I live each day. Choosing to deliberately give Him my attention helps me live in such a way that my life brings honor to Him. I am so thankful for my salvation and the infilling of the Holy Spirit and for the daily power He provides to me. The last thing I'd ever want to do is to bring pain and sorrow to the Holy Spirit because I tolerated ungodly attitudes or behaviors in my life. I declare that from this moment onward, I am going to live with the consciousness that the Spirit of Holiness lives in me! I declare this by faith, in Jesus' name!

JUNE 24

The Permanent Indweller of Your Heart

Do ye think that the scripture saith in vain, The spirit that dwelleth in us lusteth to envy?

James 4:5

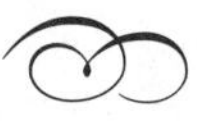

My Prayer for Today

Holy Spirit, I am so thankful that my heart is Your home! I worship You for taking up residency inside of me! The thought is almost too glorious for my mind to comprehend! I welcome Your fellowship. Teach me how to talk with You, yield to You, and cooperate with You as You pray through me, giving me guidance and direction every day. I ask You to please open my understanding to a deeper realization of Your permanent indwelling so I stay on track spiritually and continually move forward in my walk in Christ! I pray this in Jesus' name!

My Confession for Today

I am thankful to declare that the Holy Spirit is not a guest who occasionally comes to visit me. He moved into my recreated spirit to permanently abide with me. He regenerated and renovated me, and He brought His power and glory along with Him when He moved inside me. I am the permanent home for the Spirit of God. I declare this by faith in Jesus' name!

The Divine Lover

Do ye think that the scripture saith in vain, The spirit that dwelleth in us lusteth to envy?

James 4:5

My Prayer for Today

Father, I thank You that the Holy Spirit is absolutely focused on changing me, empowering me, and conforming me to the image of Jesus Christ as He helps me fulfill God's plan for my life. I am amazed by the Holy Spirit's ability to think of and concentrate on each of us all the time as He continually looks for ways to help each of us in our walk with God. I surrender every area of my life to You today, even areas I've never surrendered before. And tomorrow when You reveal other areas I need to surrender, I'll surrender those areas as well. I know the Holy Spirit wants to fully occupy my heart and my life—and I am ready to yield! I pray this in Jesus' name!

My Confession for Today

I confess that I am surrendering more and more of my life to the Holy Spirit every day I live. Every day I am seeing new areas that need to be surrendered, and with the help of the Holy Spirit and the grace of God, I am surrendering those areas. I will not stop surrendering as long as I live on this earth, because I know that every day, the Holy Spirit will show me another area I need to yield to Him. With His help, I will give Him greater access to every part of my life and being so He can have full, unhindered expression through my life to the glory of God the Father! I declare this by faith, in Jesus' name!

JUNE 26

The Holy Spirit's Desire

Do ye think that the scripture saith in vain, The spirit that dwelleth in us lusteth to envy?

James 4:5

My Prayer for Today

Holy Spirit, there is so much for me to learn about You I never knew before. Today I open my heart—as wide as I know how—and I ask You to teach me about You and Your ministry to my life. I want to be a vessel You work through, so please help me become that vessel. Jesus sent You to be with me and to indwell me. You are preoccupied with me, and You passionately and rightfully desire my affection to also be set on You. I repent for the times I allowed the cares of life or desire for other things to steal my attention and affection away from You. For each and every time I've violated my relationship with You in any way, please forgive me and know that from this day forward, I am turning toward You with my whole heart and soul. I pray this in Jesus' name!

My Confession for Today

I boldly confess that I am going to pursue a deep, intimate relationship with the Holy Spirit, and I will not stop until I've attained it. He already lives inside me, but I want to know Him and the power He continually makes available to me. I've lived my Christian life largely in my own power, but from this point forward, I want to live it fully in the power of the Holy Spirit. I declare this by faith, in Jesus' name!

Your Spiritual Interior Is Magnificent!

My Prayer for Today

Father, I thank You for the amazing work You have done inside my heart. By Your Spirit, You took my spiritually dead condition, raised me to life, and moved into my heart. My spiritual interior has been recreated and embellished so richly that You were even willing to take up residence within me. I am not a shabby shack made of dirt and sticks, but a magnificent temple that You have built for Yourself. You recreated my spirit, and then You adorned my inner self with Your revelation, holiness, splendor, righteousness, the fruit of the Spirit, the gifts of the Spirit, and the life and character of Christ Himself! Holy Spirit, help me gain a deeper revelation of what You have done inside me than I've ever had before. I pray this in Jesus' name!

What? know ye not that your body is the temple of the Holy Ghost which is in you, which ye have of God, and ye are not your own? For ye are bought with a price: therefore glorify God in your body, and in your spirit, which are God's.

1 Corinthians 6:19-20

My Confession for Today

I confess that because of the new birth, my spiritual interior has been miraculously and marvelously recreated to be a suitable residence for the indwelling presence of the Holy Spirit. I am a magnificent temple where the Holy Spirit dwells. Inside me are the power, glory, and splendor of the Holy Spirit. God's meticulous attention to detail within my inner self was so glorious and perfect that when it was all finished, He declared me to be His workmanship created in Christ Jesus. I may not see this manifested yet in my outward appearance, but inwardly this is exactly who I am. I will therefore stop speaking poorly of myself. Instead, I will honor the Lord by speaking words in agreement with the mighty work He performed in my inner self, and I will begin to speak words that honor my body as the temple of the Holy Spirit! I declare this by faith in Jesus' name!

JUNE 28

God's Investment in You

But we have this treasure in earthen vessels, that the excellency of the power may be of God, and not of us.

2 Corinthians 4:7

My Prayer for Today

Father, thank You for putting Your Spirit inside me. Yes, it's true that my body is weak, fragile, and temporary. Yet You have chosen to place Your immense, incredibly rich, inexhaustible treasure in this fragile human body of mine that is so easily broken! Help me, Holy Spirit, to understand this wonderful truth so I can more effectively yield to and cooperate with You. Open my spiritual eyes so I can truly see the wealth You have deposited inside me! I pray this in Jesus' name!

My Confession for Today

I confess that I am the repository of the Holy Spirit! When God was choosing a place for His Spirit to take up residence, He chose me! Although my physical body may be a clay earthen vessel of human frailty, He has chosen to reside deep within me so the grandeur and surpassing greatness of Christ in me, the Hope of Glory, will be shown to be arising from Your sufficiency and not from me. My spiritual eyes are being opened, and I am realizing more and more every day that God has put His greatest gift in me! I declare this by faith in Jesus' name!

The Holy Spirit Is Our Seal and Guarantee

My Prayer for Today

Father, I thank You for sending someone to preach the Gospel to me—and for giving me the faith to believe it. I am in wonder and amazement that as soon as I believed, You gave me the Holy Spirit. The Spirit's presence in me is absolute, guaranteed proof that I belong to You—and I am so thankful that You pressed the insignia of the Holy Spirit into my heart and spirit, which means "postage-paid." Because of this precious work You've done in my life, I rejoice that one day I will reach my destination to be with You in my heavenly home! I pray this in Jesus' name!

In whom ye also trusted, after that ye heard the word of truth, the gospel of your salvation: in whom also after that ye believed, ye were sealed with that holy Spirit of promise.

Ephesians 1:13

My Confession for Today

I confess that I am complete and whole in Jesus Christ. After I believed, God saw that I was truly a product of Christ's own making. God made a full examination of me to make sure all parts were complete and that I was whole in Jesus Christ. Then He gave me the gift of the Holy Spirit, who will be with me all my life as a guarantee. He is the proof that I am a child of God. He is the evidence that I am born again. And His presence in my life is the guarantee that I will make it one day to my heavenly home! I declare this by faith in Jesus' name!

The Holy Spirit Is Like the Wind

And suddenly there came a sound from heaven as of a rushing mighty wind, and it filled all the house where they were sitting.

Acts 2:2

My Prayer for Today

Father, I thank You for the movement of the Holy Spirit that comes to empower me and to make me alive to minister and represent You on the earth! So many times I do everything that needs to be done organizationally, but life and power remain missing. Today I personally ask You to blow Your wind upon me, upon my church, and upon the mission organizations I support so they will all be "moved" by the Spirit and supernaturally empowered to do the work of the ministry! I pray this in Jesus' name!

My Confession for Today

I boldly declare that I will not be satisfied until a fresh wind of the Holy Spirit has blown upon me to give me divine life and divine energy. Without this life, I can only do what human power can do, but when the Spirit blows His divine wind upon me, suddenly I am empowered to do what I could have never done before. Today—right now—I am opening myself to the rushing mighty wind of the Holy Spirit. I confess that I am a ready recipient, and I am receiving a fresh infilling of this divine wind to empower me for God's service. I declare this by faith in Jesus' name!

Study To Be Quiet

My Prayer for Today

Lord, I repent for the times I've allowed my tongue to communicate words ignited by the flesh and for giving place to devilish discussions that were not inspired by the Holy Spirit who indwells me. Words of gossip and slander proceed from a polluted heart. To speak such words destroys reputations and relationships—and taints the hearts of those who hear them. Holy Spirit, I ask You to cleanse me from all defilement and from twisted speech and inappropriate communication. Please set a watch over my lips and create in me a clean and quiet heart. I pray this in Jesus' name!

And that ye study to be quiet, and to do your own business own business…

1 Thessalonians 4:11

My Confession for Today

I declare that life and death are in the power of the tongue. Therefore, I will not use my tongue to insert hell's suggestions into people's ears, but rather speak God's will and promote God's perspective. Because out of the abundance of the heart the mouth speaks, I choose to fill my heart with God's words, and I cultivate a quiet spirit that is trained to wait upon God. I will heed His direction concerning when to speak, what to say, and when to remain silent. In that blessed quietness, confidence and discernment shall be my strength. I do not speak about or involve my opinion in matters that are none of my business. And I do not allow others to bring gossip to me wrapped in the guise of a prayer request. Like Jesus, I speak only the words I hear my heavenly Father speak. His words are love-filled and life-producing, releasing health and strength in me and in the hearts of those who hear them. I declare this by faith in Jesus' name!

Caring for the Fatherless

Pure religion and undefiled before God and the Father is this, To visit the fatherless and widows in their affliction, and to keep himself unspotted from the world.

James 1:27

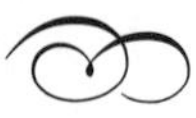

My Prayer for Today

Father, I want to demonstrate my faith in You with actions that reflect Your character. You are a Father to the fatherless and the Source of hope to the hopeless. You said that those who give to the poor are lending to You. You are watchful over the defenseless, and You take note how they are treated. I thank You for reminding me today that pure, undefiled religion is lived out by loving those who are in need. Through the demonstration of my love, I am directly participating in the expression of Your own heart toward them. And by loving them, I am offering genuine worship to You. Thank You, Father, for allowing me the privilege to be an extension of Your hands so others may know Your goodness practically through experience for themselves. I pray this in Jesus' name!

My Confession for Today

I confess that I live out a religion that is clean and acceptable before God. I give attention to the fatherless and motherless and to those people who have been abandoned in life. When I encounter the fatherless who have been abandoned, neglected, and left bereft of any support, I do not simply wish them well. I inquire of the Lord how I can personally give aid and provide help for them. I declare this by faith in Jesus' name!

Pure Religion Is a Very Good Thing

My Prayer for Today

Father, I am deeply stirred to begin formulating my long-term plan to bring real, measurable help to people in need through sincere acts of charity. You specified needy widows and orphans as people for whom I should take compassionate responsibility when their needs are brought to my attention. I ask You, Lord, to show me who and how to help. I commit to prove my faith by my works, as I live out the "clean religion" that honors You the most. I pray this in Jesus' name!

Pure religion and undefiled before God and the Father is this, To visit the fatherless and widows in their affliction, and to keep himself unspotted from the world.

James 1:27

My Confession for Today

I confess that I actively pursue a life marked by the "clean religion" that God both encourages and endorses. I do not ignore the plight of orphans and widows in need. I deliberately take action in well-planned ways to provide help and to produce change that will make a positive difference in their lives for the glory of God! I declare this in Jesus' name!

Praying for Those in Authority

I exhort therefore, that, first of all, supplications, prayers, intercessions, and giving of thanks, be made for all men; for kings, and for all that are in authority; that we may lead a quiet and peaceable life in all godliness and honesty. For this is good and acceptable in the sight of God our Saviour.

1 Timothy 2:1-3

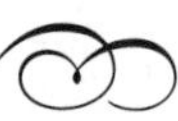

My Prayer for Today

Father, I cherish the right to vote. It is a freedom that cost the lives of many. At the appointed time, I will exercise that privilege to make my voice heard via my voting ballot. However, I realize that I don't have to wait for an upcoming election to cast my vote for righteousness. I take my place in prayer, in obedience to Your Word, and with the help of the Holy Spirit, and I pray with all manner of prayer and supplications. Seated together with Christ Jesus and by the authority of His name, I pray with confidence according to Your will, knowing that You hear me. I pray this in Jesus' name!

My Confession for Today

I confess that I exercise my rights on earth and in Heaven. I pray for those in offices of governmental authority as I exercise my authority in Christ through prayer. I operate according to the divine law of love, and I refrain from criticism and negative speech. Instead, I speak words in agreement with the will of God and the establishment of righteousness in my land. I declare this in Jesus' name!

The Lord Provides the Increase

My Prayer for Today

I have planted, Apollos watered; but God gave the increase.

1 Corinthians 3:6

Father, I see that it takes divine connections to make a project of faith come to pass and bear fruit. Many times I have felt discouraged because it seemed I had to complete a God-project alone. Father, I ask You to connect me with others who will respond to Your voice and help cause Your supernatural plan to come to pass. I receive God-ordained help to complete the assignment You have given me. I ask You to strengthen me and those with whom You will connect me so that together we can do our respective parts under Your direction to fulfill what You want each one of us to do! I pray this in Jesus' name!

My Confession for Today

I confess that I am obedient and faithful to the direction of the Lord when He gives me an assignment. And I declare that with each divine assignment He gives me, God also ordains obedient and faithful people who are positioned with me to see that assignment through to completion. Just as Paul planted, Apollos watered, but God gave the increase, we each do our part by the direction of God as we give all glory to His name! I declare this by faith in Jesus' name!

I Let Patience Have Its Perfect Work

But let patience have her perfect work, that ye may be perfect and entire, wanting nothing.

James 1:4

My Prayer for Today

Father, when You gave me the assignment I'm working on, You supplied everything that I would ever need to fulfill it! I thank You for sufficient grace, wisdom, ability, provision, help from others, and Your very own stick-to-it power! Father, I come before You now and ask You to fill me full and afresh with Your Holy Spirit. I ask You to anoint me with fresh oil and to strengthen me with a fresh touch of Your power so I can allow patience to have its perfect work in me. I am not willing to let go, loosen my grip, or grow slack. I know that I am in the right place at the right time, and I refuse to budge for any reason! Holy Spirit, I receive Your help. And by the power of God's grace undergirding me, I will hold fast and see this assignment through to the end. I pray this in Jesus' name!

My Confession for Today

I boldly confess that staying power is at work in my life! It's not a question of if I will win—it's just a matter of time until I win! No matter how long I have to stand my ground, I will not give up and quit. I will not cringe in fear or bow out because of attempted bullying, intimidation, or harassment. The enemy is the one who will have to surrender in exhaustion. And when he flees, everything I have believed to see will come together before my eyes as everything that opposed and tried to withstand my efforts falls away before the invincible greatness of my God! I declare this by faith in Jesus' name!

A Revelation!

My Prayer for Today

But God hath revealed them unto us by his Spirit: for the Spirit searcheth all things, yea, the deep things of God.

1 Corinthians 2:10

Father, I thank You for revealing the hidden things to me by Your Spirit. I repent because I recognize that too many times, I have tried to think through what to do instead of relying on You for wisdom and divine insight. Holy Spirit, You see and know everything, and You know the key to every heart. You know the secret to every success, whether in ministry, education, family, or anything else. From this day forward, I make a decision to listen to You. I know You will reveal exactly what I need to know for every situation I face in life. And now, as never before, I am listening! I pray this in Jesus' name!

My Confession for Today

I confess that the Holy Spirit not only gives me inspired ideas, but He also injects me with the courage I need to obey Him and to act on those ideas. I receive insight for the plan of God for my life, and I release my faith to move forward on that plan by the strength of the Holy Spirit within me. I declare this by faith in Jesus' name!

Be Kind To Others

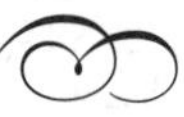

And be ye kind one to another, tenderhearted, forgiving one another, even as God for Christ's sake hath forgiven you.

Ephesians 4:32

My Prayer for Today

Father, I earnestly desire for the character of Christ to be fully formed in me. I ask that You help me cultivate the fruit of kindness Jesus displayed as He was moved by divine compassion as He went about doing good. Holy Spirit, teach me how to display the Father's heart and character to those in need of Your kindness the most. Lord, it is Your lovingkindness that leads people to repentance and draws them to You. Today I commit to love others as You have loved me by the power of Your Holy Spirit within me. I pray this in Jesus' name!

My Confession for Today

I confess that I let my roots grow down deep into Christ and that His life in me enables me to produce the fruits of righteousness that glorify His name. I choose to yield to the Holy Spirit and to let Him do His work inside me. As I surrender to the Holy Spirit's work in my life, He helps me demonstrate kindness. I allow God to do His sanctifying and transforming work throughout all my personality. Day by day, I yield to the Holy Spirit's presence to help me demonstrate the kindness of Jesus Christ in my life for the glory of God the Father! I declare this by faith in Jesus' name!

Jesus Christ–Always the Same

My Prayer for Today

Jesus Christ is the same yesterday, and to day, and for ever.

Hebrews 13:8

Father, in the midst of this ever-changing world environment, I am so thankful that Jesus Christ never changes! He was in the past exactly who He is in the present and precisely who He will be forever! Lord, I am in awe of Your unchanging love and Your unending mercy. In a society that is morally, politically, and economically shifting, I boldly proclaim: On Christ the solid Rock I take my firm stand! Truly all other ground is sinking sand. Help me, Holy Spirit, to stand strong for You, no matter who around me may abandon their position of faith. I pray this in Jesus' name!

My Confession for Today

I confess my agreement with what the Bible declares in Hebrews 13:8: Past, present, and future—Jesus is exactly the same! Today I receive the stabilizing victory and strength that His unchanging faithfulness brings to my life in every area. No matter who or what may change, my hope is built on nothing less than Jesus' blood and righteousness! I declare this by faith in Jesus' name!

Effective Fit and Function

From whom the whole body fitly joined together and compacted by that which every joint supplieth, according to the effectual working in the measure of every part, maketh increase of the body unto the edifying of itself in love.

Ephesians 4:16

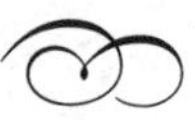

My Prayer for Today

Father, I thank You that You have placed me in my right place in the Body of Christ so every part can work effectually. I thank You, Father, that I am not alone to do the things You've asked me to do and that You have set each one of us in the Body as it pleases You for the fulfillment of Your plan and Your purposes. Although I may see certain projects that You have assigned me to fulfill, my primary function may be to join myself to another person's assignment in order to see it achieved victoriously. Regardless of whether it is my assignment or a project someone else is called to lead by Your direction, I yield myself to You and ask You to reveal to me my function according to Your design and where I fit for the purpose of Your plan. I ask You to equip me by Your grace to maintain the commitment to stay there, to provide all the mobility and support I can to make the project move forward, and to see a supernatural release of the Holy Spirit's energy to accomplish what I could never do on my own! I pray this in Jesus' name!

My Confession for Today

I declare that the Holy Spirit is clearly and regularly speaking to my heart, showing me where I am to fit and how I am to function in the Body of Christ. Regardless of how much I may want to function on my own, I realize that God has not asked me to do it all by myself. I am equipped according to the measure that has been assigned to me. I declare that I know where I fit, that I know how to function there, that I am committed to the task, and that the Spirit of God supernaturally and lavishly releases His divine power to enable all involved with the assignment to each do their part in moving forward to accomplish His will together for His glory! I declare this by faith, in Jesus' name!

Shake it Off & Get Back on the Playing Field!

My Prayer for Today

Father, I am not willing to be sidetracked by little problems that the devil has orchestrated to knock me out of the game of life. He has no new strategy. I recognize that his repeated ploy has been to insult, bully, and offend me in such a way to trigger and provoke my emotions to take over my thoughts about myself or others. The devil's goal was for me to ensnare myself in the trap of bitterness, unforgiveness, and fear so I'd remove myself from the plan or assignment that You set before me. Father, I repent for the times I have let that happen. I was so focused on the hurt I felt from a perceived wrong, I forgot that the bigger picture was Your plan and my position in it. Holy Spirit, I receive Your help to follow Jesus' instructions to forgive even when it seems to be for the same thing over and over again. When I'm confronted with a perceived wrong, help me do more than merely "grin and bear it." I ask You to strengthen me to focus on the joy of victory as I refuse to cling to offenses! I pray this in Jesus' name!

Take heed to yourselves: If thy brother trespass against thee, rebuke him; and if he repent, forgive him.

Luke 17:3

My Confession for Today

I confess that I guard my heart. I do not allow it to become hardened through bitterness because of offenses. But I keep myself in the love of God so my faith will not fail. In that position, the enemy cannot provoke me to stumble or remove myself from the game of life by choosing to walk in the flesh rather than stay in the Spirit. I follow the example of my Lord Jesus who, when He was ridiculed, chose to forgive. I follow His example and obey His command to forgive so I can live in victory above all the schemes of the enemy. I declare this by faith, in Jesus' name!

An Overcoming Attitude!

I can do all things through Christ which strengtheneth me.

Philippians 4:13

My Prayer for Today

Father, I submit my body, mind, and emotions to You as Your exclusive instruments to be filled with Your Word, Your Spirit, and Your mighty power for Your holy purposes. I yield to You, Holy Spirit, and I cease to be a slave to my body and emotions. I ask You to make me a mighty instrument in Your hand to achieve the divine destiny You have placed in my heart to be fulfilled for Your glory! I pray this in Jesus' name!

My Confession for Today

I confess that I have God's mighty power operating in me, which makes me a superior victor and champion over every trick and attack of the enemy. I let the Word of Christ dwell in me richly, and I walk in submission to the leadership of the Holy Spirit. The power of God at work within me gives me the upper hand in every situation I face and causes me to prevail in every circumstance through Christ, who fills and continuously infuses me with the strength of a whole army! I declare this by faith in Jesus' name!

No Open Doors!

My Prayer for Today

Neither give place to the devil.

Ephesians 4:27

Father, I thank You for the spiritual weapons of warfare that You have given me to resist my enemy, the devil. I see that it is essential to diligently survey my life to see if I have left any open doors that would make it easier for him to find entrance into my life and circumstances. Holy Spirit, I ask You to help me live a life of obedience so I can shut every door to deny him access. I ask You to open up my understanding as You shine the light of Your Word into my life. Help me identify and deal with areas of disobedience that may become the very entry points the devil seeks to penetrate to rob me in some way of the goodness of God manifested in my life. I pray this in Jesus' name!

My Confession for Today

I confess that the weapons of my warfare are mighty to keep my mind protected and my life secure against the onslaughts of the wicked one. I am alert, and I keep a watchful eye on myself to guard my heart and the borders of my own life with the protective barrier of obedience to the Word and to the Spirit of God. I am not negligent but diligent to keep the doors to my life open only to God and completely closed to the devil. I declare this by faith in Jesus' name!

The Old Me Is Gone!

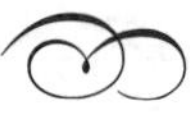

Likewise reckon ye also yourselves to be dead indeed unto sin, but alive unto God through Jesus Christ our Lord.

Romans 6:11

My Prayer for Today

Father, I thank You for the fresh breath of Your Spirit that has swept across my heart. I praise You for giving me new understanding of my identity in Christ. I am overflowing with gratitude to You as I realize that Your great plan of redemption truly caused old things to pass away and all things to become new for me in Him. Through Your great mercy, I was crucified with Christ. When I accepted that exchange, my spirit was recreated by the life of Christ that filled me and made me an entirely new creation in Him. Now with my life hidden in Christ, the old me no longer exists, and this body, once devoted to sin, is now the dwelling place of Your Spirit. My body has no right to dictate my attitudes, actions, or appetites because I am free to reckon it dead. I am forever new because of You. Holy Spirit, I ask You to help me walk in the newness of this life so that I will be an instrument You can use to demonstrate the reality of Christ's life in me, the Hope of Glory on the earth! I pray this in Jesus' name!

My Confession for Today

I joyfully confess that I am not who I once was. Today I am a new creature in Christ Jesus, and the person Christ has made me to be now is my new identity! I am forever alive unto God because of what Christ Jesus has done for me! I continually deem my old personality that existed before I was born into Christ to be as dead as a corpse with no life left in it. I am not the person I used to be. That person who once lived is dead, lifeless, gone, and buried away forever in the mind of God. I am free of my former identity forever! I declare this by faith in Jesus' name!

God Rewards Your Sacrifices

My Prayer for Today

Father, I am grateful for this reminder that You pay attention to my response to Your assignment for my life. You are very aware of where I am in life, and You see what I do to express faithfulness to You. Thank You for strengthening me with Your might in those times when I felt discouraged and wondered if my labor was in vain. I rejoice in Your all-sufficient grace that never fails to cover me in the midst of the difficulties and hardships I may encounter while obeying You. Lord, I ask You to help me be conformed more fully to Your faithful ways, so when my heavenly record is read before You, I will receive a crown to place at Your feet on that day. I pray this in Jesus' name!

Therefore, my beloved brethren, be ye stedfast, unmoveable, always abounding in the work of the Lord, forasmuch as ye know that your labour is not in vain in the Lord.

1 Corinthians 15:58

My Confession for Today

I declare that I am steadfast, immovable, always abounding in the work of the Lord, because I know that my labor in the Lord is not wasted. God is aware of all that I say and do for His glory. He openly sees my heart's motivation for what I have said and done, and He will reward me accordingly. I do not live my life for the praises of people. The prize I seek is God's approval. Therefore, I set my focus daily to live a life that will matter for eternity as I labor to see the will of God done on earth as it is in Heaven. I declare this by faith in Jesus' name!

Avoid Danger

What say I then? that the idol is any thing, or that which is offered in sacrifice to idols is any thing? But I say, that the things which the Gentiles sacrifice, they sacrifice to devils, and not to God: and I would not that ye should have fellowship with devils.

1 Corinthians 10:19-20

My Prayer for Today

Father, I ask You to help me use common sense to know the places that I need to avoid to maintain my spiritual freedom. I know that I am free. I know that Christ's power in me is greater than any force around me. But Your Word clearly teaches me to avoid those detrimental environments that once held sway in my life. So in obedience to Your Word, I deliberately choose to change my way of doing things, lest I place myself in spiritual jeopardy. Holy Spirit, I ask You to help me be sensitive to discern when I am in a wrong place or with a wrong group—and to show me how to graciously leave when I know it's time for me to be going! I pray this prayer in Jesus' name!

My Confession for Today

I confess that I will no longer intentionally place myself in positions that are too close to the edge of the cliff. Christ has set me free, but I don't need to play around or fellowship in the sinful places from which Jesus liberated me. I admit that I've made this mistake in the past, but I will not make it any longer. The Holy Spirit within gives me wisdom and common sense to recognize when I'm in a detrimental environment, and He gives me the courage to exit these situations so I can keep moving forward. I declare this by faith in Jesus' name!

Your Problem Is Nothing Special

My Prayer for Today

Father, as Your child, I am special and unique—but my problems are not. There is nothing new under the sun. Every temptation I have faced or ever will face has already been experienced by others. But more importantly, it has already been faced and overcome by the Lord Jesus Christ. Father, I rejoice that You are faithful to Your promise not to allow me to be tempted beyond what I may be able to bear, but with each temptation, You will also make a way of escape for me. Thank You for showing me the path prepared to get me out of traps that try to drain my hope and cause me to doubt and fear that I may never be free of it. I set myself in agreement with Your Word and Your Spirit to guide me out of my problems and into Your plan for me. I pray this in Jesus' name!

There hath no temptation taken you but such as is common to man: but God is faithful, who will not suffer you to be tempted above that ye are able; but will with the temptation also make a way to escape, that ye may be able to bear it.

1 Corinthians 10:13

My Confession for Today

I declare that there is no temptation that may try to overtake me that isn't already common to humankind. I refuse to see any problem as too big to solve. I confess that every situation has a solution and it can be conquered by the wisdom of God. Today I make the decision to align my thoughts, words, and attitudes with God's Word about any problem I may face. I know my Father God will always provide a way of escape for me from every temptation. Therefore, I listen to His voice and expect His Word and His Spirit to illuminate and direct my steps as I begin walking out of every trap until I arrive on the other side, free and victorious! I declare this by faith in Jesus' name!

Uncomfortable Questions To Ask Yourself

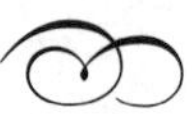

Examine yourselves, whether ye be in the faith; prove your own selves…

2 Corinthians 13:5

My Prayer for Today

Father, I come before You now and ask You to shine the light of Your Word into every hidden place of my heart to reveal to me my true motives. Disobedience produces self-deception, and, Father, I realize that actions speak far louder than words. I have often praised You with my lips, yet my heart was far from You as I rationalized and justified my self-seeking priorities making excuses for being a lover of self more than a lover of God. Holy Spirit, I ask You to help me lay aside every weight and sin that can so easily trip me up. More than anything, I desire to please You, Father, and to honor the Lord Jesus who gave His life for me. I choose Your will above my own. I yield all I am and all I possess to You for Your exclusive use. I am not my own. I belong to You. I have been bought with a price, the precious blood of Jesus Christ. Therefore, I yield to Your transforming power. On the day I stand before You and the books of my life are opened and read, I will receive a crown to set at Your feet, just as I lay my life before You now. I pray this in Jesus' name!

My Confession for Today

I declare that I examine myself in the light of God's Word and I apply what the Holy Spirit reveals. I refuse to delude myself with reasoning that is contrary to truth. I choose to be a doer and not merely a hearer who listens to the Word but refuses to internalize its meaning or to act on the truth. I respond to wisdom's voice, and I bring my life into alignment with God's purposes and plan. I choose to agree with God; therefore, I walk in harmony with His will and His ways. I don't waste my life. I keep my focus on Jesus and on eternity. On that great day when I stand before Him, my reward will be that in this life, I was fruitful for His glory because I obeyed. I declare this by faith in Jesus' name!

No Bible–No Food!

My Prayer for Today

Father, I receive what I read today as a personal exhortation TO ME to renew my commitment to consuming the Word of God on a daily basis. I need *"every word that proceeds from the mouth of God,"* for it brings healing, wholeness, deliverance, protection, and it provides all the direction I need for my life. I ask You to forgive me for letting my commitment lapse, but today I make a new commitment that the Word of God will be the highest priority in my life, more than my daily necessary food. I pray this in Jesus' name!

But he answered and said, It is written, Man shall not live by bread alone, but by every word that proceedeth out of the mouth of God.

Matthew 4:4

My Confession for Today

I make a new commitment today that the Word of God will be the highest priority in my life and that I will consume it on a daily basis. I will fill my mind with His creative, restorative substance—His very Person and nature—which will produce healing, wholeness, deliverance, protection, and all the answers I need for my life. I will put first things first and open up God's Word like a treasure to allow the Living Word who indwells the written Word to flow within me. God's Word is the light and life that will make me whole, protect my family, and help set my relationships on a blessed, right course. I confess that I will allow the life of God's Word in me to flow out to others and create a river of blessing for them to participate in and enjoy! I declare this by faith in Jesus' name!

Why Spiritual Gifts?

For I long to see you, that I may impart unto you some spiritual gift, to the end ye may be established.

Romans 1:11

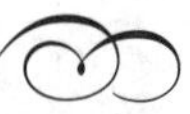

My Prayer for Today

Father, I am so grateful for the privilege of being around seasoned men or women of God. After being in their presence, I spiritually feel like an iron rod has been hammered into the soil of my heart that helps me keep growing upward in the right direction. I thank You for the blessing of being reinforced and stronger as a result of their influence. Holy Spirit, help me follow their example in Christ so I can keep my focus where it ought to be, and produce greater fruitfulness in my life. I pray this in Jesus' name!

My Confession for Today

I confess that the gifts of the Holy Spirit are at work on my behalf to establish me, to reinforce me, to make me stronger, and to help me grow. I walk with the wise, and wisdom surrounds and saturates me so that I can bear much fruit for the glory of Jesus and the furtherance of His Kingdom! I declare this by faith in Jesus' name!

Standing on the Word!

My Prayer for Today

Dear Father, I ask You to help me understand the relevance of this word I've read today. I pray that You will strengthen the present leadership of the Body of Christ to stand for the absolute truths of God's Word even if that stance places them in direct opposition to the world. I ask You to raise up strong leaders in the Christian community who will lead the way and courageously stand for truth, regardless of the price that must be paid. I pray for my pastor and for other spiritual leaders. Father, I ask You to help them hear what the Spirit is saying and grant them boldness to call the Church to a time of holiness and separation, even if it is opposed to the voice of the world around them. I pray this in Jesus' name!

Repent; or else I will come unto thee quickly, and will fight against them with the sword of my mouth.

Revelation 2:16

My Confession for Today

I boldly confess that I will stand by the truth of God's Word, regardless of what the world around me tries to dictate as morally right or wrong. A day will soon come when we will all stand before Christ's high court of reckoning and give account for how we upheld truth or how we forfeited it to accommodate the world around us. I have made my decision! Regardless of what the world says or what names it calls me, I am going to stand by the Christian values that have guided the Church for 2,000 years. Truth has not suddenly changed—it is society that has changed. I am determined to stand by biblical truth regardless of the price I must pay. I declare this by faith in Jesus' name!

Prove All Things

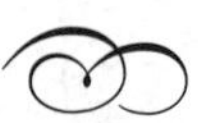

Prove all things…

1 Thessalonians 5:21

My Prayer for Today

Heavenly Father, I thank You for teaching me common sense regarding the gift of prophecy. The apostle Paul clearly told us to test all things, and I confess that I have received "words" without testing them in the past. But rather than reject all prophetic utterances because some have turned out to be false, today I assume responsibility to test and to prove what is spoken over me. I don't want to miss anything that the Holy Spirit has to say specifically to me, so I refuse to reject the gift of prophecy. But I thank You for helping me as I follow a commonsense approach to the manifestation of this gift from this moment forward. Please help me learn how to recognize what is real and what is counterfeit. I pray this in Jesus' name!

My Confession for Today

I declare by faith that I am growing in my personal discernment of spiritual things. I am not as naïve as I once was. I am learning to recognize what is real and what is counterfeit. I release every bad experience I've ever had with so-called prophetic manifestations, and I open my heart and my mind to the true gift of prophecy that comes from the Holy Spirit. God gave this gift for my edification and for the building up of the Church, and I refuse to reject it because of past bad experiences. With the help of the Holy Spirit, I am becoming wiser and more discerning in my ability to separate the false from the true. I declare this by faith in Jesus' name!

Hold Fast To What Is Good

My Prayer for Today

Heavenly Father, I thank You for speaking clearly to me about my life. I confess that there have been times when I've been tempted, out of weakness and weariness, to let go of Your prophetic utterances over my life. Today I am encouraged to wrap my arms around those promises You made to me and to not let them go until I see their fulfillment. With the help of Your Spirit, I will prove all things and hold fast to what is good! I pray this in Jesus' name!

Prove all things; hold fast that which is good.

1 Thessalonians 5:21

My Confession for Today

I declare that I will do what God has told me to do. Many forces have tried to stop me, but the Word of God is working mightily in me and it will accomplish God's will in my life. I wrap my arms around those prophetic words that I have proven to be true, and I refuse to surrender to the negative forces that try to take them away from me. I will remain steady and on course until I see the manifestation of what God has spoken to me. I declare this by faith in Jesus' name!

A New Name–A New Beginning

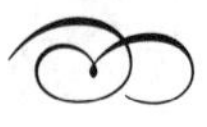

...To him that overcometh will I give...a new name...

Revelation 2:17

My Prayer for Today

Father, I thank You for the transformational change You have worked in my life since I committed my life to Jesus. You have worked so many miracles in my life and changed me so much. I give you all the honor and glory for what you have done. When I think about how my life used to be and compare it to how my life is today, I cannot imagine living without You. Thank You for redeeming me, saving me from destruction, and giving me a new spiritual status in Your family! I pray this in Jesus' name!

My Confession for Today

I declare that I am totally different from how I used to be. Since I've committed myself wholly to Christ, He has worked miracles in my life and character. I thankfully confess that since I've belonged to Jesus, I've had multiple transformational moments in my life. The Holy Spirit is working inside me continuously—to change me and to take me to a higher dimension in every aspect of my life. If anyone needs to thank God for working miracles in his or her life, it's certainly me! I thank You, heavenly Father, for the dramatic changes that You have worked in me! I declare this by faith in Jesus' name!

Always on Guard

My Prayer for Today

...abstain from pollutions of idols, and from fornication...

Acts 15:20

Father, I ask You to reveal to me the places, events, or people I specifically need to avoid in order to stay spiritually strong. I want to be a witness to the freedom You have brought into my life. But if I am not strong enough to be around the former places and people and not be affected by them, I need the courage to say no to the invitations that would negatively affect me. Give me the wisdom to know those whom I can help influence and those whom I deliberately need to avoid. I know that the Holy Spirit has the answer, and He wants to help me make the right decisions. So Holy Spirit, teach me how to be vigilant and sensible about my spiritual life, as this will affect everything about my future. I pray this in Jesus' name!

My Confession for Today

I confess that I am vigilant and fully aware when it comes to my spiritual life. I know that the devil is on the prowl, looking for an entrance into my life. Therefore, I am very sensible about where I go, what I do, and whom I see. I guard my heart carefully because nothing is more important than my spiritual life. God expects me to put distance between myself and anything that will potentially cause negative spiritual ramifications in my life. I love Jesus more than I love anything else. Therefore, I have chosen to walk the straight and narrow path, surrounding myself only with people and activities that edify my spirit. I will build close fellowship only with those who are like-minded about following Jesus Christ in a spirit of holiness! I declare this by faith in Jesus' name!

The Responsibility of Speaking for God

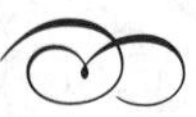

And I was with you in weakness, and in fear, and in much trembling.

1 Corinthians 2:3

My Prayer for Today

Father, I admit that I've had moments when I shook to the core when it was time for me to stand up and publicly speak, sing, testify, or to take a public position on an issue. Today I surrender to the power of the Holy Spirit. Holy Spirit, I ask You to do the supernatural part that I cannot do. I'll train, prepare, and present my body to You as a living sacrifice. As I do my part, I ask for and yield to Your help as You step forward to do the part that only You can do. I am completely and utterly dependent on You. I pray this in Jesus' name!

My Confession for Today

I confess that I have felt weakness, fear, and great trembling at times when I've been called to stand up and be counted in a significant way. But from this point onward, I will do my best to train, study, and prepare so that when my moment comes to step forward, I will lean upon the Holy Spirit and not on my preparation alone. I will make room for the Holy Spirit to work, and I declare that He will work through me with supernatural, convincing powers that are far more effective than anything I could have ever done in my own strength! I declare this by faith in Jesus' name!

What Is a Plague?

My Prayer for Today

Father, I thank You for the power in the name of Jesus. Today I use the name of Jesus to break every demonic attack against my body. I have suffered long enough with the afflictions that have assailed me. Starting today, I stand up against them with the name and the blood of Jesus Christ, and I command the devil to take his hands off my body! I pray this in Jesus' name!

And straightway the fountain of her blood was dried up; and she felt in her body that she was healed of that plague.

Mark 5:29

My Confession for Today

I confess that healing belongs to me because Jesus purchased it in my redemption! Greater is He who is in me than he that is in the world, and I authoritatively command the enemy to remove that whip that He has used to strike me and to keep me continually sick. I break the burden of its binding yoke by the power of the anointing of Jesus Christ in His mighty name! I declare this by faith in Jesus' name!

Do Not Deny My Faith!

I know thy works, and where thou dwellest, even where Satan's seat is: and thou holdest fast my name, and hast not denied my faith...

Revelation 2:13

My Prayer for Today

Father, I want to be a part of the remnant that refuses to bend to the pressures of society in these last days. Although there is pressure to modify what we believe and to be less committed, Your Word has never changed; therefore, I know that You have not asked me to change my position or what I believe. Please help me to be strong in these times and to impart strength to others who are feeling the same pressure to conform to the dictates of society in these last days. I pray this in Jesus' name!

My Confession for Today

I declare that neither society nor the courts will determine the standard by which I live and that I will live according to the teaching and dictates of the Bible. There is no doubt that society is trying to force me to change the way I think and believe, but I hold fast to the name of Jesus and to the teaching of the Word of God. It has been correct for thousands of years, and it remains the unerring guide for my life. I recommit myself to living according to the teaching and the standards of God's Word, even if it puts me at odds with what society is trying to tell me to do. I declare this by faith in Jesus' name!

Come Boldly To the Throne of Grace!

My Prayer for Today

Let us therefore come boldly unto the throne of grace, that we may obtain mercy, and find grace to help in time of need.

Hebrews 4:16

Lord Jesus, I come to You boldly with the needs I am facing in my life. I have wrongly lacked confidence and failed to be straightforward about them with You, but now I understand that You want me to be frank, forthright, and direct with You about these challenges I am facing. Thank You that You don't rebuke or scorn me for being bold—and thank You for stepping forward as a mighty Warrior to help fight my challenge with me. Today I am coming to You boldly, and I am expecting You to step forward to fight in my defense! I pray this in Jesus' name!

My Confession for Today

I declare that I obey the Lord's charge to pray boldly and forthrightly when I come to the throne of God's grace. He bids me to come, and today I accept His invitation to come boldly and to declare my each and every need. With the help of the Holy Spirit, I will lay hold of the answers that I need and my exterior circumstances must change as a result of this time at the throne of God's grace. Jesus will step forward as my Mighty Warrior to fight for me. He is just waiting for me to issue Him the invitation to step into the fray with me and to manifest His victory in this battle! I declare this by faith in Jesus' name!

Put On Christlike Attitudes

Put on therefore,
as the elect of God,
holy and beloved,
bowels of mercies,
kindness, humbleness
of mind, meekness,
longsuffering.

Colossians 3:12

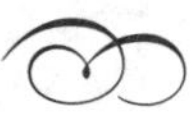

My Prayer for Today

Holy Spirit, I am so thankful that You live inside of me to produce the attitudes of Jesus Christ in my life. Today I have been convicted regarding areas in my life where I need to grow and change. I ask You to release Your divine power inside me to produce the attitudes and the attributes of Jesus' character in my life. Let Colossians 3:12 become a reality inside me as the very nature and life of Jesus becomes replicated in me! I pray this in Jesus' name!

My Confession for Today

I boldly confess that I am changing every day as I surrender to the indwelling power of the Holy Spirit. He is convicting me of areas where I need to be more Christlike, and I am responding to what He reveals to me about the areas I need to change so I can become more conformed to the image of Jesus Christ. I am not powerless. I am not a victim to my ugly old nature. The Spirit of God indwells me, and He gives me the power to change in these areas where He is speaking to my heart! I declare this by faith in Jesus' name!

5 Things To Do To Keep Yourself Strong Daily

My Prayer for Today

Father, I thank You for speaking to me today about areas where I need to be more proactive in guarding my spiritual life to make sure that I stay spiritually strong, healthy, and vibrant. I understand that to keep my spirit in strong condition will require time and energy and perhaps the sacrifice of other good pastimes. There is nothing more important than my relationship with You. How I walk with You affects every other area of my life. Help me take this seriously and apply these principles to my life. Show me how to get started, because I know that my spiritual condition is vital to the rest of my life and to the lives of those You have positioned me to influence for Your glory. I pray this in Jesus' name!

Be careful for nothing; but in every thing by prayer and supplication with thanksgiving let your requests be made known unto God.

Philippians 4:6

My Confession for Today

I confess that I am proactive in keeping my spiritual condition strong, healthy, and vibrant. I do not ignore my spiritual life. Just as I feed my body every day and have certain regimens in place to care for my physical condition, I am careful to attend to the needs of my spirit and soul. As a result, I am spiritually strong; I am spiritually healthy; and my heart is vibrant. I am disciplined, committed, and careful to keep my spiritual condition in top-notch shape! I declare this by faith in Jesus' name!

AUGUST 1

Feeling as if Hitting a Brick Wall

...we were pressed out of measure, above strength, insomuch that we despaired even of life: But we had the sentence of death in ourselves, that we should not trust in ourselves, but in God which raiseth the dead.

2 Corinthians 1:8-9

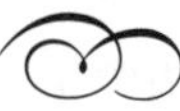

My Prayer for Today

Father, I thank You for Your marvelous plan for my life. I praise You because the devil is powerless to hijack it. I turn my attention from my failures and fix my gaze upon Jesus, who is the Author and Finisher of my faith! My victory might not be coming to me exactly as I expected—nonetheless, my victory is on the way. I surrender to the power of the Holy Spirit and allow Him to flow through me to bring me to a place of victory! I pray this in Jesus' name!

My Confession for Today

I confess that when I don't know what to do, I turn to God for direction and help, and He releases His wisdom in me. There is no such thing as a hopeless situation. When I feel that I am facing a dead end, God's power turns it into a place of a new beginning. What I am facing is not the end for me—it is, in fact, the starting point for a glorious new beginning. When the devil tries to tell me that nothing good lies ahead for me, I remind him of the future that is awaiting HIM! I confess that the resurrection power of Jesus Christ has already lifted me far above his attacks and that a brighter and better future awaits me! I declare this by faith in Jesus' name!

Grace-Given Gifts

My Prayer for Today

Heavenly Father, I am so thankful that You have placed grace-given gifts inside of me. I understand that You have made me the steward of these divine treasures. You expect me to faithfully manage these gifts that You have entrusted to my care. Father, I ask You to teach me how to use these gifts as You intended so I can meet the needs of those around me and do it in a way that gives all the glory to Jesus. Give me a pure and understanding heart so I can exercise these gifts wisely and with great responsibility! I pray this in Jesus' name!

As every man hath received the gift, even so minister the same one to another, as good stewards of the manifold grace of God.

1 Peter 4:10

My Confession for Today

I confess that God has given me gifts of His grace that are powerful and have the ability to make a difference in the lives of other people. God expects me to do something with these gifts, for He gave them to me for the purpose of building His Kingdom. I refuse to let another day pass without allowing these grace-given gifts to be expressed through me. This divine equipment has been given to me in order to help others, so I will not sit by idly while others are in need! God will move through me and use this supernatural equipment, not only to meet people's needs, but also to help them come through their situations with victory. I declare this by faith in Jesus' name!

Be Wise as a Snake!

...be ye therefore wise as serpents...

Matthew 10:16

My Prayer for Today

Heavenly Father, I take heed to Jesus' instructions to be as wise as a serpent when surveying new territory for the Kingdom of God. Father, You are the ultimate Strategist, and You leave no detail unattended in Your great plan! As I follow your specific instructions, I will be able to avoid unnecessary difficulties or destruction. Lord, I ask You to show me Your ways and grant me a wise and understanding heart. Teach me how to walk in great discretion with accurate discernment. I want to finish the assignment You've given me, so I am willing to move slow and steady to avoid harmful mistakes. Thank You for giving me the wisdom I need for each venture You have set before me. Then when the time is right, I will seize the moment by Your grace to fulfill the outcome You desire. I pray this in Jesus' name!

My Confession for Today

I confess that I am as wise as a serpent yet harmless as a dove. Your gentleness, oh, Lord, has made me great! You give me wisdom and sound counsel before I publicly act on my God-given opportunities. I pay close attention to the strategies of the Lord, and I learn the "landscape" of the environment where He wants me to establish His Kingdom. I follow the strategies of God while remaining discerning of and alert to the tactics of the enemy. I am diligent to pray out the plan of God so He can alert me to the enemy's potential attacks against me. I take time to understand my God-given opportunity, and I make sure that I am completely informed of all the facts I need to help me adjust smoothly and move forward in fulfilling my assignment without unnecessary delays or detours. I declare this by faith in Jesus' name!

The Importance of Timing

My Prayer for Today

...be ye therefore wise as serpents...

Matthew 10:16

Heavenly Father, I thank You that You are faithful to lead me in the direction I should go and in the decisions I must make. Help me recognize when it's time to lay low and blend into the landscape and when it is time to strike! I have prayed for divine opportunities, so when they present themselves to me, help me to recognize them and to have the courage to step out by faith to accept the assignment. Holy Spirit, I know that You are a faithful Leader, so today I put my trust in You to lead me in each and every step that I take! I pray this in Jesus' name!

My Confession for Today

I confess that I am wise as a serpent! I know when to lay low, how to blend into the landscape, how to learn my new territory, and how to discern and recognize when a God-given opportunity passes my way. Fear does not hold me back. Hesitation does not stop me. Because I have prayed and done my homework in advance, I am well prepared for that golden moment when God gives me the opportunity for which I've waited for so long. The Holy Spirit is my Leader, and He is leading and guiding me every step of the way. I declare this by faith in Jesus' name!

AUGUST 5

Self-Discovery—Why God Tests You

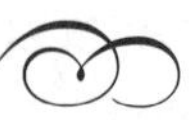

By faith Abraham, when he was tried, offered up Isaac: and he that had received the promises offered up his only begotten son, of whom it was said, That in Isaac shall thy seed be called: Accounting that God was able to raise him up, even from the dead…

Hebrews 11:17-19

My Prayer for Today

Father, I am thankful to know that You already know everything about me and that You don't need to put me through a test to find out whether or not I'm genuine. Now I understand that You are trying to show me something about myself. Help me to embrace the tests that help me to learn what kind of person I am. Holy Spirit, I ask You to help me cooperate with Your working in my life so that I will become the type of person You can use to expand and build Your Kingdom. That is my heartfelt prayer. I pray this in Jesus' name!

My Confession for Today

I confess that I am alert to recognize when God is testing me to show me something I need to know about myself. He already knows all the answers about me and nothing takes Him by surprise. But I need to know about me. I need to know that I am willing to obey and do whatever He asks me to do. I need to know that I am authentic and genuine in my faith. What He is asking me to do is for me to gain revelation about myself. It is information I need to know so that I can proceed with confidence and boldness as I push forward toward God's plan for my life. I declare this by faith in Jesus' name!

Jesus the Great Philanthropist

My Prayer for Today

Father, I ask You to help me become more like Jesus, who was the world's greatest Philanthropist! Help me not just to say I love people, but rather to show them love by my actions and deeds. Open my eyes to see the needs of those around me—and even to see how I can give of my finances to help people in other parts of the world. Since this was the heart of Jesus, it should be my heart too. Holy Spirit, I ask You to help me become like Jesus and do all that I can both spiritually and physically to meet the needs of those You bring across my path. I pray this in Jesus' name!

How God anointed Jesus of Nazareth with the Holy Ghost and with power: who went about doing good, and healing all that were oppressed of the devil; for God was with him.

Acts 10:38

My Confession for Today

I confess that God is using me to meet the physical and material needs of others. When God brings someone across my path who is hurting, I willingly respond to the Lord's direction concerning how He wants to use me to help meet his or her need. I can't help everyone, but I can and will help those He leads me to help. I obey the Holy Spirit's promptings and do what He instructs me to do. I am an extended hand of mercy to people who are hurting and disadvantaged. When the Holy Spirit needs someone to make a difference in another person's life, He knows He can count on me to be available! I declare this by faith in Jesus' name!

August 7

Embrace Your Grace!

According to the grace of God which is given unto me, as a wise masterbuilder, I have laid the foundation, and another buildeth thereon. But let every man take heed how he buildeth thereupon.

1 Corinthians 3:10

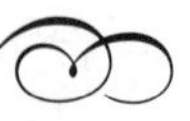

My Prayer for Today

Father, I thank You for the unique grace You have placed upon my life. I am gifted different from others, and You have called me to do what You have not called others to do. To do this job effectively, you have anointed me and equipped me in a distinctive way for the job. Today I ask You to help me surrender to the grace that you've placed on my life and to quit struggling with who You have called me to be! I pray this in Jesus' name!

My Confession for Today

I declare that I am content in the grace of God that is on my life. God has called me, anointed me, and graced me exactly for what I am doing. Who I am and what I am doing is no mistake. I have stepped into God's glorious plan for my life, and His grace has equipped me uniquely and effectively for what I am doing. Day by day, I become more comfortable with the grace of God that dominates my life! I declare this by faith in Jesus' name!

Time To Recommit To Your Promises?

My Prayer for Today

Heavenly Father, I thank You for this needed encouragement in my life today. I was nearly discouraged because I hadn't accomplished the things I promised myself at the first of the year that I would do. But I still have four months of this year left to attain some significant progress in various areas of my life. So I'm going to shake off all regret, yield to the workings of the Holy Spirit in my life, and go forward in Jesus' name. With His help, I am determined to make progress in those areas in which I know the Lord wants me to experience growth and change! I pray this in Jesus' name!

Redeeming the time…

Ephesians 5:16

My Confession for Today

I confess that I make a fresh commitment again to advance and make progress in my life and to achieve significant victories before the calendar hits December 31. The victories I long for are victories that the Lord desires for my life. He is with me. He is for me. He gives me overcoming power to accomplish these goals and dreams. I embrace His grace, and I repent for not making progress as I should have made. Today I turn my energies and my attention to the future. I plan to end this year with achievement and success! I declare this by faith in Jesus' name!

Christ's Warning To Erring Leaders

Repent; or else I will come unto thee quickly, and will fight against them with the sword of my mouth.

Revelation 2:16

My Prayer for Today

Heavenly Father, I pray for the spiritual leaders over my life. I pray that they will be quick to hear and prompt to obey Your Voice. I ask You to strengthen them with might in their inner self, that they will remain unbending in their commitment to the unchanging truths of Your Word, even if it means they must take a stand that is different from the spirit of the age around us. In this day when morals and beliefs seem to be changing on every side, give my pastor and spiritual leaders the fortitude and courage to stand firm in their commitment to the unchangeable truths of Your Word. I pray this in Jesus' name!

My Confession for Today

I confess that those who are spiritual leaders over my life walk in divine wisdom, counsel, and might. They are marked by integrity and free from compromise, standing with unwavering commitment to God's unchanging truths as revealed in the teaching of the Bible. Regardless of what society says, what the courts declare, or what the spirit of the age dictates, my leaders are led by the truth of the Bible and the Spirit of the Living God. I declare that they are sensitive to God's voice; they are quick to be corrected when it is required; and they will stand the test of time. They are anointed to minister in these last, very critical days of this age! I declare this by faith in Jesus' name!

Coming To the Lord One Step at a Time

My Prayer for Today

Father, I see now that some people—including notable people like Simon Peter—come to know You one step at a time. Help me to recognize how I can be used to bring people closer to You. Show me what to do, what to say, and what steps to take to introduce people to a knowledge of Jesus Christ that will change them at their core. Give me wisdom to lead my friends and acquaintances to a knowledge of Jesus that will transform them from the inside out. I pray this in Jesus' name!

When Simon Peter saw it, he fell down at Jesus' knees, saying, Depart from me; for I am a sinful man, O Lord.

Luke 5:8

My Confession for Today

I acknowledge that many people come to the Lord one step at a time. While only one experience is needed to bring a person to true conversion, it often takes many experiences to bring a person to that one experience that changes them forever. I confess that I am an instrument that God uses to share Christ, to bring people to a knowledge of sin, and to bring them to a place of repentance that changes them at the very core of their being. I declare this by faith in Jesus' name!

The Importance of Truthfulness

But speaking the truth in love…

Ephesians 4:15

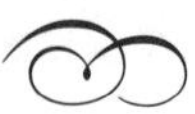

My Prayer for Today

Heavenly Father, I find speaking the truth in love to be difficult. I don't always know how to do that effectively, and at times I'm concerned that I might hurt someone's feelings or that I may be rejected. To do what I've read today will require a higher level of spiritual maturity in my life. Holy Spirit, I am asking You to help me know when to speak, when to be silent, and how to speak the truth in a way that is truthful, loving, and a blessing to those who listen to me. And help me to be open and receptive when people express the truth in love to me too! I pray this in Jesus' name!

My Confession for Today

I confess that I am honest with people about the things I express to them. I do not lie. I do not shade the truth, but I kindly and lovingly answer them in truth. Because they know I am truthful, they trust me and know that they can always depend on me to be truthful with them. Likewise, I confess that I am grateful when people speak the truth to me. God gives me the grace to listen, and He gives me the wisdom to discern what is true and what is just their opinion. I need truthfulness and honesty. Therefore, I choose to accept other people's candid relationship with me as a blessing to my life! I declare this by faith in Jesus' name!

Please the Lord Above All Else

My Prayer for Today

Father, as I serve You and Your Church, help me to always keep the balanced perspective that I am to love the people—but I am to please the Lord! As a servant of the Church, I always want to serve in a high-level, satisfactory manner, but my highest aim must be to please You above all else. Help me to find inroads into people's hearts, to give them Your Word, and to be a personal example that's so godly that they would want to imitate it. I pray this in Jesus' name!

For the appeal we make does not spring from error or impure motives, nor are we trying to trick you. On the contrary, we speak as those approved by God to be entrusted with the gospel. We are not trying to please people but God, who tests our hearts.

1 Thessalonians 2:3-4 NIV

My Confession for Today

I confess by faith that I deeply love people, but I live to please the Lord. Satisfying Jesus with my love for His people and my service to others is my highest aim. I want to be a vessel that God works through to touch others and take them higher. As a result, God gives me inroads to people's hearts and minds to pour the Word of God into them and live a godly example before them that they will want to imitate! I declare this by faith in Jesus' name!

AUGUST 13

A Cloak of Covetousness

For neither at any time used we flattering words, as ye know, nor a cloke of covetousness; God is witness.

1 Thessalonians 2:5

My Prayer for Today

Father God, everyone needs money, including me—but I ask You to keep my motivation for serving others free from the contamination of greed for money. Scripture is full of examples of people who were spoiled and suffered ruin because they let money become a motivator for ministry. I thank You for meeting my needs according to Your riches in glory by Christ Jesus. Keep my heart free from ever serving people with money as a motivator. For my own needs, I look to You, and I trust You to provide for me every step along the way! I pray this in Jesus' name!

My Confession for Today

I boldly confess that money is not and will never be my motivation for ministry. If making money is what it's all about, I need to go elsewhere and do something else. God has called me to serve people purely and to trust Him to meet my financial needs and obligations. I look to God, not people, as my Source to meet my needs! I declare this by faith in Jesus' name!

Living in the Limelight

My Prayer for Today

Father, I know what it's like to live for the honor and adulation of people, and I do not want to live in that kind of slavery ever again. It's a trap to fear people, to live constantly to please people, and to live for the praises of people. My utmost goal is to live to serve and please You. If I can live in the light of Your glory, I'll be so thankful—and that will be a glory that never passes with time. That is the true limelight my heart cries out for! I pray this in Jesus' name!

Nor of men sought we glory, neither of you, nor yet of others, when we might have been burdensome, as the apostles of Christ.

1 Thessalonians 2:6

My Confession for Today

I confess that I do NOT live for the glory and adulation of people. I appreciate being appreciated, and I am glad when people are thankful for what I do—but I live to please God. Daily I present myself before God as a living sacrifice to be acceptable unto Him, while I rely upon His grace to help me maintain a balance in my life of appreciating what others say and do while living exclusively for God and for His approval! I declare this by faith in Jesus' name!

AUGUST 15

The Heart Motive of Love

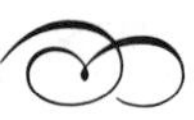

So being affectionately desirous of you, we were willing to have imparted unto you, not the gospel of God only, but also our own souls, because ye were dear unto us.

1 Thessalonians 2:8

My Prayer for Today

Father, I want my priorities to be correct about ministering to people. You deeply care for Your people, and I want that same love and compassion to be exactly what motivates me. Help me search my heart and put aside any other ulterior motive so that the care of Your people is the number-one priority on my heart. I am so thankful for the people who have genuinely cared for me and who continue to care for me. I consider it an honor to show genuine love, concern, care, and compassion for my brothers and sisters in the Christian community. I pray this in Jesus' name!

My Confession for Today

I confess that I love God's people and that I am doing all I can to help them grow in their knowledge of Jesus Christ. There are many things that vie for my attention, but I have decided that none is as important as ministering to the Lord and to His saints. Because the Holy Spirit has shed the love of God into my heart, I have a deep-seated, genuine love, concern, care, and compassion for the saints in the Christian community. I love God's people and my love for them is growing greater all the time! I declare this by faith in Jesus' name!

God's Testimony of Your Heart

My Prayer for Today

Father, I want my heart to be aligned with Your heart so I can confidently lay to rest any allegation against the truth. Holy Spirit, I ask You to help me evaluate myself to see where I stand on these issues of motivations and priorities that are so vitally important to You and to Your Church. I want my heart to be clear and clean about how I see and treat people. If there are areas where I need to change, I ask You to reveal them to me. Help me as I step forward to make things the way they ought to be. I pray this in Jesus' name!

For ye remember, brethren, our labour and travail: for labouring night and day, because we would not be chargeable unto any of you, we preached unto you the gospel of God. Ye are witnesses, and God also, how holily and justly and unblameably we behaved ourselves among you that believe: As ye know how we exhorted and comforted and charged every one of you, as a father doth his children, that ye would walk worthy of God, who hath called you unto his kingdom and glory.

1 Thessalonians 2:9-12

My Confession for Today

I confess and acknowledge that God not only observes what I say and do, but also He takes note of the intent and motivations of my heart. I am open to correction, therefore, I hear and obey the Holy Spirit when He speaks to me about changes I need to make in my life. And when the Holy Spirit speaks to me, He gives me the will and the power to make the changes He requires of me. My goal is to love God, to please Him first, and to keep my heart pure so that if God took the witness stand to testify about me, He would be able to say that I am walking worthily of His call upon me and that I am doing it by the power of His Spirit instead of the vain energy of my flesh. I establish my priorities as a believer in such a way that God Himself can testify that I pursue Him and His will for my life with all my heart, soul, and strength. I declare this by faith in Jesus' name!

The Privilege and Responsibility of Ministry

But we were gentle among you, even as a nurse cherisheth her children.

1 Thessalonians 2:7

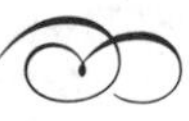

My Prayer for Today

Father, I want to be sensitive to the needs of new and younger believers. Help me to pay special attention to those who are new. Even if I didn't personally win them to Christ, help me to do whatever I can do to help them get on a strong path toward maturity if I see they are young, tender, and needy. Help me not to be self-absorbed with my personal interests but to put aside my own desires and respond to the needs of younger believers as a priority. Oh, Holy Spirit, help me to understand the great honor and privilege it is to minister to anyone, and especially to those who are young and new. I pray this in Jesus' name!

My Confession for Today

I confess by faith that I am sensitive to the needs of new and young believers. I do not see it as a burden to minister to them. I am thankful for those who ministered to me, and I count it a great privilege and responsibility to return this blessing by ministering to others who are young and new in the faith. I declare that the love of God in my heart is growing and multiplying and my concern for others is increasing. None of this is possible without the work of the Holy Spirit. So, Holy Spirit, I thank You for helping me grow in this area of my life. I declare this by faith in Jesus' name!

Love the Church as Christ Loves the Church

My Prayer for Today

Father God, I thank You for Your love which is already shed abroad in my heart by the Holy Spirit. I desire to deliberately give expression to that love more than ever before. I ask You to expand my own capacity to be filled with Your own undying love and passion for the Christian community that surrounds me. I pray that You would open the eyes of my understanding so I can comprehend how precious they are to You, and as a result, they would become so precious to me. Thank You for the example of Jesus, the apostle Paul, and others, who have gone before me and demonstrated how to love and sacrifice for others. I ask You to forgive me for the times I've been selfish and have held back on giving my time and effort to help others. Help me to grow in my personal understanding and acquaintance with Your great love for me, so that I can love others as You have loved me. I pray this in Jesus' name!

So being affectionately desirous of you, we were willing to have imparted unto you, not the gospel of God only, but also our own souls, because ye were dear unto us.

1 Thessalonians 2:8

My Confession for Today

I confess that God fills me with an undying love and passion for the Christian community. I comprehend how precious they are to God; therefore, they are precious to me. I devote myself to walk in love toward others and to willingly sacrifice for them. I repent for the times I've been selfish and have held back from giving my time and effort to help others. I commit from this moment forward to be less selfish and to be more giving, just as God gives Himself to us in the ways we need Him the most. I declare this by faith in Jesus' name!

Nurturer and Mentor

As ye know how we exhorted and comforted and charged every one of you, as a father doth his children.

1 Thessalonians 2:11

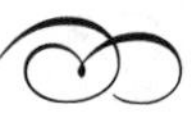

My Prayer for Today

Father, my heart is stirred as I ponder the need for and importance of nurturing and mentoring young believers as they are growing up in the Lord. How thankful I am for the Christian leaders who mentored me and who helped me mature in the Lord Jesus Christ. I think of my pastor, who led me and corrected me at the right times in order to help me grow up. Holy Spirit, I ask You to help me and other Christians to take our place and strengthen and encourage young believers who need spiritual fathers and mothers in their lives. I pray this in Jesus' name!

My Confession for Today

I confess I have wisdom from the Lord, and the Holy Spirit gives me the counsel I need to help young Christians mature in their relationship with the Lord. I find great joy in praying, teaching, serving, and helping others mature in the Lord. To see Christ formed in young believers is a priority. Therefore, I yield to the ministry of the Holy Spirit so that I can be a vessel for Him to fill and flow through in order to bless and strengthen those under my spiritual care. I declare this by faith in Jesus' name!

Deflation and Inflation

My Prayer for Today

Father, as I reflect on my life, the truth is that You have been faithful to me from the very beginning. I repent for every time I yielded to the temptation to worry and fret instead of trusting You. Father, I ask You to please help me grow up and mature in this area of my life. I have no reason to ever doubt You, for You have always been faithful to me. Help me remember Your faithfulness rather than focus on the needs that seem so large and insurmountable. Your name is Faithful—and You will be faithful to me now and always! I pray this in Jesus' name!

Therefore take no thought, saying, What shall we eat? or, What shall we drink? or, Wherewithal shall we be clothed? (For after all these things do the Gentiles seek:) for your heavenly Father knoweth that ye have need of all these things. But seek ye first the kingdom of God, and his righteousness; and all these things shall be added unto you.

Matthew 6:31-33

My Confession for Today

I confess that I do not worry about God's provision for my life. God has always been faithful to me, and He always will be faithful. Faithful is one of His names. He will always sustain all those who trust in Him and cast their burden on Him. Likewise, God will sustain me and help me. Even if my eyes cannot see the way, I know He is going to do it. Everything that I see is subject to change. Therefore, I focus my attention on the unchanging Word and the faithful character of God. I cast my burden on Him, and I trust Him to meet the needs of my life and to help me do the large tasks He has commissioned me to do! I declare this by faith in Jesus' name!

The Experience of a Lifetime!

He that findeth his life shall lose it: and he that loseth his life for my sake shall find it.

Matthew 10:39 NIV

My Prayer for Today

Father, I don't want to hold on to my life and, as a result, miss the great adventure You have planned for me and my family. Forgive me for not trusting You—and help me put all fear and doubt aside as I "kiss the ground" of my calling. Help me allow Your power and love to sink deep into my heart for what You are asking me to do. I repent for hesitating and holding back out of a sense of self-preservation and a fear of the unknown. Today I fully surrender my life and my future to You. I pray this in Jesus' name!

My Confession for Today

I confess that I will not hold back on the Lord any longer. Whatever He wants me to do, that is what I will do. In the past, fear of an uncertain future has hindered me, but now I know that God has only a wonderful adventure in store for me and my family. I rebuke the spirit of fear that has restrained me, and I put my trust fully in the Lord as I step forward by faith to kiss the ground of God's calling on my life. I declare that God will put a deep-seated love in my heart for what He has called me to do. I'll never look back in regret but will only rejoice that I finally and fully surrendered to the call with which He has entrusted to me. I declare this by faith in Jesus' name!

Why Do People Sometimes Collapse in the Presence of God?

And when I [John] saw him [Christ], I fell at his feet as dead...

Revelation 1:17

My Prayer for Today

Father, I know that You love me deeply and that Your love for me is not proven by physical manifestations such as falling down under the power of the Holy Spirit. But I want to thank You for the times I have come into contact with Your strong presence to such an extent that I could physically feel the result of it. I open my heart for You to move in my life in any way that You wish—and I ask You to forgive me for being skeptical in the past when I've heard of such experiences in others and have doubted it. From this moment onward, I am open for You to make Yourself known to me in any way You desire. I pray this in Jesus' name!

My Confession for Today

I confess that I experience the power of God in my life and that my heart and my mind are open to experiencing His presence in whatever way He wishes to manifest Himself to me. I am willing to be changed by the power of God, regardless of whether I remain on my feet or lie on the floor. I am open to the Holy Spirit, and I desire to yield fully to His divine operation inside me. I long for it; I pray for it; and I claim it! I declare this by faith in Jesus' name!

AUGUST 23

The Overcomer's Promise

...To him that overcometh will I give to eat of the hidden manna...

Revelation 2:17

My Prayer for Today

Father, You are calling me to live in overwhelming victory. Through You, I can be a conqueror who gains the mastery over all opposition. Forgive me for the times I focused more on the struggle opposing me than on the victory You have already won for me. I am a victor, not a victim. I realize that You want me to see myself as a victor, a champion, one who has completely defeated my enemies. You have made provision for me to continuously maintain that victory in my life through the Holy Spirit. I make an intentional decision to draw upon Your power in me. I'm willing and ready to jump in the fight and finish it to the end in the strength of Your might! I pray this in Jesus' name!

My Confession for Today

I confess that Christ calls me to overcome, and He gives me the power to do it. He would not ask me to do something I cannot do. But I can overcome only through the mighty power of the Holy Spirit, so I declare that I yield to the Person of the Holy Spirit who indwells me. I am a willing vessel for the Holy Spirit to release His supernatural power through me. He causes me to rise above my difficulties. His power enables me to put my foot on the enemy's neck and command him to back down. The enemies I face hear my voice of authority and see my commitment—and as a result, they back off from their attack, because greater is He who is in me than he that is in the world! I declare this by faith in Jesus' name!

A Superabundance of Heavenly Angels' Food

...To him that overcometh will I give to eat of the hidden manna...

Revelation 2:17

My Prayer for Today

Heavenly Father, I am thrilled to know that You are so concerned about my well-being. How can I do anything but praise and thank You? You have demonstrated that You care so much for me that You would provide me with the daily bread I need to keep my life strong. Today I make the decision to draw near to Your table and to eat of the heavenly bread that You have set before me—bread that never runs out! Your supernatural strength is my sustenance. I partake of Your presence as my necessary food. You have called me to overcome, and Your sustaining touch keeps me strong in the battle. I know that as You strengthen me with Your might, I will be continually replenished, sustained in times of difficulty, and enabled to move obstacles out of my way. I pray this in Jesus' name!

My Confession for Today

I confess that God provides the spiritual nourishment that I need to overcome the obstacles and difficulties that try to hinder me in life. Each day as I consciously walk with an awareness of God's presence within me, I am replenished, strengthened, and enabled to conquer any foe that shows up along the way. God's power touches me physically, spiritually, and emotionally and fills up those areas that have been depleted due to a long struggle. God's grace is available to me every day just as daily manna was available to the children of Israel during their trek across the desert. The Lord spreads a table before me even in the presence of my enemies. When I come to His table, Christ provides everything I need. With God's daily touch on my life, I am revived, refreshed, and ready to continue the fight until I can shout, "Amen! The victory has manifested because the battle was already won!" I declare this by faith in Jesus' name!

AUGUST 25

Refuse To Give Up and Quit!

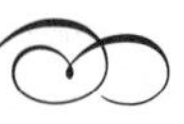

And let us not be weary in well doing: for in due season we shall reap, if we faint not.

Galatians 6:9

My Prayer for Today

Father, I have been sowing seeds and waiting for my harvest for quite some time. It is true that I have been tempted to become tired and weary of waiting. So today I thank You because You said those who wait upon You shall renew their strength! I thank You for renewing and replenishing me as I patiently wait for my harvest. Your Word promises that it will come in due season. Holy Spirit, strengthen me with Your mighty power to stay the course until my due season arrives. I receive fresh grace to remain steady and on track with the project that You have assigned to me to complete! In those moments when I'm tempted to be tired and quit, help me remember that I can grab hold of Your power and not stray from my God-assigned purpose! I pray this in Jesus' name!

My Confession for Today

I confess that I refuse to give up in times of spiritual, physical, or mental exhaustion. I will reach that point of fulfillment when I reap because I will hold tightly to what God has told me. God promised me in Galatians 6:9 that if I will remain steadfast, the manifestation of what I've been waiting for and believing to happen will come. On the basis of this promise, I REFUSE TO GIVE UP AND QUIT. I declare by faith that it's only a matter of time until my long-awaited blessing arrives. Instead of caving in to weariness and the temptation to quit, I will lift up my hands in thanksgiving. I make the choice to praise God with a grateful heart as I keep thanking God for the harvest He has in store for me! I declare this by faith in Jesus' name!

Traveling Dangers

My Prayer for Today

Father, I want to thank You for the many times You have given Your angels charge of me to protect, provide for, and guide me when I was confronted with difficulties or was completely unaware of the situations I had unknowingly wandered into or of the danger that surrounded me. I am reminded of how Your ministering spirits have met my needs; brought me help; strengthened me when I was exhausted both physically and emotionally; and kept me safe in the midst of circumstances that could have produced certain harm or even taken my life. Time after time, You've held me safe through the watchful care of Your ministering angels. Lord, I love You. You have shown me great mercy, and each day I find new reasons to praise and glorify You as a faithful Keeper of covenant in my life. I pray this in Jesus' name!

Are they not all ministering spirits, sent forth to minister for them who shall be heirs of salvation?

Hebrews 1:14

My Confession for Today

I confess that time after time, in ways I seldom realize, God dispatches angels to assist me. These ministering spirits surround me and keep me safe, and they never fail to step in to deliver me even when I don't know that I am in harm's way. Whatever my situation, and regardless of the need, angels are assigned to protect, provide, strengthen, and guide me in all my ways of obedience to the Lord. I declare this by faith in Jesus' name!

AUGUST 27

Thou Hast Left Thy First Love

Nevertheless I have somewhat against thee, because thou hast left thy first love.

Revelation 2:4

My Prayer for Today

Father, as I read how the church at Ephesus subtly shifted its focus from walking with You to working for You, I'm struck by the realization of how easily our attention can fasten on what we do for You instead of on You for who You are. Lord, I repent for how I've allowed the cares of life and my concern for other things to harden my heart and dull the fervency of my passion for You. When I compare how I am today to how I was when I first came to Jesus, I must admit that I've become doctrinally sophisticated yet spiritually powerless. I confess my sin of idolatry because I've allowed other things to become enthroned in my heart. Holy Spirit, I humbly ask You to work in me, to ignite within me a white-hot fervor for Jesus like I've never known. Bring me to a place where my chief desire is to know Him, to love Him, to walk with Him, to serve Him, and to please Him in the pure power of holiness. I pray this in Jesus' name!

My Confession for Today

I declare that I am in love with Jesus Christ. He is the center of my life. My love for Him consumes me and motivates every part of my life. I started out in the fire of God, and I will end in the fire of God. I allow the Holy Spirit to search my heart regularly to reveal my true spiritual state. I refuse to become doctrinally sophisticated yet powerless and irrelevant. I confess that I am overwhelmed with the love of Jesus. My heart is increasingly captivated by Him. Every day, every week, and every year that passes, I grow more deeply in love with Him. Soon I'll meet Him face to face. Each morning I awaken with greater determination to live my life for that moment when I look into His loving eyes. Oh, what a day that will be—but until then, I want to be consumed with His fire! I declare this by faith in Jesus' name!

Remember!

My Prayer for Today

Father, I never want to forget the amazing things You did in my life when I first came to know You many years ago. Forgive me for allowing the clutter of my life to bury precious memories that I should never forget. From the start of our relationship, You have proven Yourself faithful to me. I need not ever bury that or forget it when I get busy. Holy Spirit, today I ask You to help me "declutter" the memories of my past and revive those precious memories that I need to hold clear and dear. I pray this in Jesus' name!

Remember therefore from whence thou art fallen, and repent, and do the first works...

Revelation 2:5

My Confession for Today

I declare that I do not easily forget the things that God has done for me. I have personally experienced the faithfulness of God, and I remain thankful for all that He has done for me. Weariness, busy schedules, and a constant stream of new responsibilities do not blur God's faithfulness to me. My spiritual life is not full of drudgery, nor is it reduced into a monotonous, religious routine. I am spiritually alive, vital, and eager for God to move in my life! I declare this by faith in Jesus' name!

AUGUST 29

From Whence Thou Art Fallen

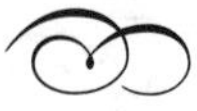

Remember therefore from whence thou art fallen...

Revelation 2:5

My Prayer for Today

Dear Father, I confess that the Church—with all of its sophistication and technology—seems to be lacking in great demonstrations of the power of God. But rather than take a critical role, I admit that I am part of this great Body of believers, and that, I, too, need to remember from whence I have fallen. Help us to remember the early days, the early passion, the early fire that burned in our hearts. Help us to do a corrective self-analysis of where we are compared to where we were. There have been so many wonderful advances, and I recognize that, but there is a simplicity and fire that is missing. Lord, restore it to us and help us burn brightly and simply as we once did. I pray this in Jesus' name!

My Confession for Today

I confess that admitting what is wrong is the first step in repentance. Therefore, I repent for allowing the busyness of life and worldliness to usurp the place in my heart that belongs only to the Lord. I press in to receive a fresh visitation of the Holy Spirit's power and the heartfelt willingness to receive it with open arms. I confess that I am open-hearted, willing, and ready for the Lord to restore His Church to the power that He destined for it to possess! I declare this by faith in Jesus' name!

Repent!

My Prayer for Today

Father, I thank You for speaking to me about my need to repent—that is, to change the way I've been thinking and living. Truthfully, I've been consumed with serving You more than I have been consumed with just loving You, as I once did in the past. I've become so busy that I don't read my Bible as I once did; I don't pray as I once did; and I've drifted from the passionate fire that once burned in my heart. I am busy and involved, but my relationship with You is distant compared to the intimate communion we once shared years ago. For all this I repent. Today I hear Your voice calling me back into meaningful fellowship. Forgive me for my spiritual lethargy, and set me ablaze with the Spirit of God! I pray this in Jesus' name!

Remember therefore from whence thou art fallen, and repent...

Revelation 2:5

My Confession for Today

I declare that I am on fire for Jesus Christ. I repent for allowing a lukewarm attitude to work inside me, and I ask God to make me a bonfire for the Kingdom of God! I confess that I burn with passion and with the power of God. I am consumed with a desire to see lost souls come to Christ. I long to see the power of God even more than I once did. I humble myself before the Lord. I hear His voice, and I submit myself to God and to His service in a fresh, new way. I declare this by faith in Jesus' name!

Do the First Works

Remember therefore from whence thou art fallen, and repent, and do the first works…

Revelation 2:5

My Prayer for Today

Father, I am deeply convicted by what I have read today. I recognize that You are calling me deeper and higher, and it is my responsibility to follow the leading of the Holy Spirit and to respond to what I have read. I repent for backsliding—for letting my once passionately intimate relationship with you slip and be replaced by other worldly concerns. I admit that I've done this, and I confess my sins and repent according to 1 John 1:9 and I receive full forgiveness. Now that I am free, I reclaim what I have lost, and I move forward to obtain what You have for me in the future. I pray this in Jesus' name!

My Confession for Today

I confess that I repent for allowing worldliness and other things to take the place that belongs only to You. I lay hold of a new level of commitment that results in renewed love for You. You are watching and waiting to see how I will respond to the dealings of Your Spirit. I profess that I return to my first love. I declare this by faith in Jesus' name!

The Solution To Offense–Forgiveness!

My Prayer for Today

Father God, I repent for the offense I have harbored in my heart toward people. I see now that offense has held me in a prison of my own making. I have been tormented by it, and it has kept me from making spiritual progress as I should. Rather than allow offense room to continue festering in my heart and soul, today I make the choice to let it go. I forgive my offenders, and I extend the same grace to them that I want others to give me. Right now I receive freedom as I choose to walk away from the offenses that have held me in bondage for so long! I pray this in Jesus' name!

...If thy brother trespass against thee, rebuke him; and if he repent, forgive him.

Luke 17:3

My Confession for Today

I declare by faith that I am an offense-free person! Others' actions, or lack of actions, do not have the power to put me into a state of bitterness and offense. To be offended requires my agreement, and I will no longer agree to stay in a state of unforgiveness and offense. I release those who have violated me in the past, and I will never bring it up again to them, to others, or to myself. I completely and freely forgive them. As a result, I am a free person with no oppressive, parasitic appendages hanging on me any longer! I declare this by faith in Jesus' name!

My Hallowed Place

And in the morning, rising up a great while before day, he [Jesus] went out, and departed into a solitary place, and there prayed.

Mark 1:35

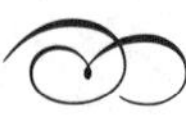

My Prayer for Today

Heavenly Father, I make a fresh commitment to start each day by lifting my voice to You. Each morning, Lord, I will rise and present my life to You, waiting expectantly for what You will speak to my heart. I ask Your forgiveness for all the times I foolishly launched into my day without having read your Word, sought Your face, or consulted the Holy Spirit whom You sent to be my Counselor, Helper, and Guide. Father, how arrogant and misguided of me to believe I could walk effectively in wisdom and truth without having submitted myself to You first. Only through rich fellowship with You can I produce fruit that remains. Forgive me for mistaking busyness for fruitfulness. I abide in You and let Your words abide in me. I treasure the words of Your mouth more than my necessary food. Holy Spirit, I ask You to help me order my day and to keep it set around giving my time with the Father first place from this day forward. I pray this in Jesus' name!

My Confession for Today

I confess that I do not neglect my time in a "solitary place" with God. I deliberately designate an off-limits time and place where I can have deep, meaningful, and uninterrupted fellowship with the Father, the Son, and the Holy Spirit. Just as Jesus arose a great while before day to meet with the Father and then emerged from His solitary times renewed in power, I come forth from my daily times refreshed, reinvigorated, filled with new ideas, and empowered for my day. These moments of solitude with the Father keep my heart sensitive and yielded to Him while equipping me to possess my daily victory in the power of His might! I declare this by faith in Jesus' name!

Jesus Always in Our Midst

My Prayer for Today

Father, I thank You for the promise Jesus made in Matthew 18:20 — that if two or three gather together in His name, there He would be in the midst of them. There is nothing even remotely comparable to the sweet presence of Jesus in the midst of Christian fellowship. It makes me want to ask You to forgive me for the times that I haven't made a better effort to gather with other believers. I really need that sweet presence of Jesus that is experienced in Christian fellowship — and I'm so thankful that Jesus manifests Himself to those who gather in His name. Help me to be more consistent about my commitment to gathering in Jesus' name with other brothers and sisters. And thank You for revealing and manifesting Yourself to us in such a precious way! I pray this in Jesus' name!

For where two or three are gathered together in my name, there am I in the midst of them.

Matthew 18:20

My Confession for Today

I confess that I need the sweet presence of Jesus that is manifested specially as brothers and sisters gather together in the name of Jesus. The Lord Jesus promised that He would be there among us as we gather in His name — and I commit to gathering regularly with others who are also seeking His face. Thank You, Lord, that You did not say we had to all be in the same room at the same time. You said simply that we had to gather at the same time in Your name, and Your precious presence would be there with us. I declare that I need that "corporate" presence of Jesus and that I will therefore take advantage of every opportunity to gather with other believers in Jesus' name! I declare this by faith in Jesus' name!

SEPTEMBER 4

6 Suggestions for Finding Your Faith Place

But without faith it is impossible to please him…

Hebrews 11:6

My Prayer for Today

Father, I thank You for helping me know how to get started on finding my place of faith. I want to know Your will; I want to follow it; and I want to stay "in" that place of faith until I hear You tell me that I've faithfully finished the task You've assigned to me. Help me know where to start, where to serve, what to sow, and where to sow my seed. So Holy Spirit, let's do it—I am ready to get started today! I pray this in Jesus' name!

My Confession for Today

I confess that I am not a person who just sits around, wondering about God's will for my life. Until He speaks to me, I will implement these six suggestions in my life: I will start; I will know how and where to serve; I will determine the level of commitment I can make right now; I will sow my seed; and I will not stop. I fully expect to see harvests coming back to me from every direction. I refuse to sit idly and wonder what I should do. I will find a place to serve and sow, and I will get started. As I take these steps of faith, I'll begin to hear God's voice speak to me specifically about my own place of faith—and when I hear it, I'll obey and stick with it until I hear the Lord say the job is done. I declare this by faith in Jesus' name!

Spiritual Curb Appeal

My Prayer for Today

Father, I repent for thinking that other people's opinion of me is unimportant. Help me live such a powerful, balanced, godly, dependable life that others will look to me as a tower of strength they can rely on. My life is my pulpit, and how I live before others will determine whether or not they respect me. If they do hold me in respect, the door will stay open for me to lead them and to influence them with the Gospel of Jesus Christ. So starting today, I am changing the way I think and embracing the truth that other people's opinions about me are very important! I pray this in Jesus' name!

Moreover he must have a good report of them which are without...

1 Timothy 3:7

My Confession for Today

I confess that I have a positive influence on the people around me. I have a testimony that I am a cheerful, optimistic, faith-filled, dependable, and hardworking team player who is enjoyed by others. Because I do my best to live according to the Word of God, I have a good reputation with others in both the non-Christian world and in the Christian community. People respect me, honor me, believe me, trust me, and want to follow me because they have witnessed that I am solid, dependable, and reliable. Because the Holy Spirit is working in my character to transform my mind and conform me to the image of Jesus Christ, I have a good testimony with everyone I know and meet. I declare this by faith in Jesus' name!

SEPTEMBER 6

Jesus Christ, Ruler of Earthly Kings

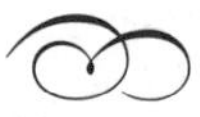

...Jesus Christ, who is the faithful witness, and the first begotten of the dead, and the prince of the kings of the earth...

Revelation 1:5

My Prayer for Today

Father, I am so thankful that Jesus is Lord over all, and that includes my life! Your Word is coming to pass at a rapid pace in these end times: Darkness is increasing; morals are sliding; laws are changing for the worse; and society is rapidly degenerating. But seated above them all is Jesus—the King of kings of the earth. When all is said and done, rulers may have a temporary say-so in the affairs of humankind, but Jesus ultimately rules over all. Help me not to despair when I see evil prosper and to remember that Jesus has not lost His grip on the situation. He really IS Lord over all! I pray this in Jesus' name!

My Confession for Today

I boldly confess that Jesus Christ is not only the King of kings, but the Ruler of all the kings of the earth (see Revelation 19:16; 1:5). There is no higher power or authority than Jesus Christ. His throne is exalted above all others. Human powers come and go, but the Kingdom of Jesus Christ endures forever. I declare that 2,000 years of Church history have proven that Jesus is highly and forever exalted, and that He will have the ultimate say-so in the affairs of humankind. I may not see how His hand is moving, but none is greater than or equal to Him. Jesus Christ rules over all, and He is directing the affairs of humankind to fulfill His divine purpose! I declare this by faith in Jesus' name!

Faithfully Doing the Small Things

My Prayer for Today

Father, I am amazed by Your design for the Body of Christ, with each of us interdependent upon the other. Alone we can do our small parts, but together we can accomplish a greater goal. I ask You to help me really see and understand this truth. I repent of the pride that has tried to creep in to make me despise small things or to hinder me from cooperating with others to fulfill my part in Your plan. I confess that these are areas where I need to grow. Father, You resist the proud, but You give grace to the humble. I ask You for Your grace to help me reach new levels in these areas so I can glorify You and be a true blessing to others. I pray this in Jesus' name!

For by the grace (unmerited favor of God) given to me I warn everyone among you not to estimate and think of himself more highly than he ought [not to have an exaggerated opinion of his own importance], but to rate his ability with sober judgment, each according to the degree of faith apportioned by God to him.

Romans 12:3 AMPC

My Confession for Today

I confess that I am well aware of my interdependence with others in the Body of Christ. You called us as a whole Body so that we may work properly and accomplish greater goals. I am not willing to be independent in the way I operate. By the grace of God working in me, I submit myself to God and resist the temptation to overestimate myself. I will appreciate those who are called alongside me to work, and I will humbly esteem their great value to God and also to me. The visible and less visible members are equally important, and as I walk with God, I am becoming ever more aware of my need to do my part, along with those who are called by God to do their own part. I declare this by faith in Jesus' name!

Are We Too Busy Serving That We Miss What Matters?

I know thy works, and thy labour, and thy patience, and how thou canst not bear them which are evil: and thou hast tried them which say they are apostles, and are not, and hast found them liars: And hast borne, and hast patience, and for my name's sake hast laboured, and hast not fainted.

Revelation 2:2-3

My Prayer for Today

Father, I desire to retain the fire in my heart that I had when I first came to know You. Life has become busy, and I confess that somewhere along the way I allowed the busyness of it all to dim the fire in my heart. Although I've become more experienced and professional, I am less passionate than I used to be. I repent for this, and I confess that it is wrong. Holy Spirit, I ask You to help me return to the place of my first love. I have lost sight of loving You more than anything else. For this I repent, and I ask You to forgive me. Purify my heart so that Your presence will ignite a flame in me until You are the highest priority and goal in my life. I pray this in Jesus' name!

My Confession for Today

I confess that I refuse to allow my productivity for God to take precedence over my passionate love for Him. I will not offer diligence toward duty as a substitute for devotion toward Him as I approach my God-given assignment. I return to the place of my first love. I commit to pull away often from the busyness of life and ministry so I can be still in the presence of the Lord in order to maintain a vital connection with Him. I will not attempt to serve God without a fresh touch of His Spirit upon me. In the morning I will lift up my eyes, my heart, and my voice unto the Lord while I wait until His Word speaks to my heart in a fresh way for each new day. From that place of union with Him, I will stay focused on what really matters. I declare this by faith in Jesus' name!

Stand Together To Overcome Darkness

My Prayer for Today

Heavenly Father, I ask You to help me assume my role in prayer as we charge forward into the last of the last days. In these last days, everything that can be shaken will be shaken. Holy Spirit, since judgment begins at the house of God, I ask You to help me as I examine myself. I want to be certain that I live my life worthily as I ought so that after having preached to others, I myself won't become a castaway. Lord Jesus, I embrace my divine duty to build the Kingdom of God until You return and to lead others in taking a righteous stand to actively withstand the forces of darkness by the power of Your mighty name! Strengthen me with Your wisdom, counsel, and might to accept my responsibility to pray and to live with unflinching conviction. Father, although spiritual darkness seems to blanket the nations, You promised that the knowledge of the glory of the Lord would cover the earth as the waters cover the sea. So I refuse to allow fear to grip my heart. The darker the hour, the greater the opportunity for Christ in me—the Hope of glory—to shine brightly and be revealed to a dying world that needs Him! I pray this in Jesus' name!

This know also, that in the last days perilous times shall come.

2 Timothy 3:1

My Confession for Today

I confess that I live a life of increased prayer and consecration to God. In moments when I may be tempted to think I'm too busy to pray, I will recognize that something else has to go—but it won't be my time in the Bible or in prayer! As the days grow darker spiritually, I will become even more accountable to my church and to fellow believers because we are stronger together. I receive the wisdom of God that protects me from either a ditch of legalism or of lawlessness. I keep myself in the love of God and find new avenues to work with other Christians to build God's Kingdom. Because I increase my time in the Word of God, my faith increases regardless of circumstances, and I continue to pray for those in authority. It is an honor to help gather in this end-time harvest of souls. Therefore, I confess that I take my place to drive back spiritual darkness with the light of the Gospel so Jesus can be exalted and the transforming power of God can be displayed to this generation as never before. I refuse to slow down or weaken my stance of faith until the nations come to His great light. I declare this by faith in Jesus' name!

The Power of Agreement

Again I say unto you, That if two of you shall agree on earth as touching any thing that they shall ask, it shall be done for them of my Father which is in heaven.

Matthew 18:19

My Prayer for Today

Father, I am so grateful that unity reflects Your heart and causes the anointing of Your presence to saturate us and manifest Your blessing in our midst. Enormous power exists when believers get in agreement with You and with each other. Holy Spirit, I ask You to teach me and the body of believers You have planted me in how to operate just like a symphony orchestra. I ask this also for the Body of Christ at large. As many instruments combined with a wide array of sounds, help us yield to Your direction as a skilled Conductor so that all those sounds blend together into a beautiful musical masterpiece. Help us symphonize in faith and unity more and more so we may have greater power in prayer and action and make a phenomenal impact on the listeners that extends far beyond what any one instrument could achieve on its own. I pray this in Jesus' name!

My Confession for Today

I confess that I contribute to the unity the Father desires the Body of Christ to operate in. I refuse to adopt an adversarial role when He has called me to do everything I can to achieve unity. We have more that unites us than divides us, so I choose to focus on the things that bring us together instead of the things that drive us apart. I thank You for the support I've found from other believers and ministers, and I ask You to help me be a support to others who are stepping out in faith to do what You have asked them to do. I declare this by faith in Jesus' name!

Five Different Crowns of Reward

My Prayer for Today

Father, Your Word clearly teaches that when we see Jesus in Heaven, He will have a special "reward" in His hand—a victor's crown—to place upon our heads. But more important to me than receiving a crown is that I please You. To receive a crown from You will be a blessing, as it is Your recognition of what I have done, and it will be a treasure that I can lay at Jesus' feet on that day. But the greatest reward for me will be knowing I have run a race that brought You pleasure! I pray this in Jesus' name!

Henceforth there is laid up for me a crown of righteousness, which the Lord, the righteous judge, shall give me at that day: and not to me only, but unto all them also that love his appearing.

2 Timothy 4:8

My Confession for Today

I declare that I will run my race of faith all the way to its final conclusion. There will be no dropping out of the race halfway along the God-ordained course of my life. I'm in this to finish it and to bring glory to the name of the Lord Jesus Christ. I am thankful that because I will be faithful to the end, on the day I see Jesus, He will give me a victor's crown. But most of all, I want to see the satisfaction in His eyes that I've run a race of faith that has brought glory to His name. His glory is my highest goal and the reason I am running in this race of faith! I declare this by faith in Jesus' name!

Do Things Right the First Time!

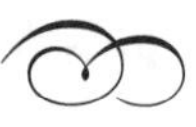

For which of you, intending to build a tower, sitteth not down first, and counteth the cost, whether he have sufficient to finish it? Lest haply, after he hath laid the foundation, and is not able to finish it, all that behold it begin to mock him.

Luke 14:28-29

My Prayer for Today

Father, I thank You for your common-sense approach to life. I know that You have called me to do significant things with my life, so I accept the challenge to sit down and calculate the costs before I get started. The last thing I want is to start something I can't finish and give others a reason to mock me or to deride Your holy assignment. I do not want to create an opportunity to hear the accusing voice of the devil or the mocking voices of doubters or nonbelievers. So help me use my mind, seek wise counsel, and take each step of faith carefully and methodically. I receive Your supernatural assistance to do every natural thing You've called me to do. I pray this in Jesus' name!

My Confession for Today

I declare that I start every project by first sitting down to seriously contemplate the cost and the effort it will take to complete it. I ask You to help me think through every step that is required to finish this project. I will start this assignment with the full assurance that this is correct. I am confident and persuaded that I will finish what I have started because I fasten my attention and take my direction from Jesus, who is both the Author and the Finisher of my faith! I declare this by faith in Jesus' name!

We Have the Answer To Difficult Days!

My Prayer for Today

Father, there is no doubt in my mind that we are living in the last of the last days. The challenges in our future are unlike any faced by the previous generations. Jesus warned of impending calamities as we approach the end of the age. He did not warn us of these difficulties to scare us but to prepare us. Holy Spirit, I trust You for the wisdom I need in order to plan and be prepared in every area of my life for what lies ahead. I ask You to make me Your hand of deliverance and provision for others as You equip and enable me to meet the severe needs of those who are suffering in these difficult times. I pray this in Jesus' name!

Then the disciples, every man according to his ability, determined to send relief unto the brethren which dwelt in Judaea.

Acts 11:29

My Confession for Today

I confess that God has not given me a spirit of fear, but of power, love, and a sound mind. Therefore, I am well organized and prepared for any dark days that lie ahead. I rise up in faith and boldly seize the hour for the spreading of the eternal Gospel. I remain sensitive to and in touch with the Spirit of God, and He teaches me how to prepare as He leads me according to truth and shows me things to come. God has blessed me so I can be a blessing to others. I have resolved to be an expression of God's hope and blessing; therefore, He will bless me with resources and provisions that I can share with those who are in need. I declare this by faith in Jesus' name!

God's Law of Giving and Receiving

But this I say, He which soweth sparingly shall reap also sparingly; and he which soweth bountifully shall reap also bountifully.

2 Corinthians 9:6

My Prayer for Today

Heavenly Father, I thank You that the law of sowing and reaping works regardless of what is happening in the current world economy. Your Word commands me to give tithes and offerings, and I obey what Your Word tells me to do. You said that if I love You, I will keep Your commands. By giving, I am demonstrating my love to You. It is a part of my worship. I thank You for keeping Your promise that if I give, it will be given to me again. It is part of Your personal promise to me, and I thank You for being faithful to perform Your promise in my life. I pray this in Jesus' name!

My Confession for Today

I confess that I am consistent and faithful when it comes to giving tithes and offerings to the work of the ministry. People need to hear the Good News of Jesus Christ—and I commit to using my money to preach the Gospel and to mature new believers in their faith. When it comes to my contributions, I declare that God can count on me. If there is any area that needs to be cut back in my expenses, it will not be in the area of my tithes and offerings. I will be faithful, and God will multiply my seed back to me. My time of harvest will come, and it will never be late. God is well aware of my situation, and He will keep His promise of sowing and reaping to me! I declare this by faith in Jesus' name!

Busting Through Every Barrier!

My Prayer for Today

In journeyings often, in perils of waters, in perils of robbers, in perils by mine own countrymen, in perils by the heathen, in perils in the city, in perils in the wilderness, in perils in the sea, in perils among false brethren.

2 Corinthians 11:26

Father, I thank You for the power of God that sustains me when I am in rough places. The devil has tried to hinder me, oppose me, and thwart Your plan for my life. But I've kept my eyes focused on the goal that You have given me—and as a result, You have empowered me to keep going forward regardless of the opposition that I have encountered. Today I ask You to empower me by the Holy Spirit to tackle and overcome every hindrance that I am facing. I thank You for this divine power that always helps to make a way! I pray this in Jesus' name!

My Confession for Today

I confess that greater is He who is in me than He that is in the world! The devil and the world itself may try to limit and hinder me from fulfilling God's plan for my life, but I declare that I will not be defeated, nor will I allow the devil to have delight in mastering my life. With the name of Jesus, the power of God, and the endurance of the Holy Spirit, I will press forward by faith until I have gone where I am supposed to go and have done what I am supposed to do! I declare this by faith in Jesus' name!

SEPTEMBER 16

Have Ears "To Hear"!

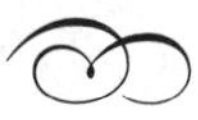

To all that be in Rome, beloved of God, called to be saints…

Romans 1:7

My Prayer for Today

Father, I thank You for opening my spiritual ears to hear the call You first issued to me when You called me to repentance and salvation. I understand that I "heard" that call only because You opened my spiritual ears to hear. How I thank You for that divine act of grace in my life! And now, Father, I ask that my spiritual ears remain open so that I can continue to hear the invitations You extend to me when You call upon me to do new tasks and assignments. Help me not to be so busy that I don't hear You. It is my sincere prayer that my spiritual ears remain open to hear You, and that when You speak, I am quick to obey what You have called and invited me to do! I pray this in Jesus' name!

My Confession for Today

I joyfully confess that God speaks to me and that I hear Him when He speaks. He has opened my spiritual ears, and I have the ability to hear when He calls and invites me to do something new and special. When God asks me to do something or beckons me to a new task, I do not argue. I choose to quickly agree with God so that I can walk continually with Him. I consider it an honor and a privilege whenever God allows me the opportunity to do something in His service. I declare this by faith in Jesus' name!

Lifting Holy Hands

My Prayer for Today

Father, You are stirring my heart today to offer myself to You as a holy instrument to do Your will. I realize now that the lifting of my hands to You represents bringing my life to You in yielded surrender. You are calling me to a higher level of dedication, and when I lift my hands to You, that action represents a life lifted in consecration to Your glory. When I look at my hands, help me think seriously about the adjustments I may need to make so I can lift up my life to You in worship with confidence and without compromise. I pray this in Jesus' name!

I will therefore that men pray every where, lifting up holy hands...

1 Timothy 2:8

My Confession for Today

I proclaim that every day I dedicate myself more and more to Jesus. Today I make a fresh decision to live a life that is consecrated to the purposes of God. Every day I choose to set my attention and affection on Jesus and to allow the Holy Spirit to reveal to me areas of my life that Jesus longs for me to surrender. I release those areas to His control and submit them to the lordship of Christ. When I raise my hands in worship, I raise hands that represent purity, dedication, consecration, and total surrender to the will of God! I declare this by faith in Jesus' name!

SEPTEMBER 18

What Are You Doing With Your Time?

Redeeming the time, because the days are evil.

Ephesians 5:16

My Prayer for Today

Father, I ask You to help me understand what my top priorities should be and then give me the discipline to live according to those guidelines. Help me discern when something is actually a distraction that will pull me off task so I don't become entangled in activities that are either unnecessary or possibly even a hindrance to the main thing You want me to accomplish. I repent for the times I have allowed procrastination and laziness to waste valuable time. Those are not habits that I want to continue in my life. Teach me to focus and prioritize as You help me cultivate new habits and patterns that produce Your desired results in my life. Today I make a fresh commitment to steward my time with diligence and to trust You to guide my choices so I can make the most of every moment. I pray this in Jesus' name!

My Confession for Today

I confess that I am diligent, productive, and undistracted as I give my time and attention to the most important priorities in my life. I maintain keen focus on the assignment before me. I keep my ears open to the Holy Spirit's guidance to follow His wisdom in all I set out to do. Therefore, I am productive and organized. I believe that I receive lasting fruitfulness as the reward of how I invest my time. I declare this by faith!

Your Most Valuable Partner

My Prayer for Today

Dear Father, I thank You for reminding me again today that even as I do my part, I have to always remember that I must trust You to do Your part or no increase will come to what You have called me to do. I promise to nurture the soil, plant the seed, pull the weeds, and water what is planted—but I look to You to provide the sunshine and proper weather conditions to produce the increase I need. I understand that one plants, another waters—but only You give the increase. Thank You for bringing this back to the forefront of my mind today and for encouraging me to remember that You are the crucial ingredient in all that I do! In the end, we can do all our parts, but the increase is totally dependent on You! I pray this in Jesus' name!

So then neither is he that planteth any thing, neither he that watereth; but God that giveth the increase.

1 Corinthians 3:7

My Confession for Today

I boldly confess that I will do what God has asked me to do. I will nurture the soil, plant the seeds, pull the weeds, and water what has been planted—and I will do it faithfully with others who work alongside with me. But no results will be gained if God does not join Himself to what we are doing. So today I look to God as the great Provider of increase. He will provide the sunshine and weather necessary to make these seeds and acts of faith grow. Without Him, I can do nothing, but with God as my primary Partner, it is guaranteed that I will see and experience increase! I declare this by faith in Jesus' name!

Special Mercy for the Overwhelmed

To Timothy, my dearly beloved son: Grace, mercy, and peace, from God the Father and Christ Jesus our Lord.

2 Timothy 1:2

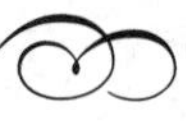

My Prayer for Today

Father, I am so grateful that when You call me to do something difficult and it tempts me to feel inadequate, You insert extra mercy between the grace and the peace in my life. Holy Spirit, I receive a special measure of mercy to undergird me in the times when I feel overwhelmed by the trials of life. I pray this in Jesus' name!

My Confession for Today

I confess that when my heart is overwhelmed, I go to the Rock of my salvation to partake of His mercies that are new for me every morning. I confess that His mercy is at work in my life right now. Today I walk with a renewed sense of courage, persistence, and inner toughness because God's all-sufficient grace, mercy, and peace are being multiplied to me. I declare this by faith in Jesus' name!

Riches Are Not Always Measured in Dollars and Cents

I know thy works, and tribulation, and poverty, (but thou art rich)...

Revelation 2:9

My Prayer for Today

Heavenly Father, I thank You that spiritual riches go beyond dollars and cents. Financial wealth can be obtained and lost, but spiritual riches are enduring. Although I am thankful for the ways You have blessed me financially, I know the riches of this life are fleeting. Therefore, I ask You to help me walk worthily of my rich spiritual inheritance that possesses a value exceeding anything this world can offer. I rejoice in knowing that spiritual riches outlast this life and that this is the wealth I can take with me to Heaven. I pray this in Jesus' name!

My Confession for Today

I confess that God meets my financial needs according to His riches in glory by Christ Jesus. But in addition to having my financial needs met, I am also spiritually enriched by the gifts of the Holy Spirit and by the love of God within me that makes me more than a conqueror—no matter what I may face. I have right standing with God Himself by the blood of Jesus; an abiding peace that surpasses natural understanding; and a wellspring of joy that provides me with an endless source of strength. I boldly confess that I am spiritually rich and superabundantly blessed by the riches of God in my life. I declare this by faith in Jesus' name!

SEPTEMBER 22

All Scripture Is Given by God's Inspiration

All scripture is given by inspiration of God...

2 Timothy 3:16

My Prayer for Today

Dear Lord, I am so thankful that the Bible is filled with your power and life. When I pick it up and read it, I am receiving the very life of God into my being. Father, help me to become more disciplined when it comes to reading Your Word. Each word contains Your very life, essence, energy, and dynamism in it. It contains the power and answers that I need for every situation that I am facing in my life. Please forgive me for not reading it as often or as much I should. Holy Spirit, I receive Your strength today to make and to stay faithful to a new commitment to take the Word of God into my heart EVERY DAY so that it can nourish and sustain my heart and my soul. I pray this in Jesus' name!

My Confession for Today

I confess that I value the Word of God as the most important priority in my life. I keep it before my eyes, I put it in my ears, and I speak it out of my mouth. The Word of God dominates my life decisions and guides my path. I hide it in my heart so that I do not sin against God. As I read the Bible, it releases the essence, energy, and dynamism of God Himself into my spirit, soul, and body. God's Word revives me, rejuvenates me, and replenishes me. The very force of heaven invades my life as I take the Word of God into me! I declare this by faith in Jesus' name!

Navigating Stormy Last-Days Seas

My Prayer for Today

Father, I thank You that the Word of God thoroughly furnishes me to rise above the perils of this hour. There is no doubt that turbulent waters are in front of us, but the Word of God makes me well-equipped and outfitted to sail through the densest darkness and to sail across the greatest storms. Without Your Word, I am ill-equipped to travel long distances or to survive strong storms, but with Your Word working in my life, I have all the spiritual gear I need to make it all the way to my ultimate destination. Thank You for giving me Your Word—for equipping me with everything I need to sail through rough waters and to survive even the worst of storms! I pray this in Jesus' name!

All scripture is given by inspiration of God, and is profitable for doctrine, for reproof, for correction, for instruction in righteousness: That the man of God may be perfect, thoroughly furnished unto all good works.

2 Timothy 3:16-17

My Confession for Today

I acknowledge that we are living in a season of storms in these last days. Like it or not, times have become turbulent, the waves are getting higher, and only those who are adequately equipped will make it to the other side. I boldly confess that I will not only begin the journey, but in Christ I am "thoroughly furnished" and will complete it. Because the Word of God is hidden in my heart and is a light unto my path, I will not fall, I will not stumble, and I will not sink. The Word of God enables me to ride high above the waves, and it will take me all the way to the other side to God's ultimate destination for my life. I declare this by faith in Jesus' name!

The Healing Power of Jesus Christ

How God anointed Jesus of Nazareth with the Holy Ghost and with power: who went about doing good, and healing all that were oppressed of the devil…

Acts 10:38

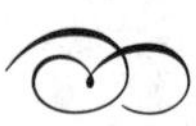

My Prayer for Today

Father, I thank You for the healing power of Jesus Christ. Whether it works instantaneously or progressively, healing is miraculous, and I am so thankful that You heal those who believe. Help me embrace the fact that although many are healed instantaneously, many are also healed progressively. Rather than be moved by what I see in front of me, help me to believe that when I pray in Jesus' name and release my faith for a person's healing, divine power is released into that person, and day by day they will progressively be restored to health. I pray this in Jesus' name!

My Confession for Today

I confess that God uses me in the healing ministry. Some people are healed instantly when I pray, while others are healed progressively over a period of time. Regardless of whether the healing is instantaneous or progressive, it is miraculous, and I am thankful for God's healing touch. I will lay my hands on the sick, fully expecting divine power, like divine medication, to enter their bodies and work inside them until their condition is reversed and they are restored to health again. I declare this by faith in Jesus' name!

Remain Steady and Ready

Preach the word; be instant in season, out of season…

2 Timothy 4:2

My Prayer for Today

Father, I hear You saying, "Stay at your post, and don't budge an inch! Stay there, and do what I have told you to do. Be faithful when times are good—and if times turn bad, remain steady and unflinching." I know that if I'll remain faithful to the call and to the place where You have called me, You will empower me with inner strength and sufficient grace that will enable me to see my calling through to a glorious conclusion! So, Holy Spirit, I receive Your fortitude to withstand the pressure to give up, give in, and throw in the towel. Strengthen me with the might I inwardly need to stay put and see my assignment through to completion! I pray this in Jesus' name!

My Confession for Today

I confess that God strengthens me with His might to be faithful, steadfast, and persevering. When times are good or when times are tough, I am consistently constant. I stay put, no matter what. I will not be moved in my committed stance. The grace of God is teaching me how not to be provoked or lured to move away from my post. I keep my focus fastened on Jesus, and my roots grow down deep into Him. His stability keeps me grounded and enables me to be faithful to the call and to the place where God has planted me. I declare this by faith in Jesus' name!

Last-Days Deception

For the time will come when they will not endure sound doctrine; but after their own lusts shall they heap to themselves teachers, having itching ears; and they shall turn away their ears from the truth, and shall be turned unto fables.

2 Timothy 4:3-4

My Prayer for Today

Father, I thank You that the Holy Spirit warned the Christian community about error seeking to secure a foothold inside the Church in the last of the last days. This motivates me to become even more committed to the solid teaching of the Word of God than ever before in my life. I ask You, Holy Spirit, to help me listen with a discerning ear to what I hear and take into my spiritual ears. What I spiritually digest determines my spiritual health, so please help me consume spiritual teachings that are wholesome and profitable to my spiritual life. I pray this in Jesus' name!

My Confession for Today

I confess that I am excited God has chosen me to be part of this last-days' generation! The Holy Spirit inside awakens me to what teaching is right and what teaching is wrong—and I have a spiritually discerning ear to know what I should accept and what I should reject. I further declare that I will NOT be part of the "itching-ear" generation. Instead, I have a heart for the solid, time-tested teaching of the Word of God. On this Word of Truth I stand, and I will not move or even budge. Where God's eternal Word is concerned, I will allow no room for negotiation! I declare this by faith in Jesus' name!

Be an Immovable Pillar for God

My Prayer for Today

Lord, I ask You to help me know the place where I am supposed to serve and to use my gifts and talents. Help me accept Your assignment with joy, regardless of what it is or where it is, and to keep my eyes fixed on my heavenly reward. In times when it gets tough and my flesh screams to be released from my assignment—or in those moments when the devil tries to tell me that my part is insignificant—please help me dig in my heels and refuse to move from that place where You have called me. I pray this in Jesus' name!

Therefore, my beloved brethren, be ye stedfast, unmoveable, always abounding in the work of the Lord, forasmuch as ye know that your labour is not in vain in the Lord.

1 Corinthians 15:58

My Confession for Today

I declare that I am of value to God and to His plan to touch people. I am reliable, steadfast, and immovable in what God has asked me to do. Even if the devil tries to tell me that I'm not making a difference, I declare that I am making a difference in the lives of others. My time, talents, and gifts are a blessing to others. And I boldly confess that nothing I ever do for Him is wasted! I declare this by faith in Jesus' name!

Ministering Spirits

Are they not all ministering spirits, sent forth to minister for them who shall be heirs of salvation?

Hebrews 1:14

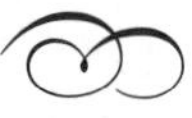

My Prayer for Today

Father, I thank You for assigning angels to protect me from harm. I am grateful for Your promise to send angels on a special mission to protect, minister to, and help the heirs of salvation. Since I'm an heir of salvation, I qualify! I am so thankful to know that I have angels assigned to keep watch over me and that they will serve me with the highest-level service possible. So rather than let fear try to grab hold of me in times of hardship or potential danger, I will give thanks to You for the angels who are present and on active duty—sent on a mission to protect and minister strength and help to me when I need it most! I pray this in Jesus' name!

My Confession for Today

I confess that God sends His angels to guard me. These ministering spirits are as flames of fire and they are on a specific mission to protect the children of God. Wherever I go, angels are on assignment to go with me and to surround me and keep me safe. Because these angels hearken to the voice of God's Word, I speak the Word and believe in its power—knowing that angels watch over those words to perform them. Although I cannot visibly see them, I have angelic traveling companions who are with me all the time in every situation I face. According to Psalm 34:7, I am surrounded by the angels of the Lord, and He delivers me from harm! I declare this by faith in Jesus' name!

Feeling Like a Scapegoat?

My Prayer for Today

...we are made as the filth of the world, and are the offscouring of all things unto this day.

1 Corinthians 4:13

Father, I am so glad that Jesus understands what I am going through when I suffer verbal abuse or ridicule or when I experience unjust discrimination. It is so emotionally difficult to be blamed for things that have nothing to do with me, yet I face this from time to time. Instead of becoming bitter and hardhearted toward those who wrong me in this way, I ask You to give me a heart full of love for them. In my own flesh, I am unable to forgive and love them as I must, but with Your Spirit's help, I can love even the most unlovely person. So today I'm asking You to fill my heart with forgiveness, love, and compassion for those who have dealt unfairly with me. I pray this in Jesus' name!

My Confession for Today

In Jesus' name I confess that I forgive the people who have deliberately misused me, abused me, and falsely accused me. If they really understood what they were doing, I believe they would never have done such a terrible thing. Instead of letting my heart get hard and bitter, I am turning to the Holy Spirit for help. He will soften my heart; He will help me forgive; and He will fill me with love and compassion for those who have tried to victimize me. Just as Jesus forgave those who crucified Him, today I am choosing to forgive those who have done wrong to me. With the help of the Holy Spirit, I can do this and I WILL do it. I declare this by faith in Jesus' name!

September 30

It's Time To Use Your God-Given Gifts and Talents

As every man hath received the gift, even so minister the same one to another, as good stewards of the manifold grace of God.

1 Peter 4:10

My Prayer for Today

Lord, thank You for placing spiritual gifts in my life. These gifts were given by You, and my heart's desire is to use them as You intend for them to be used. Forgive me for the time I've wasted waiting for the perfect moment before I got started. Help me now as I step out in faith to start using these gifts in ways that will benefit those around me. I know that Your gifts have power, so as I release these precious treasures, I ask that Your power will also be released to meet the needs of the people whose lives I touch. Today I willfully recognize the gifts You have placed inside me, and I make the choice to let these gifts begin to operate through me! I pray this in Jesus' name!

My Confession for Today

I confess that God's grace works mightily in my life and those mighty gifts have been placed in my life through this divine grace. Although in the past I have put myself down and lightly esteemed my value in the Body of Christ, I have made the decision to recognize, embrace, and take ownership of the marvelous gifts inside me! God expects me to be responsible in my stewardship of these gifts, so I will be meticulous and faithful in the way I allow these gifts to operate through me! I declare this in Jesus' name!

God Makes the Impossible Possible!

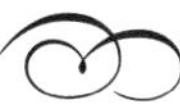

My Prayer for Today

Father, I am so thankful that You are our Great Provider, Great Quickener, Great Physician, Great Redeemer, and Great Restorer. There is absolutely nothing that You cannot do. I ask You to breathe new life into my visions and dreams that have been on the verge of death. You are the great power of the Resurrection, and I ask You to release Your resurrection power into my situation and turn it around. I know this is impossible in the natural—but with You, I know that all things are absolutely possible! I pray this in Jesus' name!

(As it is written, I have made thee a father of many nations,) before him whom he believed, even God, who quickeneth the dead, and calleth those things which be not as though they were.

Romans 4:17

My Confession for Today

I confess that the resurrection power of Almighty God is working in me to reinvigorate my visions and my dreams and to bring them back to life again. Despite what seemed to be against me and against the fulfillment of what God promised He would do with my life, God will show me His greatness and His glory. I will see the miracle come to pass. I boldly declare it will come to pass. God's quickening power is at work on my behalf, and it's at work inside me right now! I declare this by faith in Jesus' name!

OCTOBER 2

The Humility of Christ

Who [Jesus], being in the form of God, thought it not robbery to be equal with God: But made himself of no reputation, and took upon him the form of a servant, and was made in the likeness of men: And being found in fashion as a man, he humbled himself, and became obedient unto death, even the death of the cross.

Philippians 2:6-8

My Prayer for Today

Dear Heavenly Father, I am left speechless when I consider the humility that Christ demonstrated when He left the realm of eternal glory. To know that He was made in the likeness of a man, and then died the death of a Cross—and that He did it all for me—leaves me in awe of Your goodness and love. If Christ had not been willing to lay aside His glory and to come to earth as a man, I would have remained lost and unsaved. Father, how I thank You for sending Jesus—and for the example that Christ has set for me and for all believers to cultivate the characteristic of humility as evidence of Your love in our lives. I pray this in Jesus' name!

My Confession for Today

I confess that Almighty God, clothed in radiant glory from eternities past, came to this earth to die a horrible death on the Cross to purchase my eternal salvation. This required humility beyond anything I could ever comprehend, yet this was the reason Jesus came. Jesus now sits at the Father's right hand, arrayed in splendor beyond human imagination—but His humility remains intact, consistent, and unchanged. He was, He is, and He will always be humble, just as Hebrews 13:8 says, *"Jesus Christ the same yesterday, today, and forever."* I confess that I am yielding to the Holy Spirit's work to produce this same Christ-like humility in my life as well. I declare this by faith in Jesus' name!

A Promise To Overcomers

My Prayer for Today

Father, I hear what Your Spirit is speaking to me today. You are calling me to jump into the race and stay in the race until I reach the finish line. You are calling me to fight the good fight of faith—and to maintain the victory once it has been won. I recognize that for me to do this, I will need to be permanently and consistently undeterred to overcome and obtain victory in every sphere of my life. Father, this is a level of commitment far greater than I've ever demonstrated in my life. Holy Spirit, I ask You to help me forge ahead. By Your strength, I know I can and will do it. I pray this in Jesus' name!

...To him that overcometh...

Revelation 2:7,11,17,26; 3:5,12,21

My Confession for Today

I declare by faith that I am an overcomer in Jesus Christ. He has given me His Spirit. I have His Word. And He overcame the devil at the Cross and the resurrection—then He gave me His name to use. There is no reason I can't overcome the troubles I've had in my relationships, my weight, my health, my finances, or any other struggle that I've had. With the Spirit's help, I am strong; I am stable; I am undeterred. In Him I win and maintain the victory! I declare this by faith in Jesus' name!

OCTOBER 4

The Devil Can't Curse What God has Blessed!

How shall I curse, whom God hath not cursed? or how shall I defy, whom the Lord hath not defied?

Numbers 23:8

My Prayer for Today

Father, I rejoice that because I am in Christ, I am the blessed of the Lord and protected by the blood of Jesus Christ. The devil does not have the power to curse what God has blessed. Holy Spirit, I receive Your help to walk in obedience to the Word of God and to shun anything that would violate the supernatural shield of protection that surrounds my life. I pray this in Jesus' name!

My Confession for Today

I confess that I am safe and shielded by the blood of Jesus Christ. When God placed me in Christ, He surrounded me with divine protection that cannot be breached. No demon, no devil, no evil worker has the power to speak any kind of curse on my life. I am curse-free because Jesus Christ bore the curse for me in every form, that I might become the blessed of God forevermore. I do not live in fear of the devil, and I rejoice that greater is He who is in me than he that is in the world! I declare this by faith in Jesus' name!

Waiting for That Last Person To Repent

My Prayer for Today

Heavenly Father, my heart is stirred today to pray for my unsaved friends, family, and acquaintances. The Bible has long foretold that a day of judgment is coming, but I've never thought about it so deeply as I've thought about it today. Thank You for being patient with the world—and for being so merciful that You are waiting for more people to repent before the clock stops ticking and time runs out. Father, I want to be open and available for You to use me to share the witness of Jesus with those who are unsaved. And if I was the one You used to bring the last person to Christ, I would be overwhelmed by the privilege of doing so! I pray this in Jesus' name!

The Lord is not slack concerning his promise, as some men count slackness; but is longsuffering to us-ward, not willing that any should perish, but that all should come to repentance.

2 Peter 3:9

My Confession for Today

I confess that we are living in the last days. The time is soon coming when the prophetic clock will stop for this age. When it does, the Church will be caught away, and the judgment cycle will begin on the earth. I declare that from now until then, I will do all that I can to share Jesus with my unsaved friends, family, and acquaintances. God's longsuffering causes Him to wait for one last person to repent, and I will do all I can to bring as many souls as I can to the Lord before this age ends and the next age begins. I declare this by faith in Jesus' name!

OCTOBER 6

The Holy Spirit Removes Obstacles

Likewise the Spirit also helpeth our infirmities: for we know not what we should pray for as we ought: but the Spirit itself maketh intercession for us with groanings which cannot be uttered.

Romans 8:26

My Prayer for Today

Father, I thank You for the insight I've gained into how the Holy Spirit comes to my aid. When it seems that I have fallen headlong into a hole, I can call out to the Holy Spirit for help and He will meet me in my experience. Thank You, Holy Spirit, for moving on my behalf to rescue me. At the bottom of every pit, You take hold together with me in prayer against the hindrances that attempt to prevent my deliverance until they move out of my life. Father God, I thank You for assuring my victory through the power of Your Spirit at work in me. I pray this in Jesus' name!

My Confession for Today

I confess that each time I say, "Holy Spirit, I need You to help me," He answers, "That's what I'm here for. I am here to bear the responsibility of helping you in prayer." If ever I happen to fall into a hole, or if I feel discouraged and confused about why I fell into that trap in the first place, the Holy Spirit meets me right where I am in the midst of my trouble and begins to help me in my weakness. The Holy Spirit is always here with me, and He grabs hold of my problem together with me. We press against it together until it moves out of my life completely! I declare this by faith in Jesus' name!

Our Partner in Prayer

My Prayer for Today

Heavenly Father, I simply don't know how to pray as I ought! I have to acknowledge that I don't even know what the deepest desire of my heart is. Thank You for the Spirit of God who searches, investigates, examines, and sifts through my heart to discover the will of God that is embedded deep within my innermost being. Holy Spirit, it is my will to cooperate with You as You search to find the deeply laid plans of God inside me and to pray about them according to God's will. Thank You, Holy Spirit, for interceding effectually on my behalf. I cannot even begin to calculate the value of Your great intercessory work in my prayer life. I pray this in Jesus' name!

Likewise the Spirit also helpeth our infirmities: for we know not what we should pray for as we ought: but the Spirit itself maketh intercession for us with groanings which cannot be uttered. And he that searcheth the hearts knoweth what is the mind of the Spirit, because he maketh intercession for the saints according to the will of God.

Romans 8:26-27

My Confession for Today

I confess that I am grateful for the work of the Holy Spirit in my life. He makes intercession on my behalf to strengthen me in my weakness when I face crossroad moments and don't know what to do. Just as the Holy Spirit hovered over the waters when God created the earth, He hovers over my life to help me pray about the deep, God-given desires of my heart. The Holy Spirit knows better than I do what the plan of God is for my family, for my job or business — and for all the dreams He has placed inside me. He knows all the secret places of my heart. I simply ask Him, and the Holy Spirit helps me discover the precise wisdom I need to know in prayer about my life and my future! I declare this by faith in Jesus' name!

OCTOBER 8

A Father's Bad Influence

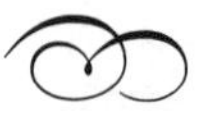

Then certain of the vagabond Jews, exorcists, took upon them to call over them which had evil spirits the name of the Lord Jesus, saying, We adjure you by Jesus whom Paul preacheth. And there were seven sons of one Sceva, a Jew, and chief of the priests, which did so.

Acts 19:13-14

My Prayer for Today

Father, in this critical hour, it is so important for parents to adhere closely to the Word of God in order to guide this young generation along the path that fulfills Your plan for their lives. I pray for myself and for other fathers and mothers who represent Your Kingdom—that our hearts will remain steadfast and strong in the truth of Your Word. We will not be like Sceva, who led his sons astray because of his own wayward and hardened heart. Instead, we will be true spiritual leaders in our homes so that we can not only teach our children with right words, but also train and lead them by the example of our lives in the direction of a deep commitment to Christ and an authentic, intimate relationship with the Person and power of the Holy Spirit. I make a fresh commitment today to be a godly influence in my children's lives, always pointing them to the path that leads to life! I pray this in Jesus' name!

My Confession for Today

I confess that I accept my divinely ordained responsibility as a parent to lead as a godly influence for my children and the younger generation in my life. I have the potential of changing young lives as I live an authentic example of the character and the ways of God the Father before them. I continually rely upon Heaven's wisdom to help me teach my children to walk in obedience to Jesus and the Word of God. I make a fresh commitment today to be a consistent example of obedience and love who leads my children in one direction only: God's good path! I declare this by faith in Jesus' name!

Demonic Intelligence—No Match for the Power of Jesus!

And the evil spirit answered...

Acts 19:15

My Prayer for Today

Father, I am inspired and thankful to learn I have authority that is given to me because of my relationship with Jesus Christ and His matchless name that He has entrusted to me. When I encounter situations where demonic power is present, I thank You for giving me the boldness to take authority and to expel those powers in Jesus' name! I pray this in Jesus' name!

My Confession for Today

I confess that greater is Jesus in me than the devil that is in the world. The devil is minor compared to the awesome power of Christ that indwells me. When I speak the name of Jesus, empowered by the Holy Spirit, the spirit realm listens and obeys. I am in Christ, and Christ is in me. When I speak in Jesus' name against demon powers, it is like Christ is speaking through me! I declare this by faith in Jesus' name!

OCTOBER 10

A Demonic Recognition

And the evil spirit answered and said, Jesus I know, and Paul I know; but who are ye?

Acts 19:15

My Prayer for Today

Father, I am thrilled and grateful to learn of the authority that I have in the name of Jesus Christ. I am so thankful that I am a real, born-again child of God—and that You have authorized me to use Your power and Your name at any moment that it is required. I need never be afraid of the devil because demons recognize that the power of God inside me is greater than all of them put together. Thank You for encouraging me to be bold when I sense the devil is trying to manifest his presence or wage an attack! I pray this in Jesus' name!

My Confession for Today

I declare that the Son of God lives inside me—and I am in Him—and when I am required to speak to an evil presence and command it to go, that evil spirit recognizes Jesus' voice speaking through me. I am not afraid. I do not give way to fear. I do not listen to communication that would incite anxiety or fear. I receive from strong, Word-based teaching resources, like this one today, in order to build my faith and prepare me to take action when it is needed! I declare this by faith in Jesus' name!

Illegitimate Authority and a Demonic Attack

And the man in whom the evil spirit was leaped on them, and overcame them, and prevailed against them, so that they fled out of that house naked and wounded.

Acts 19:16

My Prayer for Today

Father, what an awesome thing to realize that the demons not only recognize Jesus' authority—they also recognize the authority of those who know Jesus. Of course, Jesus stripped Satan of all his powers (Colossians 2:15) and it should be no surprise to me that he is terrified of Jesus' name and those who had been authorized to use it. But I am especially thankful to You for bringing me out of the bondage of darkness, for translating me into the Kingdom of Your dear Son, and for giving me authority in the name of Jesus Christ! I pray this in Jesus' name!

My Confession for Today

Demons may have authority over unsaved people, but I boldly confess they do not have authority over me and others who are in Christ Jesus. I never have to fear a demonic attack like the seven sons of Sceva experienced because the devil is the one who is running from me when I use the Spirit-empowered name of Jesus! I refuse to shrink in fear, and I refuse to let the devil intimidate me, because I have the presence of the Greater One living inside me! I declare this by faith in Jesus' name!

OCTOBER 12

Jesus Is Glorified

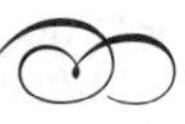

And this was known to all the Jews and Greeks also dwelling at Ephesus; and fear fell on them all, and the name of the Lord Jesus was magnified.

Acts 19:17

My Prayer for Today

Father, I want to see Your divine power unleashed in my city, in my church, and in our ministry. Nothing brings glory to the name of the Lord Jesus like a miracle or a supernaturally heaven-sent manifestation of divine power. Forgive me for restraining the manifestations of the Holy Spirit when He has longed to demonstrate the power of God. I am sorry and so wrong for fearing what people will think—when in fact, this is the very thing that will make the greatest impression on people. I ask You to help me from this moment forward to surrender to the great working of Your power and that this type of manifestation will cause the name of the Lord Jesus to be magnified! I pray this in Jesus' name!

My Confession for Today

I admit that the fear of people—and what other people think—has caused me to hinder the power of God from operating as God wants it to operate in our city, in our church, and in our ministry. However, from this moment forward, I confess that I am throwing open my arms to receive the supernatural assistance that Heaven wants to give in terms of signs and wonders. Such signs and wonders were sent to draw people to Jesus, not deter people from Jesus—so I am going to stop wondering what people think and I'm going to become an instrument for the power of God to bring signs and wonders into manifestation! I declare this by faith in Jesus' name!

Whose Law Do You Ultimately Obey?

My Prayer for Today

Father God, I realize that it is better to obey You than man. I didn't realize the pressure that early Christians faced just to meet together. Because we have so much freedom, I often forget that there are Christians around the world today who are persecuted simply for attending church. As we face the days ahead of us—when laws passed by high courts may conflict with the law of God—give us the courage to stick by Your law and do what You say. This will take great strength of will, so I ask You, Holy Spirit, to give me the inward fortitude to do what is right, regardless of what the world around me says. I pray this in Jesus' name!

Not forsaking the assembling of ourselves together…

Hebrews 10:25

My Confession for Today

I confess that I am committed to carrying out the instructions outlined in the Word of God. The thinking of the world and society may change, but God's Word is unchanging—and I will stick by the Word of God, regardless of the way the world around me tries to dictate my actions or influence my beliefs. I am filled with courage; I am overflowing with confidence; and I have the power of the Holy Spirit. The Lord is my strength and my personal bravery. The Word of God is a high tower of strength to me. Regardless of what man says or the price it will cost to obey, I will do what God's Word commands. I declare this by faith in Jesus' name!

OCTOBER 14

Put on Love

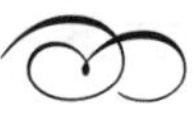

And above all these things put on charity, which is the bond of perfectness.

Colossians 3:14

My Prayer for Today

Lord, I thank You for the love of God that has been shed abroad in my heart by the Holy Spirit who was given to me. Releasing this love is a choice, and I repent for the times I've chosen to walk in anger, frustration, or intolerance instead of choosing to put on love as You've instructed me to do. I thank You for Your great love for me. Jesus said I will prove to be His disciple when I release His love toward others. Thank You, Lord, for the gift of a free will. I honor You with it by choosing to put on agape love. I will give no place to the devil by keeping myself clothed in the love of God. I pray this in Jesus' name!

My Confession for Today

I confess that the incorruptible seed of God's Word is sown into my spirit. Therefore, God's agape love is planted within me. I deliberately choose to put on that love as a garment. Clothed in the love of God, I walk into each situation covered with the God-kind of love that never fails, fades out, or comes to an end. In every situation I face, I am equipped to love others as God has loved me—purely from the heart, with no strings attached! I declare this by faith in Jesus' name!

From Truth To Fables

My Prayer for Today

Heavenly Father, I know that we are living in the last days. I ask You to help me keep my head on straight when it comes to the preaching and teaching of the Bible. This is a day when truth is being traded for motivational messages, and many in the Church don't even know the basic tenets of the faith anymore. I ask You to help me stay on track with solid Bible teaching. Keep me rooted and grounded in the Word of God, I present myself to You to use as a source of strong teaching for people who are new in the Lord or who are simply hungry for deeper and balanced teaching! I pray this in Jesus' name!

And they shall turn away their ears from the truth, and shall be turned unto fables.

2 Timothy 4:4

My Confession for Today

I confess that I have been taught the Word of God and that I stand on a strong, stable doctrinal foundation. My spiritual senses are so exercised that I am able to discern true teaching from myth-like teaching. My heart goes out to those who are not able to discern the difference, and I will do everything in my ability to help put people on a strong doctrinal foundation that will hold them up in the times ahead. I am thankful for the Word of God that has been placed in my life. I honor it. I cherish it. And I accept the responsibility to help share it with others. I declare this by faith in Jesus' name!

OCTOBER 16

Do What Is Honorable in Jesus' Name

Now I pray to God that you do no evil, not that we should appear approved, but that you should do what is honorable…

2 Corinthians 13:7 NKJV

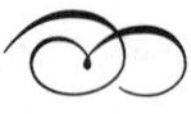

My Prayer for Today

Holy Spirit, I am more determined than ever before to yield to You—the Spirit of Truth—in every area of my life. I commit to be honest and forthcoming in all my dealings with people in my life. If I've ever caused harm to a fellow Christian or hurt the reputation of Jesus' name, I ask You for forgiveness. As I look back on my life, I can't think of a time when I've done this intentionally. But perhaps I have a poor memory. So just in case I've been guilty in some way of dishonoring the name of Jesus or grieving the Person of the Holy Spirit by my poor actions and behavior, I repent and ask You to forgive me so the slate will be clear in my life! I pray this in Jesus' name!

My Confession for Today

I declare that I will not be involved in any type of sinful shenanigans that would hurt the testimony of Jesus' name or that would cause people to retreat from fellowshipping with His Church. I will walk worthily of the calling that has been given to me. I will walk in integrity and be forthright, even if it costs me personally to be honest and truthful. I declare that I will not deliberately do evil to anyone, but I make it my aim to represent the Lord Jesus Christ in a noble and honorable manner in all things! I declare this by faith in Jesus' name!

The Cross!

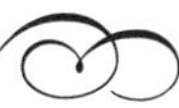

My Prayer for Today

Heavenly Father, I am thankful for the life-saving, transforming power of the Cross of Christ. Thank You for sending Jesus to die on that Cross to pay the price for my freedom. Thank You that the Holy Spirit opened my spiritual ears to hear and that my heart believed the message. I gratefully rejoice that the Cross is still the power of God to us who believe. I pray this in Jesus' name!

For the message of the cross is foolishness to those who are perishing, but to us who are being saved it is the power of God.

1 Corinthians 1:18

My Confession for Today

I confess that my life has been changed by the power of Jesus Christ and His death on the Cross. That Cross has become the wisdom and power of God to me. Because of the Cross, I am freed from sin, bondage, sickness, and disease. It has been, is now, and will always be the power of God to me and to all those who believe. I am not ashamed of the Gospel of Jesus Christ that proclaims the power of the Cross. I am attentive and available to the Spirit of God so He can use me as He desires—both to proclaim and to demonstrate the power of the Cross so that men may receive the saving knowledge of its truth! I declare this by faith in Jesus' name!

OCTOBER 18

What Impression Do You Make on Others?

Look not every man on his own things, but every man also on the things of others.

Philippians 2:4

My Prayer for Today

Heavenly Father, how many times have my thoughts, words, and actions been focused on me, my problems, or my preferences? Whether I did this privately or even more regrettably with others, I repent for such selfishness. Father, my utmost desire is to reflect You to others, just as Jesus did when He walked on the earth. You are Love, my Father. Therefore, I ask You to help me leave the undeniable fragrance of Your goodness and love upon every life that I touch. I pray this in Jesus' name!

My Confession for Today

I confess that the love of God is shed abroad in my heart by the Spirit of God who dwells within me. Therefore, I am not haughty, arrogant, conceited, or inflated with pride because I walk in humility, patience, and kindness that God's own loving nature reproduces in me. I choose to walk in God's love, and that sets me free from fear, which includes carnal craving for self-exaltation, self-protection, self-promotion, and any attitude that exalts fleshly preference above godly character and priorities. When others leave my presence, they sense that God's love has encouraged and lifted them higher than they were before. And when I encounter people who are so self-absorbed that they cannot see beyond themselves, God's love shines so brightly through me that their hearts are touched and stirred to seek Jesus more deeply and to be like Him. I declare this by faith in Jesus' name!

The Queen of All Virtues

My Prayer for Today

But let patience have her perfect work...

James 1:4

Father, I draw upon the might of Your invincible life within me, and I ask You to help me cultivate Your character trait of this never-give-up kind of patient endurance in my life. Help me rely upon and release the power of the Holy Spirit so that I do not bend or surrender in the face of pressure—or capitulate to the forces that have tried to conquer me. I ask You, Holy Spirit, to infuse me with Your mighty power in my inner self so that I will be strong and enduring. Fill me with Your staying power—Your divine hang-in-there power—to outlast the odds and to eventually win the battle that has been arrayed against me. It's just a matter of time until the opposition folds and goes away, but I need patience to stay in the fight until that glorious moment of victory occurs. I receive Your help today! I pray this in Jesus' name!

My Confession for Today

By faith, I declare that I have the inner fortitude to outlast every skirmish that the enemy has tried to array against my life. Because the Holy Spirit is inside me, I am tougher than any circumstances I face. I do not bend. I do not break. The Lord is my Strength and my impenetrable Shield; therefore, I do not yield to the pressures that try to move me from His promises for my life. Patience works in me—and that means I have been fortified with God's very own hang-in-there power that never surrenders an inch of what He has promised to me. I declare this by faith in Jesus' name!

OCTOBER 20

Time for a Personal Evaluation?

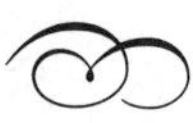

For unto every one that hath shall be given, and he shall have abundance: but from him that hath not shall be taken away even that which he hath.

Matthew 25:29

My Prayer for Today

Father, I pray that You will help me honestly evaluate myself and my performance. Even more, I ask for Your grace to help me see where I need to change. I receive Your empowerment to make the necessary adjustments so You can trust me with more responsibility. In those areas where I have not done well, I ask You to forgive me, and I receive Your forgiveness. With the power of the Holy Spirit and my decision to change, I believe that I'll make forward progress in my life and that You will put more on my plate because You've seen that I am faithful with what I'm doing right now. I pray this in Jesus' name!

My Confession for Today

I confess that I am faithful with what God assigned me to do right now. God is watching me; He is evaluating my performance; and He sees that I am doing the best I can with the knowledge and experience that I possess. I confess that I am willing to grow and change in the areas where I have not done well. I refuse to shut my eyes to the truth, and I will be honest with myself about the areas I need to change. God's Spirit is helping me—and with His help, I will become a vessel that God knows He can depend on and use. I declare this by faith in Jesus' name!

Stop Murmuring and Disputing With God

My Prayer for Today

Father, as I surrender to the lordship of Christ, my act of obedience triggers a release of power and a supernatural flow of divine energy to produce change and transformation until I am shaped into the image of Christ. Lord, I ask You to make my thoughts agreeable to Your will while Your mighty power is trying to effect a deep and permanent character change within me. I make a decision right now to be compliant and to obey You as You work in me by Your Spirit to make me be the person You created me to be! I pray this in Jesus' name!

For it is God which worketh in you both to will and to do of his good pleasure. Do all things without murmurings and disputings.

Philippians 2:13-14

My Confession for Today

I confess that God is working in me to will and to do according to His good pleasure. The power I need to change is already inside me, just waiting for my compliance and obedience. When I stop moaning and muttering and disputing with God about what He is asking me to do, I see His hand at work in my life. When I stop putting up a fight and surrender to the power that is at work in me at this very second, I can conquer any character flaw as God's mighty power changes me to become more like Him. I declare this by faith in Jesus' name!

OCTOBER 22

In What Race Is God Asking You To Run?

Being confident of this very thing, that he which hath begun a good work in you will perform it until the day of Jesus Christ.

Philippians 1:6

My Prayer for Today

Father, I hear You beckoning me to step forward by faith, and I am inspired to do what You are telling me to do. I've been in a preparation season for a long time. I thank You that you are finally telling me it's time to step forward, to put my feet into the river's waters and to see Your supernatural power make a way for me to enter into the land You promised to me and that You've been speaking to me about. Thank You for having confidence in me. With the Holy Spirit living inside of me, the two of us together can challenge the impossible and do the unthinkable! By faith, I am stepping forward—and I thank You for carrying me toward the finish line and helping me complete what You have put into my heart! I pray this in Jesus' name!

My Confession for Today

I declare that the impossible is moving out of the way for me. God has been preparing me a long time to do more than I've been doing. He has tested me, watched me, prepared me, and now it's time for me to take the big leap of faith and move forward toward the goal He's put in my heart. It's a miracle, but He is carrying me toward the finish line and He will make sure I get all the way to the conclusion. I give God all the praise and glory, for He prepares me, empowers me, and carries me toward that place He has ordained for me to be! I declare this by faith in Jesus' name!

God's Applause

My Prayer for Today

Father, You see everything. You are not unjust. You know how I have worked for You and how I have shown my love for You by caring for other believers. When I am tempted to be discouraged and to think that no one appreciates me, remind me that You know exactly what I am doing and why I am doing it. I know that You take note of what I do for Your Kingdom, and Your approval is what I desire. Holy Spirit, You are my Helper. I receive Your wisdom, counsel, and might to do my work for Jesus in the most excellent, professional manner possible. Thank You for Your power that enables me to serve the Lord in such a manner that one day He'll rise to give a round of applause for what I've done and how I've done it. I pray this in Jesus' name!

Therefore judge nothing before the time, until the Lord come, who both will bring to light the hidden things of darkness, and will make manifest the counsels of the hearts: and then shall every man have praise of God.

1 Corinthians 4:5

My Confession for Today

I confess that I work as unto the Lord, whether or not men see my labor. Although it is nice to be thanked, I don't work for the people's applause. Rather, I am laboring to please the Lord, and my priority in life is to serve Him in a manner that is honoring of Him. I devote 100 percent of my energy and efforts to glorify Jesus in all I do. With the help of the Holy Spirit, I purpose to satisfy His heart with my service and my heart motives behind my service. On that day when I am called to give an account for my works, I will stand boldly and unashamedly before Jesus because I will know I've given my best here in this life. I declare this by faith in Jesus' name!

OCTOBER 24

Who Is an Apostle?

And He Himself gave some to be apostles…

Ephesians 4:11 NKJV

My Prayer for Today

Father, I ask You to help me recognize those who are apostolic gifts—those who have apostolic callings—in the Body of Christ. We need all fivefold ministries—apostles, prophets, evangelists, pastors, and teachers—for the building up of the Church. If one of these is missing, there will be a certain portion of Christ's impartation missing from the Church. I ask You to help me be open-minded to the reality of the apostolic ministry gifts and to honor them in our midst. I pray this in Jesus' name!

My Confession for Today

I confess that apostles, prophets, evangelists, pastors, and teachers are all present and active in the Body of Christ. I am open to each of these impartations of Christ. Because I am open to them, I will be a recipient of the grace of God that is delivered through each of these. I will receive ministry from apostles, prophets, evangelists, pastors, and teachers—and it will contribute to my edification, growth, and to the building up of the Body of Christ! I declare this by faith in Jesus' name!

The Historical Meaning of the Word "Apostle"

My Prayer for Today

And He Himself gave some to be apostles…

Ephesians 4:11 NKJV

Father, I thank You for accurate knowledge in the Bible that reveals the enormity of Your great plan and the significance of every distinctive part of the Body of Christ. Lord, I ask You to open the eyes of my heart to see and understand more about the role and value of this fivefold ministry gift overall and to me personally, because I want everything You have to offer me and Your Church! I pray this in Jesus' name!

My Confession for Today

I confess that I believe in and honor the ministries of prophets, apostles, evangelists, pastors, and teachers according to Ephesians 4:11, which says that each ministry gift, including the apostolic ministry, is essential for the growth and the building up of the Church. So I will embrace in my life this aspect of Christ's character and function that He expresses in His Body through each ministry gift to the Body of Christ! As a result, I grow strong in my own identity in the part I am ordained to fill as a member of the Body. I declare this by faith in Jesus' name!

OCTOBER 26

Apostles Named in the New Testament

And He Himself gave some to be apostles…

Ephesians 4:11 NKJV

My Prayer for Today

Lord, I am amazed at this list of people who were sent forth as apostles in the New Testament. I now wonder about and have a new desire to better understand the gifts You have set in Your Body as it pleases You. Help me, Holy Spirit, to understand not only my own spiritual gift but also the authentic gifts in those around me—including the apostolic gift whom You've sent to build up, draw forth, speak out, align, govern, strengthen, and establish Your Church as Your unique agent on the earth. I want to humbly and completely cooperate with and draw from the apostolic anointing that rests on those You have genuinely called to this ministry so that I can experience the fullness of Your intent when You gave gifts to us. I pray this in Jesus' name!

My Confession for Today

I confess that my appreciation for and knowledge about the valuable apostolic ministry is expanding. My perspective is adjusting concerning the supernatural function of authentic ministry gifts—and of the apostle in particular. I see that it is worthy of my study and consideration. I want everything that God has for me, and if this is part of God's plan for the Church, my heart is longing for it too. I declare this by faith in Jesus' name!

Supernatural Patience and Endurance

My Prayer for Today

Lord Jesus, thank You for giving the gift of the apostle to Your Church to establish and strengthen us in doctrine and in the personal and practical knowledge of Your wisdom and ways. I thank You, Lord, for the divine endowment of patient endurance that You impart to the apostle to be able to build and advance the Kingdom of God. Holy Spirit, since this supernatural quality of endurance and staying power is mine also as a child of God, I place my trust in You and fully expect You to lead me in triumph through every obstacle and challenge. By the power of Your anointing within and upon me, I ask You to spread the fragrance of the knowledge of God through my life everywhere I go, to the praise and honor of my Lord Jesus Christ. I pray this in Jesus' name!

Truly the signs of an apostle were wrought among you in all patience…

2 Corinthians 12:12

My Confession for Today

I confess that I have staying power! This divine impartation is part of my inheritance as a child of God! I have within me the supernatural ability to endure difficulties and to persevere through challenges while holding fast to my faith. When I encounter hostility or obstacles, the Lord Himself is my strength and personal bravery. The Lord steadies and directs my steps, enabling me to make progress in times of trouble, testing, suffering, or great responsibility. Amid all these things, no matter what I may face, I am more than a conqueror through Jesus Christ, and I always triumph in surpassing victory through Him! I declare this by faith in Jesus' name!

October 28

The Signs of a True Apostle

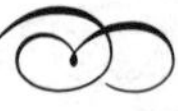

Truly the signs of an apostle were wrought among you...

2 Corinthians 12:12

My Prayer for Today

Father God, I praise and magnify You, for You alone are the God of miracles. Your mighty wonders cannot be contained or explained by any natural power or force of nature. Lord Jesus, You said supernatural signs would follow the preaching of Your Word. I pray that ministers and believers everywhere who proclaim Your Word will also walk in mighty demonstrations of Your awesome power to authorize them as they enforce Your will. Lord Jesus, as we approach the day of Your returning, I expect an increase in signs, wonders, and miracles—not only through Your people, but also on behalf of Your people to protect them and to prevent their assignments from being cut short as they live in consecrated service to Your divine will. I pray this in Jesus' name!

My Confession for Today

I confess that Jesus Christ is the same yesterday, today, and forever; therefore, I know that He continues to confirm His Word with signs following just as He said He would. The supernatural power of my Almighty God is still on display today through miracles, signs and wonders that manifest outside the realm of ordinary events—and they do so both through me and on my behalf to the glory of God the Father! I declare this by faith in Jesus' name!

Falsely Claiming To Be an Apostle

And He Himself gave some to be apostles…

Ephesians 4:11 NKJV

My Prayer for Today

Father, I thank You for keeping me safe from influence of imposters and spiritual predators. Thank You for helping me to be wise and to keep my eyes wide open about who I receive as a spiritual authority in my life. I realize that I must be accountable to someone in my life, but I ask You to give me discernment about who that person should be! I pray this in Jesus' name!

My Confession for Today

I confess that my natural and spiritual eyes are wide open, along with my natural and spiritual ears. I am sensitive to the voice and leading of the Holy Spirit and I do not fall victim to unscrupulous people who flatter others for personal gain. I pay close attention to what I hear and see. If anyone has ulterior motives for wanting spiritual authority in my life, the Spirit of Truth illuminates my understanding so I can see and recognize it. The Spirit of God within my spirit will bear witness to alert me so I will know when I have come across the real deal! I declare this by faith in Jesus' name!

Apostolic Authority–Relational, Geographical, Territorial

And He Himself gave some to be apostles…

Ephesians 4:11 NKJV

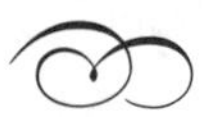

My Prayer for Today

Father, I ask You to help me use my head and not just react according to my emotions, when it comes to who is leading me spiritually. You have given me a mind that You expect me to use, and I pray for the wisdom to think carefully and clearly about those to whom I give the right to lead me spiritually. I thank You for my pastor and for my church. Nonetheless, I know that I must keep my eyes open and my heart in tune with Your Spirit about anyone to whom I yield oversight in my life. I pray this prayer in Jesus' name!

My Confession for Today

I confess that I have a good head on my shoulders! My heart is open to the Spirit of God, and my mind thinks soundly and clearly. I rely on God's wisdom and counsel, and He causes my thoughts to be in agreement with His will. I have a strong foundation of God's Word in my heart and mind; therefore, I am not easily misled because that Word illuminates my understanding. When something is wrong, an alert goes off inside me that warns me to be careful. I am not suspicious or quick to accuse, but I am sensitive to what is happening spiritually. I thank God that the Holy Spirit produces in me the mind of Christ, and the mind of Christ helps me to think soundly and accurately. I declare this by faith in Jesus' name!

False Apostles and Deceitful Workers

For such are false apostles, deceitful workers...

2 Corinthians 11:13

My Prayer for Today

Father, help me trust those who are over me in the Lord to know how to test and try those who come to minister to our congregation. I trust my pastor and the leadership of our church. Nevertheless, I pray for You to guide them and to give them wisdom as they open the doors of our church to ministers who are new to us. I ask You, Lord, to heighten their spiritual discernment so that they can clearly distinguish when everything that glitters is not gold, and everything that looks spiritual is not necessarily of God. Help our overseers to have the wisdom of God in whom they invite to minister to our congregation. I pray this in Jesus' name!

My Confession for Today

I confess that my pastor and the leadership team of our church are spiritually sensitive about those whom they invite to minister to our congregation. They are diligent to pray and seek the Lord; therefore, I can rest at peace that whomever may be invited to stand in our pulpit is anointed to impart something from Heaven that will strengthen and establish us to do the will of God from the heart. I am so thankful that this responsibility is not mine, but I pray for them. I declare that those who are called and equipped to exercise stewardship and give an account for my soul in the Lord walk in the wisdom and spiritual fortitude they need to make right choices for our congregation, so when they stand before You they can hear You say, "Well done!" I declare this by faith in Jesus' name!

NOVEMBER 1

More End-Time Ministry Advice

But watch thou in all things, endure afflictions, do the work of an evangelist, make full proof of thy ministry.

2 Timothy 4:5

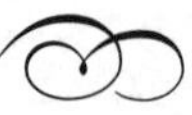

My Prayer for Today

Father, I thank You for this reminder of the dire need to guard my heart and spirit against the whims of the times that have adversely affected the Church. I don't feel fear because of this teaching; I feel prepared by it. I am thankful to You for loving me so much that You put such clear, sound warnings in Scripture to protect us in these last days. Help me be open to what You are doing and closed to what leads away from the pure teaching of doctrinal truth. I pray this in Jesus' name!

My Confession for Today

I confess that I exercise discernment when it comes to my consumption of spiritual teaching. I know that what I put into my eyes and ears affects what I believe and what I receive—so I put a filter upon my eyes and ears to make sure only truth finds access to my mind and heart. Lord, I am thankful that You have chosen me to live in these last days, and I count it an honor that You trusted me with this privilege. While so many people struggle to know what is right or wrong—doctrinally or morally—I declare that Your Word is burning and alive in my heart and will keep me walking in the light, enabling me to bring answers to people in a way that will offer them spiritual help and relief. I declare this by faith in Jesus' name!

Do What You Do in the Name of Jesus

My Prayer for Today

Father, I examine my life to see if I am living in a way that honors the indwelling Spirit and the name of Jesus. Help me recognize the attitudes and actions that don't honor the Holy Spirit or exalt the name of Jesus in my life. I ask You to forgive me and to help me to become sensitive in spirit if I have hardened my heart through unbelief and disobedience. Lord, as honestly as I know how, I am serious about my walk with You, so I ask You to please help me to turn away from anything that grieves You. I pray this in Jesus' name!

And whatsoever ye do in word or deed, do all in the name of the Lord Jesus...

Colossians 3:17

My Confession for Today

I confess that I make it my aim that whatever I do in word or deed, I do all in the name of the Lord Jesus. I take every thought captive to do His will, and I endeavor to think, speak, and act in a way that only gives honor to my Lord Jesus Christ. I declare this by faith in Jesus' name!

NOVEMBER 3

Plotting To Entangle

Then went the Pharisees, and took counsel how they might entangle him [Jesus] in his talk.

Matthew 22:15

My Prayer for Today

Father, I ask You to forgive me for the times I've allowed myself to be affected by people I knew were in the crowd or by whom I was talking to in a moment. Help me stand fearless and true to You, to Your Word, and to who I am. I have no reason to be embarrassed or ashamed or to squirm from fear of what man thinks of me. Just as Jesus boldly spoke to the Pharisees who tried to catch Him, help me be bold in moments when I am tempted to be weak or to draw back. Your soul takes no pleasure in those who draw back, so I refuse to be intimidated! Your righteousness makes me as bold as a lion. Therefore, since God is for me, I will not fear any mere person who may come against me! I pray this in Jesus' name!

My Confession for Today

I confess that just like Jesus, I will not change how I present myself or what I believe when I know opponents are listening to me, looking for something negative to say about my faith. I have no need to shrink down or apologize for what I believe or for the power of God that works through me. I will stand forth boldly and pour out what I really believe with the anointing of the Holy Spirit empowering me. I will be true to the Word of God, steadfast in my convictions, and unashamed as I present the Gospel by the power of Christ in me! I declare this by faith in Jesus' name!

God Can Reach Anyone!

My Prayer for Today

Heavenly Father, I thank You that Your saving power can reach any person, regardless of how deep they are in sin, how hardhearted they are, or how far from You they may have wandered. Your mercy extends to every person, and Your salvation was meant to save every person! I thank You for giving me hope for my friends and loved ones through the testimony of the apostle Paul. Today I pray for my friends, acquaintances, and relatives who are far from God. I pray that the Holy Spirit will direct their paths into an encounter with the living Christ that will suddenly transform their lives for eternity! I pray this in Jesus' name!

I [Paul] was formerly a blasphemer, a persecutor, and an insolent man...

1 Timothy 1:13

My Confession for Today

I boldly confess that my friends, acquaintances, and relatives are on a collision course with Jesus Christ—and that they are going to be saved and changed in a split-second experience with Him. Although they are not walking with God and seem hardhearted right now, God is working mightily to invade their lives and to bring His saving power into their spirits. They may not know it, but they are on the verge of salvation! By faith I call them out of darkness and into the light of God's Kingdom, where His righteousness, peace, and joy will cause them to increasingly yield to the lordship of Jesus Christ until their lives fully manifest His glory on the earth. I declare this by faith in Jesus' name!

Behavior in the House of God

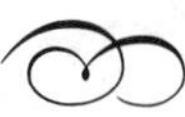

But if I tarry long, that thou mayest know how thou oughtest to behave thyself in the house of God, which is the church of the living God, the pillar and ground of the truth.

1 Timothy 3:14-15

My Prayer for Today

Father, I ask You to help me behave appropriately when I am in the house of God—not only when I am in a service, but also to behave appropriately as a Christian. May my lifestyle and behavior bring glory to the Lord Jesus Christ. Forgive me for the times I have acted out of order or done things that were inappropriate or disruptive. Help me develop a personal discipline in the way I conduct myself not only when I am in the house of God but also in every area of my life because I am, in fact, Your temple, and Your Spirit resides within me. Therefore, I desire to conduct myself worthily as I ought at all times in a dignified manner that reflects You, giving both You and the sanctuary where Your people gather the full respect that is due according to Your will. I pray this in Jesus' name!

My Confession for Today

I confess that I am mannerly, honoring, and respectful when I am in the house of God. I listen attentively, and I do not disturb others who are trying to hear the Word. I honor God in my behavior. When I see others, either young people or adults, who are disruptive and dishonoring, God shows me how to respectfully teach them how to behave and to conduct themselves in church. Because I am serious about my life with Christ, I behave seriously when I am in the house of God! I declare this by faith in Jesus' name!

An Astounding Miracle

My Prayer for Today

Father, first of all, I repent for each and every time I've been where the Word is preached, yet I disrespectfully allowed myself to be distracted by other things in my mind by writing notes, by sending text messages, or by visiting with my neighbor. Father, Your words are life. Each one contains the power to save, to heal, to deliver, to transform, and to make all things new. Forgive me for not giving Your Word the full esteem and utmost regard. I've been wrong for not totally focusing on the message being preached. For this, I truly ask You for forgiveness. I ask You to help me discipline my mind to focus as I respond with ears to hear and a heart to receive what is being preached so that the message will impart faith to my heart! I pray this in Jesus' name!

Then Philip went down to the city of Samaria, and preached Christ unto them. And the people with one accord gave heed unto those things which Philip spake, hearing and seeing the miracles which he did. For unclean spirits, crying with loud voice, came out of many that were possessed with them: and many taken with palsies, and that were lame, were healed. And there was great joy in that city.

Acts 8:5-8

My Confession for Today

I boldly confess that each time the Word of God is preached, I give it my full concentration. I refuse to be dull in my hearing or to negatively influence the atmosphere of a meeting with hardness of heart and unbelief. Instead, I shove all other thoughts aside, and I fixate on the Word being declared to me. As a result, faith is ignited in my heart, for faith comes by hearing—really hearing—the Word of God. As I mix my faith with what I hear, I not only see and experience supernatural results in my life, I also affect the atmosphere and help create an environment for the supernatural power of God to explode around me so others can hear and be healed, saved, or transformed by the Word of God. Such supernatural occurrences were not meant just for Bible times. They are for anyone in any generation who will draw near to the Word, focus on it, and receive an influx of faith. And I confess that this is a description of me! I declare this by faith in Jesus' name!

God's Spirit Forewarns and Prepares

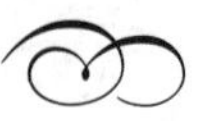

Fear none of those things which thou shalt suffer: behold, the devil shall cast some of you into prison…

Revelation 2:10

My Prayer for Today

Father, I thank You that Your love for the Church is so strong that You forewarn and prepare us for the days ahead. Please forgive me for the times when You tried to warn me but I didn't listen—and help me open my heart to hear what You are saying to me now about the times to come. Regardless of what the future holds, I know that You are Lord of all and that You made me to be an overcomer. I pray for a flood of the Holy Spirit's power to be unleashed in my life in these last days so that I will have everything I need to brave any storm and emerge victorious on the other side! I pray this in Jesus' name!

My Confession for Today

I confess that my spiritual ears are open and I am attuned to what the Holy Spirit is telling me about the present and the days ahead. The future will not take me by surprise, because I am listening to the Holy Spirit, and He reveals to me what I need to know. Jesus promised that the Holy Spirit would show us things to come, and I declare that my spirit is wideawake and alert to hear the Spirit's forecast about the future. I am filled with the Holy Spirit; therefore, He gives me all the strength and energy I need to outlast any storm the devil ever tries to send my way. With the help of the Holy Spirit, I will come out on the other side of any difficulty as an overcomer! I declare this by faith, in Jesus' name!

Jesus has Overcome the World!

My Prayer for Today

Father, I thank You that You sent Jesus—and that Jesus has overcome the world in every respect. Regardless of what the devil tries to do, Jesus has already overcome it. I do not have to lose heart or be discouraged. I can lift my head, throw my shoulders back, and rejoice, because Jesus has overcome the world and deprived it of its power to harm me. I am more than a conqueror through Jesus Christ, who has given me His overcoming power to make me triumphant in this life! I pray this in Jesus' name!

...In the world ye shall have tribulation: but be of good cheer; I have overcome the world.

John 16:33

My Confession for Today

I boldly confess that Jesus Christ is Lord over all! Jesus is Lord over every foe and every enemy I face in my life. Jesus didn't partially overcome the world; He completely overcame it. And because I am in Christ, I share in this glorious victory! Jesus said to take heart and to be courageous, so today I take heart and face the future with courage. I am not a victim to my circumstances because Jesus died on the Cross, defeated the enemy, and rose from the dead victorious over all. He has literally overcome everything that needs to be overcome, and now He shares that glorious victory with me! I declare this by faith, in Jesus' name!

NOVEMBER 9

Friends To the Rescue

And when Paul would have entered in unto the people, the disciples suffered him not. And certain of the chief of Asia, which were his friends, sent unto him, desiring him that he would not adventure himself into the theatre.

Acts 19:30-31

My Prayer for Today

Heavenly Father, I acknowledge and repent for being stubborn. I admit that my decisions have not always been right, and there have been moments when You have used friends and associates to stop me from acting in a way that might harm me. At the time, I didn't like their advice and their actions, but after I calmed down I came to realize that You had intervened in my life by using them to help redirect my steps. Thank You for loving me so much that You would use others to help navigate me through difficult moments. I am so grateful for the friends and influences You've positioned along my path in life who have helped me when I didn't even know I was going the wrong way. My heart is filled with thanksgiving for this today! I pray this in Jesus' name!

My Confession for Today

I confess that I walk among the wise, and I give attention to the voice of wisdom. God loves me so much that He will place people around me who speak truth to me and help me when I don't even know that I need help. When I am about to make a wrong decision or take an action that could be detrimental to me, they speak up and I listen to what they have to say. I declare that I will be open-hearted to them and will hear the voice of God speaking to me through friends when I need His voice to come to me in that way! I declare this by faith, in Jesus' name!

Jesus Is Not Ashamed of His Church!

My Prayer for Today

Father, I thank You for reminding me of Your great love for the Church in spite of all of its present blemishes, flaws, and imperfections. Forgive me—and forgive others—when we have been judgmental of Your precious Church and have been ashamed or embarrassed of it. We have actually been judgmental of ourselves because we are Your Body, the Church, members one of another. You are right in the midst of the Church; therefore, I refuse to criticize what You have given Your life for and invested Yourself in so completely. I thank You for bringing correction and encouragement to my heart today. I repent for any judgmental attitude about your Church or its leadership, and I receive Your forgiveness. Help me keep a right heart attitude. I pray this in Jesus' name!

...And being turned, I saw seven golden candlesticks; and in the midst of the seven candlesticks one like unto the Son of man...

Revelation 1:12-13

My Confession for Today

I boldly confess that I love the Church of Jesus Christ, and I am thankful to be a member of it. I regret holding a critical attitude, and I repent of it right now. I make the decision to change the way I see the Church and how I speak about the Church. Most of all, I make the decision to pray for the Church. Christ loves the Church as His own Body; therefore, I refuse to despise Christ Himself by ill-esteeming His own Body—of which I, too, am a part! Since Christ is in the midst of the Church, I set my affection and devotion in the midst of the Church. With the help of God's Spirit working in my heart and mind, I will maintain a good, positive, faith-filled attitude toward the Church and its leadership, especially when I see imperfections that seem glaringly obvious to me. Who am I to judge another's servant? God is able to make him stand. My responsibility is to pray so that I am not judged in the same critical way. I declare this by faith in Jesus' name!

NOVEMBER 11

Jesus' High Priestly Ministry

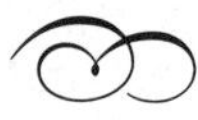

And in the midst of the seven candlesticks one like unto the Son of man, clothed with a garment down to the foot, and girt about the paps with a golden girdle.

Revelation 1:13

My Prayer for Today

Father, I thank You that Jesus is in Your Presence as my Great High Priest, where He ever lives to make intercession for me and for those who belong to Him. I thank You that I have no need to be ashamed or embarrassed when I come to You through Him, because He has thrown open the door and invited me to come boldly to the throne of grace to receive help and assistance in my time of need. I am so thankful for this high priestly ministry of Jesus—that He was, is, and forever will be my Great High Priest! I pray this in Jesus' name!

My Confession for Today

I declare that Jesus is my Great High Priest. Seated at the right hand of the Father, He lives to make intercession for me. Jesus, my High Priest, is touched with the feeling of my infirmity. I have no need to be ashamed or embarrassed when I come before the Father through Him, because He has given me unrestricted access and invited me to come boldly to the throne of grace to obtain help in my time of need. I pray this in Jesus' name!

Eyes as a Flame of Fire

My Prayer for Today

...his eyes were as a flame of fire.

Revelation 1:14

Father, I thank You that Your love for me is so intense that You want to burn up the chaff in my life. Your highest will is for me to surrender these problem areas to You so I do not have to experience that chaff-burning fire. Instead I would experience the holy fire that comes to purify me and take me higher in my walk in the Spirit. So today, Holy Spirit, I ask You to help me examine my heart and willfully surrender those chaff-areas of my life that do not reflect Your character or Your purpose for my life. Open my heart to Your holy, purifying fire, oh God, that I may be cleansed to ascend into the high places of Your glory! I pray this in Jesus' name!

My Confession for Today

I purpose in my heart to respond humbly to the dealing of God so that His fire that kindles upon me will ignite me into a burning flame for His glory. Daily I choose to walk before the Lord in a way that His holy fire will purify and take me to a higher level in Him. I know that the fire of God will burn up the chaff of self-willed works and ways that I wasn't willing to surrender on my own. The choice is mine, and I choose to yield to the refining fire because I know that, whether I like it or not, divine fire will come. And when its fires try the metal of my life, I want all that remains of me through the flames to be found before Him as pure gold. I declare this by faith in Jesus name!

NOVEMBER 13

The Similarity Between Pastors and Stars

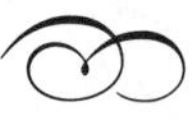

And he had in his right hand seven stars...The seven stars are the angels of the seven churches: and the seven candlesticks which thou sawest are the seven churches.

Revelation 1:16,20

My Prayer for Today

Heavenly Father, I thank You for what I have learned today about pastoral ministry. I specifically pray for my pastor—that he will have sufficient spiritual fuel in the core of his being for a long-lasting ministry; that my pastor's ministry will be more stable and strong the older he gets; that my pastor will take his unique role among all pastors; that he knows the "orbit" designed and laid out for his pastoral ministry; and that he will fulfill the divine destiny that You have planned for his life. I thank You for the way my pastor serves, and I ask You, Father, to bless him abundantly. Give him the wisdom, power, and strength that is needed for a long-term ministry that brings forth much fruit for the Kingdom of Heaven. I pray this in Jesus' name!

My Confession for Today

Today I release my faith for my pastor. I specifically confess that my pastor has sufficient spiritual fuel in the core of his being for a long-lasting ministry; that my pastor's ministry will be stable and stronger the older he gets; that my pastor will take his unique role among all pastors; that my pastor knows the orbit designed for his pastoral ministry; and that he will fulfill the divine destiny that You have planned for his life. I confess that You, Father, give my pastor the wisdom, power, and strength that is needed for a long-term ministry that brings forth much fruit for the Kingdom of Heaven. I declare this by faith in Jesus' name!

Moving On in Life at the Right Time

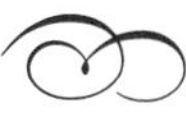

My Prayer for Today

Father, I needed this word today. I do feel that I'm beginning a new season in my life. Knowing how to move on has been the challenge for me. I ask You to give me wisdom to know what steps to take, discernment to know what to say and what not to say, and understanding as to how to do this in a manner pleasing to Jesus. For me to do this correctly, I need Your help and guidance. So, Holy Spirit, I open my spiritual ears to hear You, and I extend my hand for You to lead me through all the steps I need to take—until I land securely in the next place and the new season that You have ordained for my life. I pray this in Jesus' name!

And he [Paul] went into the synagogue, and spake boldly for the space of three months, disputing and persuading the things concerning the kingdom of God. But when divers were hardened, and believed not, but spake evil of that way before the multitude, he departed from them, and separated the disciples, disputing daily in the school of one Tyrannus.

Acts 19:8-9

My Confession for Today

I confess that God, by His Spirit, is leading me into the next season of my life. Although it is difficult to leave the present season, I know and declare that God is opening a new door for me and that the next season will be the most wonderful time I have ever known in my life thus far. Because I lean upon the Holy Spirit and I follow His voice, He will show me what to say, what not to say, what steps to take, and how to transition from where I am to where I am headed. The Holy Spirit is speaking to me and leading me, and I will end up in the next God-ordained place for my life. I declare this by faith in Jesus' name!

NOVEMBER 15

Healing with Handkerchiefs and Aprons

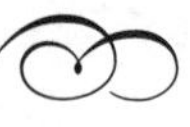

So that from his [Paul's] body were brought unto the sick handkerchiefs or aprons, and the diseases departed from them, and the evil spirits went out of them.

Acts 19:12

My Prayer for Today

Father, I ask You for the grace to step out of my comfort zone and into the place You have designed for me. I've been reluctant to let go of what is known and comfortable—but without faith, it is impossible to please You! I know that You are calling me onward and upward. I receive the courage I need to release the familiar and to step out by faith to enter the next season of my life. And, Father, just as Paul experienced miracles he had never known once he obeyed, I pray that my life will explode with miraculous answers to prayer as I step forward to obey what You are telling me to do. I pray this in Jesus' name!

My Confession for Today

I confess I have the grace to step out of my comfort zone and into the place God has designed for me. I am not afraid to let go of what is known and comfortable, because I know that God is calling me onward and upward. He gives me courage to step out in faith to enter the next season of my life. Just as Paul experienced miracles he had never known once he obeyed, my life will explode with the miraculous as I step forward to obey what the Holy Spirit is telling me to do. I declare this by faith in Jesus' name!

The Judgment Seat of Christ

My Prayer for Today

Father, since the day is coming when I will stand before the judgment seat of Christ to be rewarded or not rewarded according to my works, please help me take a serious look at my life now and evaluate where I need to make changes. On that glorious day, I do not want to look into Jesus' eyes while feeling regret and sadness—I want to look into His eyes, knowing that I did all He asked of me to fulfill His plan for my life. Holy Spirit, help me examine my heart and my actions to see what I need to change now. And Holy Spirit, I ask You to remind me continually that a day is coming when I will stand before Christ to answer for my life. Please keep me in remembrance of this so that I will live at all times with eternity at the forefront of my mind. I pray this in Jesus' name!

...we shall all stand before the judgment seat of Christ.

Romans 14:10

For we must all appear before the judgment seat of Christ; that every one may receive the things done in his body, according to that he hath done, whether it be good or bad.

2 Corinthians 5:10

My Confession for Today

I acknowledge that I live each day with an awareness that I will stand before the Judgment Seat of Christ one day. As a result, I take a serious look at my life regularly to see where I need to make changes. I am determined that I will look into His eyes on that glorious day without regrets, knowing that I did my best to fulfill His plan for my life. Hence, I will live in obedience and yieldedness to the direction of the Holy Spirit so that I can be ready for that great and notable day. I declare this by faith in Jesus' name!

NOVEMBER 17

Unhindered Access To God's Throne

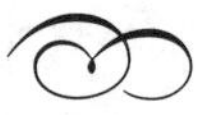

For through him we both [Jew and Gentile] have access by one Spirit unto the Father.

Ephesians 2:18

My Prayer for Today

Father, I give glory, honor, and praise to You that through Jesus Christ, I have instant, unhindered access to Your throne. Because Your Spirit lives inside me, the door to Heaven is open above me and Your ears are attentive to hear and answer me. Furthermore, because my heart is an open door to you, this same connection gives You access through me to others. Holy Spirit, teach me how to live every moment in an active, engaged faith that pleases You and keeps me continually aware of my connection with You. I pray this in Jesus' name!

My Confession for Today

I confess that my life is hidden with Christ in God. According to Ephesians 2:18, I have instant access to God through Christ Jesus. Furthermore, the Father has access through me to reach those around me because my heart is an open door to Him. I do not need to fear that God won't hear me. I thank my God that He always hears me! When I pray in faith, the Holy Spirit enables me immediately to connect with the Father to access His wisdom and His power with no delay! I declare this by faith in Jesus' name!

Embrace a "No Strife" Policy

My Prayer for Today

Father, I thank You for instructing me so vividly about the consequences of strife and the confusion that will ensue. I can remember moments in my own life when I allowed strife to escalate and produce chaos and confusion in a foul situation that should have never been permitted. Thank You for reminding me how important it is to submit to the Holy Spirit and to resist the attempt of my own flesh to control me or those around me by giving place to strife. In moments when I am tempted to fall into a rage about something, help me remember that such attitudes open the door for the devil's attack. Help me be controlled and vigilant about my attitudes so the devil cannot attack me and bring chaos into my life. Holy Spirit, I look to You for Your help! I pray this in Jesus' name!

For where envying and strife is, there is confusion and every evil work.

James 3:16

My Confession for Today

I confess that I do not allow strife to throw me into moments that result in chaotic events or ugly situations. Strife simply has no place in my life, and I refuse to be a participant in anything that even hints of it. From this moment onward, I operate with a "no strife" policy in my life. When I am tempted to get into anger or to yield to an ugly, strife-filled attitude, I will turn from it before it releases negative consequences in my life. The Holy Spirit is at work inside me, and I choose to cooperate with Him in order to prevent this from occurring in my life! I declare this by faith in Jesus' name!

Allow God To Prepare You

But now hath God set the members every one of them in the body, as it hath pleased him.

1 Corinthians 12:18

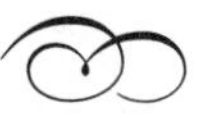

My Prayer for Today

Dear Father, as I walk through this time of transition, I know that You are preparing me for the next steps. I thank You, for I know that You are committed to preparing me for the next season of my life. You are helping me get ready by placing me with the right people in the right places to receive the training I need. Please help me yield to and follow Your leading. I fully trust You to order my steps according to what pleases You. My times are in Your hands, Father. Help me be flexible and pliable toward the work You are doing in me as You faithfully complete what You have begun in me. I know that if I am obedient and follow Your voice, You will empower me to see and to fulfill the high calling You've placed on my life! I pray this in Jesus' name!

My Confession for Today

I confess that I know the voice of my Good Shepherd and the voice of a stranger I will not follow. My heavenly Father is ordering and directing my steps so that I will walk with the wise and be wise. As He positions me to stand among the right people, with great ease He is directing my steps to receive the training I need so I can do what the Lord has called me to do. I do not falter; I do not fear. He who has called, equipped, and justified me is near to me and has clothed me with His very own self. Therefore, having done all to stand in this time of testing, I will pass every test and stand fully approved before Him! I declare this by faith in Jesus' name!

Desire Gets You To the Top

My Prayer for Today

Father, I ask You to stir up desire in my heart that is strong enough to make me yearn to be the best possible me and achieve all that I can achieve. I know that You expect me to perform to my fullest potential, but I admit that my desire needs an upgrade in order for me to reach that highest level. You have given me the talents I need, and I have ideas that I've never taken the time to develop. Now I see that I need greater desire at work in my life. So today, Father, I ask the Holy Spirit to stir desire deeply inside me so that I'll never again be satisfied with mediocrity or the status quo! I pray this in Jesus' name!

This is a true saying, if a man desire the office of a bishop, he desireth a good work.

1 Timothy 3:1

My Confession for Today

I confess that a strong, God-given desire propels me forward, energizes me, and compels me to be the best I can be at whatever I set my hand to do. I reject laziness; I reject any idea that just doing "what's required" is enough for me; and I put forth whatever effort is required to reach the top of the mountain God has set before my life. I intend to scale that mountain, shout the victory—and rejoice that God has done such a wonderful work in my life and granted me the desires of my heart! I declare this by faith in Jesus' name!

NOVEMBER 21

Stand Strong

Preach the word; be instant in season, out of season...

2 Timothy 4:2

My Prayer for Today

Father, I hear You saying, "Stay at your post, and don't budge an inch! Stay there, and do what I have told you to do. Be faithful when times are good—and if times turn bad, remain steady and unflinching." I know that if I'll remain faithful to the call and to the place where You have assigned me, You will empower me with inner strength and sufficient grace that will enable me to see my calling through to a glorious conclusion! So, Holy Spirit, I receive Your fortitude to withstand the pressure to give up, give in, and throw in the towel. Strengthen me with the might I need inwardly to stay put and see my assignment through to completion! I pray this in Jesus' name!

My Confession for Today

I confess that God strengthens me with His might to be faithful, steadfast, and persevering. When times are good or when times are tough, I am consistently constant. I stay put, no matter what. I will not be moved in my committed stance. The grace of God is teaching me how not to be provoked or lured to move away from my post. I keep my focus fastened on Jesus, and my roots grow down deep into Him. His stability keeps me grounded and enables me to be faithful to the call and to the place where God has planted me. I declare this by faith in Jesus' name!

You Are What You Are by the Grace of God

My Prayer for Today

But by the grace of God I am what I am…

1 Corinthians 15:10

Father, I ask You to help me really see and realize that the way You made me is not a mistake. You have fitted me exactly for the call that You have placed upon my life. Although I may be different from others around me, it is okay, because my call is different from that of my neighbors and friends. I confess that I've struggled with myself, but today I surrender it all—and I thank You that I am what I am by the grace of God. I ask You to help me understand it and receive it. With the help of Your grace, any self-imposed self-rejection I have lived under comes to an end. I receive Your grace; I accept who You have made me to be; and I confidently shine as a trophy of Your masterful making! I pray this in Jesus' name!

My Confession for Today

I confess that I am made exactly as God intended for me to be made. He fitted with me thoughts, gifts, and talents that may be different from others, but they are essential for what God has called me to do. These differences will be precisely what is needed when I fully step forward into the plan that God has designed for me and my family. I have battered myself long enough—and starting today, I accept who I am and what the grace of God has made me to be! I declare this by faith in Jesus' name!

NOVEMBER 23

Hold Your Position and Refuse To Move!

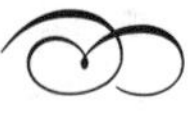

But continue thou in the things which thou hast learned and hast been assured of, knowing of whom thou hast learned them.

2 Timothy 3:14

My Prayer for Today

Lord, I recommit myself to the Word of God. Society is changing what it believes all the time, and it is drifting further and further away from the truths found in the Word of God. But according to Your commandment, I will "continue" in the teachings of the Holy Scriptures that have the power to make me "wise" for living in these times. Holy Spirit, I ask You to stir my heart with a new passion for the Word of God—that I would hunger and thirst for it continually—and then empower me not only to devour it but also to do it steadfastly. Teach me to draw my strength and nourishment from the Word of God in order to strengthen my spirit, soul, and body so that I will stand strong and victorious in these last days! I pray this in Jesus' name!

My Confession for Today

I confess that I hunger and thirst for God's Word more than my necessary food and drink. I make a deliberate decision to abide in the Word of God and to allow it to abide in me. I will not budge from my position on the Word as final authority in all manner of life. Therefore, as the world and its practices grow darker and darker beneath the sway of the wicked one, the Word of God shall remain a lamp unto my feet and a sure guide to my path. I will not be moved when I see governmental legislation and even some church leaders make drastic shifts in defiance of God's Word. I will "stay put" and hold the course of my commitment to God's ways, as I continue to occupy until He comes! I declare this by faith in Jesus' name!

What Is Delaying the Coming of the Lord?

My Prayer for Today

Father, thank You for helping me see as You see. Thank You for giving me Your heart for those who are lost and headed for hell. More and more, I sense Your compassion and Your longing that every person would receive the free gift of salvation as we approach the end of this age. Help me stay sensitive and obedient to Your Spirit so that I never miss an opportunity to share the Good News of Jesus with a heart that is ready to receive. I pray this in Jesus' name!

The Lord is not slack concerning his promise, as some men count slackness; but is longsuffering to us-ward, not willing that any should perish, but that all should come to repentance.

2 Peter 3:9

My Confession for Today

I confess that I am regularly spending time with my heavenly Father and becoming more and more sensitive to what is important to Him. The Father loved people so much that He gave His only Son to die on the Cross to redeem them. He doesn't want even one person to be lost and eternally separated from Him. More and more, the desires of my Father's heart are becoming the desires of my heart. Therefore, I live every day endeavoring to stay sensitive to the leading of the Holy Spirit. And every day He gives me divine opportunities to share the life-changing Gospel of Jesus Christ with those I encounter whose hearts are ready to receive. I declare this by faith in Jesus' name!

NOVEMBER 25

Why the Promise of a White Stone?

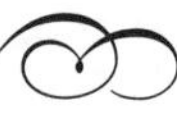

...To him that overcometh...I will give him a white stone...

Revelation 2:17

My Prayer for Today

Father, I thank You for the blood of Jesus Christ, which has cleansed me from all sinful actions of the past. Although I admittedly did wrong in the past, it is not held against me, because the blood of Christ has made me free. You have officially declared me clean. I stand before You as a born-again individual, free from the offenses of my past. A white stone has been cast in my favor. I am cleansed and free, and You are voting for me and my success! I pray this in Jesus' name!

My Confession for Today

I confess that I refuse to wallow in condemnation over my past sins that even God Himself doesn't remember. Instead, I focus my attention on the blood of Jesus as I remember all He has done for me. When the devil—or anyone, for that matter—tries to throw a stone of judgment against me by mentally tormenting me about past actions that I've already been forgiven for, I boldly answer: "Christ has reviewed all the evidence and already cast His vote. He has found me innocent!" I toss aside any garments of despair, and I put on the garment of praise because Jesus' blood has purged my conscience from dead works to serve the living God. Since God is for me, who can be against me? Jesus has cast His vote of a white stone in my favor—and that is the only vote that matters! I declare this by faith in Jesus' name!

A Simple Command That Requires Strict Obedience

Let us therefore follow after the things which make for peace, and things wherewith one may edify another.

Romans 14:19

My Prayer for Today

Father, I now have a clearer understanding of the enemy's well-planned attacks to incite Christians to wage war among ourselves and ultimately fall prey to his divisive tactics. I ask You to help me apply a more meticulous approach to pursue peace and to preserve it. Father, I receive Your specific wisdom in this very intentional endeavor. I can no longer allow any room for sloppy, last-minute thinking about how to construct relationships that need to last for generations. Thank You for strengthening each member of Your Body internally so that externally we can build the Christian community by prayer and with peace, love, and serious consideration of the high priority that we edify one another so that the world may truly know we are Yours by our love. I pray this in Jesus' name!

My Confession for Today

I confess that I engage an intentional pursuit of those things that make peace. I see to it that my words, attitudes, and actions edify and build others up rather than injure or put them down. I obey the Lord's command to make it my premeditated objective to edify others. Therefore, I give no place to the devil by allowing distrust, suspicion, or contempt to spring up and manifest in my life. I choose to follow the great plan of the Chief Architect, the Holy Spirit, and I refuse to deviate from it so He can build us into the glorious design the Father envisioned before the foundations of the world! I declare this by faith in Jesus' name!

NOVEMBER 27

Where Are We in Time?

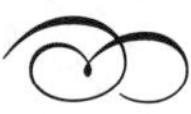

...what shall be the sign of thy coming, and of the end of the world?

Matthew 24:3

My Prayer for Today

Father, I ask You to help me do all I can to prepare my heart for the soon return of Jesus. Times are changing—and I'm thankful to know what Jesus had to say about the end of the age in Matthew 24:3. Help me comprehend the significance of the fact that I've been chosen to be a part of a very special generation. Help me find my role, get in my place, and do all I can to help advance the Gospel and its message before the age ends and Jesus returns. And especially help me to reach my family, friends, acquaintances, and coworkers with the message that the Cross has the power to save them, forgive them, and transform their lives! I pray this in Jesus' name!

My Confession for Today

I confess that I am blessed to be part of the wrap-up of the age before the return of Jesus Christ. It is no accident that I am alive at this time. God made me for such a time as this—and I will step into my place, fulfill my role, and do all I can to shine the light of the Gospel to those who are sitting in darkness. God will use me to remove the blinders that are on the eyes of unbelievers and bring them into the Kingdom of His dear Son! I declare this by faith in Jesus' name!

Supernatural Peace

My Prayer for Today

Father, I thank You for Philippians 4:6,7. Starting today, I ask You to help me fulfill the conditions in verse 6. And as I do, I expect You by faith to start performing the promise in verse 7 on my behalf. I thank You that Your peace will bring tranquility and rest to my soul and serve as a sentinel to prohibit detrimental, damaging, and negative thoughts from entering my heart. Jesus fought the battle for me; the war is won; and now it's time for peace to express its full power in me! I pray this in Jesus' name!

Be careful for nothing; but in every thing by prayer and supplication with thanksgiving let your requests be made known unto God. And the peace of God, which passeth all understanding, shall keep your hearts and minds through Christ Jesus.

Philippians 4:6-7

My Confession for Today

I boldly confess that I refuse to worry as I let my requests be made known unto God. I give God thanks for working in my life. As a result, I will experience the peace of God, and it will work for me to produce supernatural tranquility and rest for my soul. That peace will surpass any thoughts, which are trying to make me fearful. That peace will act as a guard to keep wrong thoughts from entering my heart—and it will throw open the door for positive, faith-filled thoughts to find entrance instead. I declare this by faith in Jesus' name!

All Things Are Possible

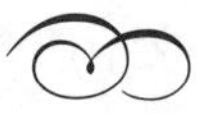

Jesus said unto him, If thou canst believe, all things are possible to him that believeth.

Mark 9:23

My Prayer for Today

Father, I realize that I have let some things slip regarding my walk of faith. Lord, I repent for being so carnal that I was moved by what I saw and what I felt. I commit afresh not to be provoked by circumstances that are subject to change. By Your grace, from this moment onward, I will be moved to take action only on the Word and by the Spirit of God. Thank You for strengthening my resolve to make a quality, lasting decision to step it up and get my faith in gear! You empower me by Your Spirit to stay consistent with my intake of the Word of God so my faith can remain fresh, current, and active and I can be strong in spirit to receive what I need. I pray this in Jesus' name!

My Confession for Today

I confess that my faith is alive and well and that I remain "in faith" to receive what I need! I keep my fellowship with the Lord intimate, fresh, and vibrant by spending time in His Word and in prayer daily. I keep myself in the love of God, and as a result, my faith does not fail. I give my attention to God's words and His desired end results; therefore, the Lord Himself keeps my thoughts in agreement with His will. I speak and act in agreement with God's words; therefore, I walk in and release the peace, wisdom, and supernatural ability of God everywhere I go. According to Jesus' promise in Mark 9:23, anything and everything is possible to me! I declare this by faith in Jesus' name!

Not Ashamed of the Gospel of Christ

My Prayer for Today

Father, I thank You for the Person of the Holy Spirit who resides within me. I acknowledge that His presence within me has imparted to me *dunamis* power—the strength of an entire army. Therefore, with confident assurance I boldly proclaim: the Greater One in me is mightier than any force that opposes me in this world! Father, I ask You to forgive me for times when I've retreated and acted in shame about the Gospel. I know I should have engaged my faith and released a flood of divine energy to empower me and overwhelm the enemy. So from this moment on, I make a firm decision that I will not be ashamed of the Gospel of Christ, but I will allow its strengthening might to flow through me, no matter what opposition or obstacle I face! I pray this in Jesus' name!

For I am not ashamed of the gospel of Christ: for it is the power of God unto salvation to every one that believeth...

Romans 1:16

My Confession for Today

I declare that there is a whole army of divine power at my disposal because the Holy Spirit indwells me. I believe the Gospel and its claim; therefore, I am strong and courageous knowing that divine signs of God's presence and approval are manifest in my life. I am not confounded, confused, or embarrassed when others poke fun at my faith. I don't shrink back or cringe in terror or intimidation. Instead, I simply draw from the supply of the Holy Spirit within me, engage my faith, and let His power strengthen me for what I am confronting at that moment. It is absolutely true that greater is He who is in me than he that is in the world! This *dunamis* power in me lifts me above any foe around me, and as I continually activate God's power by faith, I am an overcomer over every challenge that I'll ever face in this life! I declare this by faith in Jesus' name!

DECEMBER 1

Preparing for Christmas

Wherefore, beloved, seeing that ye look for such things, be diligent that ye may be found of him in peace, without spot, and blameless.

2 Peter 3:14

My Prayer for Today

Father, I ask You to help me look truthfully at my own spiritual condition to determine if I am doing all I should to prepare for the coming of the Lord. There is no doubt that He is coming and He is coming soon. But am I living in a way that will bring Him pleasure when He comes? This is a hard question to ask and pray, but I feel the need to be honest with myself and with You about it today, Lord. Speak to my heart, Holy Spirit, and reveal to me the areas where I need to put forth more effort into my spiritual life. I ask You to strengthen me with might in my inner self to be courageous, persistent, and diligent until it is done. I pray this in Jesus' name!

My Confession for Today

I confess that how I adorn and decorate my life with godliness and holiness is more important than how I physically decorate my house for Christmastime. I want to be found pleasing to the Lord when He comes. Therefore, to get myself ready for His coming—and to stay prepared for His coming—is the chief goal of my life. Whatever changes I need to make, I am willing to make. Whatever God is calling me to lay aside, I am willing to lay aside. More than anything else, I want to be a vessel that is found pleasing to Jesus when He comes for His Church. Lord, if there is any hint of anything in me that is unwilling to yield to this as my chief desire, I declare that it's moving out and being replaced by an unrelenting desire to be pleasing to You as the chief desire of my life. I declare this by faith in Jesus' name!

What To Do When Someone Needs Your Help

My Prayer for Today

Heavenly Father, in the midst of this season when many are happy and joyfully celebrating Your gift of love to humankind, I realize that this is also a time of year when some people feel a profound sense of loss or sadness. Father, I ask You to let me be a hand of help to those who are in need. Help me bring encouragement to those who feel loss, who are disempowered, or who feel like they are struggling beyond their natural capacity to overcome. I know that You want to use me to reach them. I surrender myself as an instrument You can use to bring strength to the weak, hope to the hopeless, and support to those who need it the most. According to Romans 15:1, I commit to being a source of power and support to those who are in need. I pray this in Jesus' name!

We then that are strong ought to bear the infirmities of the weak, and not to please ourselves.

Romans 15:1

My Confession for Today

I confess that I look beyond my own needs to see the needs of others. I am not self-consumed, but I am concerned about those about me who are suffering in all sorts of ways. The Holy Spirit uses me as I surrender to His sanctifying power so I can effectively undergird those who feel weak, especially in this holiday season. The Holy Spirit opens my eyes so I can see and feel what they see and feel and help them through their current struggle! I pray this in Jesus' name!

December 3

The Attraction of Something Special

And Jesus went about all Galilee, teaching in their synagogues, and preaching the gospel of the kingdom, and healing all manner of sickness and all manner of disease among the people. And his fame went throughout all Syria: and they brought unto him all sick people that were taken with divers diseases and torments, and those which were possessed with devils, and those which were lunatick, and those that had the palsy; and he healed them. And there followed him great multitudes…

Matthew 4:23-25

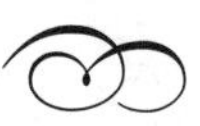

My Prayer for Today

Father, I thank You for encouraging me today. I have discounted myself as being too insignificant to make a large impact in Your Kingdom. But today I see that I could make a huge and eternal impact with something as small as a gift of candy or an encouraging word. Rather than look at what I can't do, help me look around to see what I have and what I could do that would make a difference in bringing others to Christ, especially during this Christmas season. I pray this in Jesus' name!

My Confession for Today

I confess that I am an instrument that God will use to touch others with the Good News of Jesus Christ. I have judged myself as being small and insignificant for too long. From this moment forward, I make the decision to look around me to see what I have to offer others that will cause the love of Jesus and His name to become a reality to them. I am not insignificant or too minor to be used by God in a big way. God wants to use me to reach people—even those who will themselves later impact multitudes for the Kingdom of God! I declare this by faith in Jesus' name!

Sharing the Message

My Prayer for Today

Father, I ask You to help me be creative in the ways I introduce the message of Jesus to those who are unsaved. Help me think "outside the box" and plan new and creative ways to present this eternal message. I know people who need salvation, but I need to think of new ways to present the message to them. Lord, You are the ultimate creative force in the universe, so I ask You to release Your creativity in me and help me as I take this greatest message of all to those I love and am praying for to receive Christ. I pray this in Jesus' name!

Go ye therefore, and teach all nations, baptizing them in the name of the Father, and of the Son, and of the Holy Ghost.

Matthew 28:19

My Confession for Today

I confess that I am filled with the power of the Holy Spirit, and He empowers me with strength and creative ideas on how to present the message of Jesus Christ to my family, friends, and acquaintances. I have no excuse to say I am lacking ideas, because the greatest source of ideas lives inside me. So, Holy Spirit, I open myself to You—and I ask you to unleash Your creative flow to show me how to be on the "go" to take this saving message to those who are in need of it. I declare this by faith in Jesus' name!

DECEMBER 5

Christ—the Focus of Christmas

Set your affection on things above, not on things on the earth.

Colossians 3:2

My Prayer for Today

Father, I ask You to help me purposefully and deliberately lift my thoughts to a higher realm than where they've been in past holidays. Yes, the season is joyful and full of festivities, but help me remember that it is Your commandment that my thoughts go to a higher place than short-lived, seasonal experiences. I will meditate on what really matters at this time of the year, and I will grow spiritually as a result! I pray this in Jesus' name!

My Confession for Today

I confess that I am not fixated on low-level, temporal concerns that won't even matter a year from now. I refuse to allow myself to become swamped in festivities, holiday events, and the giving and receiving of gifts. Instead, I choose to meditate on the real reason for the season. This year I lift my thoughts to a higher realm, and as a result, this will be the best Christmas season I've experienced in my life thus far! I declare this by faith in Jesus' name!

Stay Connected to Christ

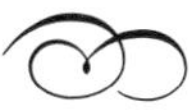

My Prayer for Today

Father, I refuse to be beautiful but lifeless, having a form of godliness but denying the power that only comes through a vital connection with my Life Source, Jesus Christ. Holy Spirit, I ask You to reveal to me how I can let my roots grow down deeper into Him in every way. Please help me remain deeply connected to Jesus by hearing, receiving, loving, and obeying His Word so my roots will grow down deep into Him. And as I become more deeply rooted in Christ, I thank You for helping me flourish and remain vibrant in every season of life. I pray this in Jesus' name!

As ye have therefore received Christ Jesus the Lord, so walk ye in him: Rooted and built up in him...

Colossians 2:6-7

My Confession for Today

I confess that I put my roots deep into Christ and that His presence fills me with everything I need to be refilled and "reflourished," so I keep growing outward and upward as a Christian. I ask You, Holy Spirit, to assist me in remaining rooted and built up in Jesus Christ. I refuse to allow any event in life to cause me to behave as if I've been cut off from my roots in Christ Jesus. With my root structure based firmly in Him, I will continue to flourish as a growing Christian! I declare this by faith in Jesus' name!

Selecting Gifts to Bless–An Act of Love

...in lowliness of mind let each esteem other better than themselves.

Philippians 2:3

My Prayer for Today

Father, I see now that money is a great revealer of my heart and how I use it to bless others reveals the level of my esteem for them. I thank You for this encouragement. Instead of selfishly spending all my money on my own needs, I will pay attention to my opportunities to demonstrate selflessness for the sake of others. And help me remember that Jesus gave the greatest gift of all when He could have called twelve legions of angels to deliver Himself in the Garden of Gethsemane, but He surrendered to the arresting forces and gave his life so we could receive salvation. How I thank God that Jesus esteemed us better than Himself! I pray this in Jesus' name!

My Confession for Today

I confess that because the love of God rules my thoughts and actions, I deliberately live more focused on others' needs than on my own needs, wants, and desires. The law of sowing and reaping works, and I am fully confident that as I sow into the needs and desires of others before I take care of my own desires, God will be faithful to multiply it back to me and will meet my needs in a far greater way than I could ever imagine! I declare this by faith in Jesus' name!

A Grateful Heart

My Prayer for Today

Father, I confess that I have moments when I am tempted to moan and complain that I don't have more than I currently have to spend on myself and on others. Especially during this Christmas season, I am facing the frustration of wishing I could do more than I can do. I repent for the times when I've yielded to emotions stemming from ingratitude. I ask You to help me always be grateful for what I have rather than to focus on what I don't have. Let me never forget the gifts I can give—such as lovingkindness, thoughtfulness, and investments of time and attention. These are gifts that are not held in our hands, but they leave the lingering fragrance of Your goodness long after this season is past. I pray this in Jesus' name!

In every thing give thanks: for this is the will of God in Christ Jesus concerning you.

1 Thessalonians 5:18

My Confession for Today

I confess that I am a grateful and thankful person. In moments when ingratitude and an unthankful attitude try to rule me, I reject it and deliberately adopt the posture of a grateful heart. Not only am I blessed and thankful for what I can give to others, but I am also thankful for what I receive. Everything is an act of grace; therefore, I choose to have a grateful attitude for anything I am able to give or receive! I declare this by faith in Jesus' name!

DECEMBER 9

Broken Hearts Healed

... he hath sent me to heal the brokenhearted...

Luke 4:18

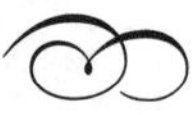

My Prayer for Today

Father, my family grapples with the aftereffects of different situations that have caused fracturing of relationships. I have felt pain and cried many tears over the brokenness in my family. Yet I can also see Your faithfulness to me and to each one of us through the years. No matter who may fail, forsake, or disappoint us, You have always kept Your Word to intervene and lift us up. Today as I read about the anointing of Jesus that comes to release us from feelings of hurt and brokenness, I am greatly encouraged. I throw open my arms to receive His healing and delivering power! Although things can never be as they once were—or perhaps never were but should have been—I ask that the peace of God and the anointing of God release me and my family members from the pain that has hurt each one of us so badly in different ways as a result of these failed relationships. I pray this in Jesus' name!

My Confession for Today

I confess that I am not an emotional slave to the dysfunctional ordeals my family has been through over the years. Although there may have been times when I felt trapped by the pain of hurt and misunderstanding, the anointing of God has set me free and I am now liberated from these past wounds and inner hurts. I am not shattered, fractured, or inwardly torn to pieces. Regardless of what the enemy tried to do, I am whole, free, and full of love for every member of my family! I declare this by faith in Jesus' name!

The Sustaining Power of God

My Prayer for Today

God, I thank You that Your presence is constantly available when I go through hardship and trials. When it seems that emotions will overwhelm me, You are there—sustaining me and giving me the power I need to overcome each hardship. Just as you sustained the apostle Paul, you will sustain me—regardless of what I am facing in my life. You will step forward as my personal Helper to strengthen and assist me in my time of need. I am so thankful for this, and I praise You for it today! I pray this in Jesus' name!

Blessed be God...who comforteth us in all our tribulation, that we may be able to comfort them which are in any trouble, by the comfort wherewith we ourselves are comforted of God.

2 Corinthians 1:3-4

My Confession for Today

I confess that I am more than a conqueror through Jesus Christ! On my own, I would suffer endless loss, but because Jesus lives BIG inside me, I have the power to overcome every single obstacle that I face in life. There may be some events that I thought I would never face, but God's power has stood at my side and has strengthened me to make it to victory. God has ordained victory for my future. I latch hold of it and refuse to let go until I've experienced the total victory that Jesus Christ has planned for my life! I declare this by faith in Jesus' name!

December 11

Shaking the Gifts!

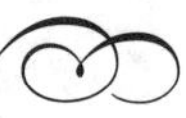

For ye have need of patience…

Hebrews 10:36

My Prayer for Today

Father, I repent for my impatience as I wait for the fulfillment of what I've asked You to do for me. In a certain sense, I've been "shaking the gifts" and not trusting that You would do what You said You would do. Waiting a little longer won't hurt me. In fact, it will help me develop my character and learn patience. For this, I say thank You. And for my impatience, I ask You to forgive me and to help me keep growing in this aspect of my life. I pray this in Jesus' name!

My Confession for Today

I confess that patience is a strong force in my life. As I walk with Christ and learn to trust in Him ever more dearly, the attribute of patience is growing stronger and stronger in me. I don't have to mistrust the Lord or check Him out to see if He is really doing what I asked. If I have asked for something in faith, it's only a matter of time until what I've prayed for comes to pass! I declare this by faith in Jesus' name!

Volatile Emotions

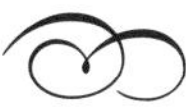

My Prayer for Today

For the wrath of man worketh not the righteousness of God.

James 1:20

Dear Father, I confess that I've had moments when I've exploded, lost my temper, and said things that I later regretted. I ask You to forgive me—and I ask You to help me learn how to submit my emotions to the control of the Holy Spirit. Whether it's me, my family members, or my friends who are acting in ugly ways, help me realize that such behavior is irrational. Thank You for Your grace to help us upgrade our emotional responses to the various situations in life we encounter each day. I pray this in Jesus' name!

My Confession for Today

I confess that my emotions and reactions are controlled by the Holy Spirit. When my flesh tries to act up, the Spirit of God inside me helps me regain control and bring my flesh into subjection to the Word of God and the behavior of Christ. My mind, my emotions, my reactions, my mouth—they are all tools to be used by the Holy Spirit, and I will NOT use them in explosive ways that could damage and hurt the people whom I love and respect. I declare this by faith in Jesus' name!

December 13

Make Time for Christmas Carols

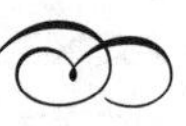

Speaking to yourselves in psalms and hymns and spiritual songs, singing and making melody in your heart to the Lord.

Ephesians 5:19

My Prayer for Today

Father, I appreciate everything I know about ministering in music and Christmas carols at this time of the year. Help me not to focus on my own needs and problems but to take a day or two to focus on people who are living lonely and solitary. If possible, help me gather a group of people who will join with me to creatively bring the praise and glory of God to people who need a lift! I pray this in Jesus' name!

My Confession for Today

I confess that I have a voice to glorify the Lord and that this holiday season, I am going to use it to bring emotional encouragement and spiritual exhortation to people who need a lift from the cares of life. I may not be the best singer, but I can sing with others. I choose to obey Ephesians 5:19 and speak and sing to one another in psalms, hymns, and spiritual songs this Christmas season. God will join me with a group of praisers with like-minded hearts, and together we'll become a "musical troupe" to bring joy to people who need encouragement! I declare this by faith in Jesus' name!

Refuse Greediness

My Prayer for Today

Father, I ask You to forgive me for wanting everything all at one time. I didn't realize this was greed trying to get a foothold in my life. Help me know how to dream without falling headlong into greed at the same time. As I set my sights toward things on the earth, help me to recognize which desires are pure and inspired by You and which are just my own carnal lusts or worldly desires. I truly want to please You, Lord, so I ask You to help me conform my thoughts to Your will. I pray this in Jesus' name!

Now the works of the flesh are manifest, which are these... lasciviousness.

Galatians 5:19

My Confession for Today

I confess that I am moderate in the way I live and in the things I desire to obtain. I refuse to allow greediness to rule me. I live by the law of the Spirit of life in Christ Jesus that works mightily in me. His love in me enables me to focus on what others need more than what I want for myself. I am thankful for this work of Christ that helps me to esteem others more highly than myself. I declare this by faith in Jesus' name!

Christmas Table Talk

And let us consider one another to provoke unto love and to good works.

Hebrews 10:24

My Prayer for Today

Father, this year when we gather around the Christmas table, I ask You to set a watch over my lips and a guard over my mouth. I make the decision now that my words will glorify You and bless and edify others. If the conversation turns negative and those around me begin to talk about various individuals, help me to be bold and courageous enough to lovingly say, "Enough of that" — and then shift the conversation toward the positive. I refuse to be negative and give way to sarcasm. The carnal mind enjoys that, and so does the devil because it gives him an opportunity to interject his lies. But I thank You, Holy Spirit, that You are my Counselor, and with Your help, my heart deeply ponders and guides what my mouth speaks before I ever say a word. I pray this in Jesus' name!

My Confession for Today

I confess that I am a source that provokes others to love and to good works! My mouth is a life-spring of good works that encourages others to do what God would have them to do. I do NOT speak critical words, nor am I a source of negative talk. When my family or friends are together as a group, I see myself as a moderator who keeps the conversation on course. I will influence the group to speak of things that are praiseworthy and of a good report. I am a positive force, and because of me, others are stimulated to love and to good works! I declare this by faith in Jesus' name!

Holiday Fellowship

My Prayer for Today

Father, I thank You for the fellowship that exists in the Body of Christ. Because of fellowship, we are made stronger. Fellowship with close friends and family—and the Holy Spirit—makes us stronger and gives us a sound foundation of relationships in the Body of Christ! Help me to use my home to help build stronger relationships in the Christian community to whom I belong! I pray this in Jesus' name!

...breaking bread from house to house, did eat their meat with gladness and singleness of heart.

Acts 2:46

My Confession for Today

I confess that I am a stronger Christian because of my fellowship with other believers over the years. Their fellowship has strengthened me, encouraged me, and taken me to a higher level in my walk with Christ. When I fellowship with other believers, it becomes an opportunity for iron to sharpen iron as we grow in Him together and allow the love of God to bring out the best in one another. I readily acknowledge that I need Christian fellowship, and I cherish it as a treasured gift in my life. I declare this by faith in Jesus' name!

DECEMBER 17

Special Christmas Offerings

And he said, Of a truth I say unto you, that this poor widow hath cast in more than they all.

Luke 21:3

My Prayer for Today

Father, so often I've given of my excess and never really dipped into an amount that would cause me to have to use my faith. I am corrected today, and I will change. Today I make a deliberate decision to exercise my faith in a greater way by choosing not to refrain from giving even when my offering is small. Like the widow's mite, my offering will please and honor Jesus because it is a gift from my heart that requires more faith than if it were merely a token from a surplus supply. Without faith it is impossible to please You, Father. And I seek to please You above all else. Holy Spirit, help me to know how much to stretch my faith, how much to give, and where to sow my seed so it will make a difference. I am sincerely asking for and receiving Your wisdom in this matter. I pray this in Jesus' name!

My Confession for Today

I confess that from this moment onward, I will not casually give offerings out of my excess. Rather, I will dip deeper and truly give sacrificially to the Lord. I thought I was doing what was right, but I am convicted by what I have read today. I am going to make a change in my manner of giving. I am going to give on a level that requires more faith on my part. I affirm this day that whether I am giving of my time, my talent, or my finances, faith and love will be evident by the manner in which I give. I declare this by faith in Jesus' name!

Reading the Christmas Story

My Prayer for Today

Father, concerning the story of Christmas, give me the courage and boldness to tell my family that we're starting with God's Word first—and then we'll dive into the gifts and presents. I ask You, Holy Spirit, to honor this commitment to bring special wisdom and insight to my children—and to us—as a result of giving the Word of God first place in our Christmas Day. I pray this in Jesus' name!

But continue thou in the things which thou hast learned and hast been assured of, knowing of whom thou hast learned them; and that from a child thou hast known the holy scriptures, which are able to make thee wise unto salvation through faith which is in Christ Jesus.

2 Timothy 3:14-15

My Confession for Today

I confess that this year will mark a Christmas that's very different from those we've experienced in previous years. This year we are starting a new tradition with eternal significance—one that we'll continue year after year. We will begin our Christmas morning with the reading of the Christmas story together as a family. This will teach us all patience, and it will put the most important element of Christmas—Jesus—right in the center of the day just as He ought to be. And as a result, we will all grow in wisdom and insight regarding the significance of that special day, for the One whose birth we are celebrating has been made unto us wisdom! I declare this by faith in Jesus' name!

DECEMBER 19

Christmas Morning

My Prayer for Today

But continue thou in the things which thou hast learned and hast been assured of, knowing of whom thou hast learned them; and that from a child thou hast known the holy scriptures, which are able to make thee wise unto salvation through faith which is in Christ Jesus.

2 Timothy 3:14-15

Father, I realize that continual, godly habits build stability into a life and a family. Traditions can help cultivate godly character through the good habit of placing God's Word first before natural enjoyment. I can see the benefits of starting and continuing wonderful traditions for my family. Help me be a voice of loving influence in getting a godly Christmas tradition started and then to help sustain it through the years with my family. I pray that all of us who share our Christmas mornings together—no matter how young or how old—will grow in our knowledge of the Lord Jesus Christ because we have made the commitment to start the tradition of reading the Christmas story! I pray this in Jesus' name!

My Confession for Today

This Christmas I will start a new tradition with my family and my loved ones. BEFORE anything else on Christmas, we will begin the day by reading the Christmas story from the Bible. I am confident that the Holy Spirit will help us make this a happy and joyful time in the Word of God as a family. Afterward, we'll enjoy the rest of our Christmas festivities together. But from this year on, we will begin our Christmas Day focused on the reason we are even celebrating this holiday in the first place! I declare this by faith in Jesus' name!

Teach Your Children and Grandchildren

My Prayer for Today

Father, I continue to be stirred by this exhortation on the importance of deliberate traditions and habits to place God's Word first on a daily basis. Teach me how to make practical applications of Deuteronomy 11:19 every day in every area of my life beyond this holiday season. I ask You to show me how to start new traditions for our family that can be passed down to ensuing generations. I also ask You to help our family really think through what kind of Christian tradition we can start and continue year by year to keep You and Your Word the focal point of all that we do. Once we get started, give us the strength of will to keep it up perpetually and pass it on to other generations. Most of all, we want not only a Christian tradition but also a daily lifestyle that will honor Christ and bring Him glory! I pray this in Jesus' name!

And ye shall teach them your children, speaking of them when thou sittest in thine house, and when thou walkest by the way, when thou liest down, and when thou risest up.

Deuteronomy 11:19

My Confession for Today

I confess that I create deliberate habits to bring God's Word into my daily life and the lives of those around me. This year I'm going to seriously consider what kind of Christian traditions I can begin in my family and will move forward to initiate a godly heritage in my home. There's no better time to start than now, so I plan to get started this Christmas season! I declare this by faith in Jesus' name!

DECEMBER 21

Christmas Cleanup!

Let all things be done decently and in order.

1 Corinthians 14:40

My Prayer for Today

Father, I accept the challenge to keep things decent and in order as we celebrate and have fun together. There's no reason to let piles of trash build up and make it really hard for someone to clean up later in the day. Show me every opportunity to demonstrate kindness and consideration and to help my family do likewise so that no one gets their feelings hurt because they feel left alone in the task of bringing order back to the house. Lord, help me to set the standard, and to set the rules. And help us do things in a way that makes it a joyful day for everyone involved! I pray this in Jesus' name!

My Confession for Today

I confess that I am going to lead my family in keeping things decent and in order this Christmas season. Rather than let the house go and allow stacks of trash and piles of messes to build up that could later cause strife, I will rid my house of the problem before it ever gets started. I'll set the example and ask others to help me keep the house looking nice before it descends into a mess that looks horrible. This sounds simple, and it IS simple. With God's help, this year we're going to keep things looking decent and orderly around our house! I declare this by faith in Jesus' name!

Be Kind

And be ye kind to one another…

Ephesians 4:32

My Prayer for Today

Father, I'm embarrassed by how often I have failed simply to "be kind" toward others — especially those closest to me. I feel almost silly that I've overlooked it or counted it as unimportant. Help me start where I am and, day by day, become more focused on the special needs and special days in other people's lives. I know this is what You would do, so help me to be more like You! I pray this prayer in Jesus' name!

My Confession for Today

I confess that God never overlooks any detail about our lives. He is Love, and He goes out of His way to show honor and esteem so others will know they are valued. I am determined to be thoughtful of others. I confess that I will work harder on this than I've ever worked on it before, and I will show care and kindness to people who have special days in the month of December. I declare this by faith in Jesus' name!

DECEMBER 23

Holiday Confusion and the One Constant That Remains

But made himself of no reputation, and took upon him the form of a servant, and was made in the likeness of men.

Philippians 2:7

My Prayer for Today

Father, I thank You that regardless of what day it happened—Jesus took on the form of a servant and was made in the likeness of men. He stooped to the level of His creation and died the death of a Cross, all because He loved me and wanted me to become a part of His eternal family. Help me not to get stuck on "what" day it actually happened, but rather to rejoice in the fact that it did happen! Because Jesus came to earth in the form of a man and died for me, today I am a child of God. For this, I can say thank You for the greatest gift. I am so glad I am redeemed! I pray this in Jesus' name!

My Confession for Today

I understand that the exact day on which Jesus' birth occurred is not so important—but what is important is that He put aside His glorious attributes and took on the form of a human being and a servant, and humbled Himself to die the death of a Cross. Because of the price He paid, I have been permanently saved and set free. For this, I declare my thankfulness at Christmastime! I declare this by faith in Jesus' name!

Christmas Eve Traditions and Relationships

My Prayer for Today

Father, I thank You for the fellowship of the Spirit that we have with other Christians who mutually share faith with us. What a fellowship, what a joy, and what a blessing—to build years of fellowship and Christian traditions with other believers. I ask You to help me start thinking about how to build Christian traditions for myself and my own family, especially in moments like Christmas Eve. I am so thankful for fellow believers who share the same hope I possess. I'm so grateful we can spend cherished times together in our mutual love for the Lord and for each other. I pray this in Jesus' name!

If there be therefore any consolation in Christ, if any comfort of love, if any fellowship of the Spirit, if any bowels and mercies, fulfil ye my joy, that ye be likeminded, having the same love, being of one accord, of one mind.

Philippians 2:1-2

My Confession for Today

I confess that I will work on building traditional Christian events for myself and my family in order to deepen the true significance of this beautiful season. God has given me friends that I can spend those moments with—and if I haven't developed those friends yet, I declare by faith that I'm going to step out of my comfort zone and begin to connect with other Christian believers. I need this, my family needs this—and I will look for ways to do it. I declare this by faith in Jesus' name!

DECEMBER 25

The Real Gift That Keeps Giving

But seek ye first the kingdom of God, and his righteousness; and all these things shall be added unto you.

Matthew 6:33

My Prayer for Today

Father, I don't want to be on-again, off-again in my pursuit of You. But as You command, I want to be habitual and constant in the way I seek You and Your Kingdom. There are many other things I need in life, but You promised that if I seek Your Kingdom first, all these other things will eventually be added unto me. So today I ask You to help me focus on the Kingdom of God and to keep my focus there for as long as I live on this earth! I pray this in Jesus' name!

My Confession for Today

I confess that nothing in the world is more important to me than seeking the Kingdom of God and His righteousness. God's Word promises that if I'll remain focused and constant in seeking God's Kingdom and His righteousness first, before anything else, He'll make sure every other need is met in my life. So I confess by faith that starting today—and for every day following this new commitment—I am going to make God's Word, His Kingdom, and His righteousness the chief priority in my life. I declare this by faith in Jesus' name!

Eating Leftovers!

My Prayer for Today

Lord, I am hungry for fresh revelation of the Word of God. How could I be anything but thankful for the foundational truths that I've already received, yet my spirit is crying out to know You better and to receive revelatory truths that unveil aspects of Your character and Your ways yet unknown to me. I ask You to help those who teach me to be like a good scribe, knowing when to emphasize the old and when to introduce the new. Then You will equip them to bring forth new truths that my spirit is crying to hear and to know. I pray this in Jesus' name!

Then said he unto them, Therefore every scribe which is instructed unto the kingdom of heaven is like unto a man that is an householder, which bringeth forth out of his treasure things new and old.

Matthew 13:52

My Confession for Today

I boldly confess that I am grateful for every teaching I've ever received and that each one has added to the foundation of my life. But I am hungry for more of the Lord. I want more of His Word, more of His revelation. I want to learn new things, based on the teaching of the Bible, that will feed my spirit in a way I've never been fed before. I thank God for my pastor and for those teachers who teach me—but I purpose to keep an open ear and an open heart so I can also receive fresh heavenly revelation from the Spirit of God to feed to my spirit! I declare this by faith in Jesus' name!

DECEMBER 27

Being Thankful!

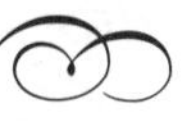

In every thing give thanks: for this is the will of God in Christ Jesus concerning you.

1 Thessalonians 5:18

My Prayer for Today

Heavenly Father, I've been through rough times, but the truth is, those times could have been a lot rougher. When I consider what You have brought me through—and the place of peace and rest You've brought me into—I can only say THANK YOU. Please forgive me for often quickly forgetting the good things You have done for me, and help me cultivate this attitude of thankfulness in my heart, for this is Your will in Christ Jesus concerning me! I pray this in Jesus' name!

My Confession for Today

I declare that I have a lot to be thankful for. Yes, it's true that there are things I need and desire, but compared to where I used to be and how I experienced lack, I am living in the land of superabundance. I will not be forgetful of the good things God has done for me. I purpose to keep a grateful attitude for all the things He has done and is doing for me, both great and small. And when others ask me how I'm doing, I will confidently answer them, "THANKFUL!" I declare this by faith in Jesus' name!

Preparing for a New Year

My Prayer for Today

Father, I admit that I've failed to fulfill some of the things You definitely told me to do in the past year. I confess it, I admit it, and I walk free of it. You do not hold it against me, because I am making a heartfelt confession about it. In fact, You take my failure and remove it from me as far as the west is from the east! And Your resurrection power helps me pick up right where I am to start anew and to gain those victories that belong to You and that You long to impart to me! I thank You, too, for helping me reset the start button to gain new victories in these areas of my life. I pray this in Jesus' name!

If we confess our sins, he is faithful and just to forgive us our sins, and to cleanse us from all unrighteousness.

1 John 1:9

My Confession for Today

I confess that God's mercies over me are new each day. Therefore, each day is a brand-new opportunity to forget those things which are behind me as I press toward the prize of God's calling that is drawing my attention to focus more and more upon Him. As I prepare my heart and mind to evaluate this past year, while giving attention to what God desires of me for the next year, I consider my ways and evaluate myself in the light of God's Word. I trust in the Lord to reveal to me throughout the coming year how to stay on track with His plan for me. I receive fresh grace to do whatever it takes to discipline my body and mind, and to order my days so I don't waste precious time. I am diligent and I am faithful; therefore, I abound with blessing and I live free of regrets! I declare this by faith in Jesus' name!

DECEMBER 29

Spiritual Hoarders

...I have suffered the loss of all things, and do count them but dung, that I may win Christ.

Philippians 3:8

My Prayer for Today

Father, I confess that there is spiritual trash in my life—and I've just tolerated it and let it grow deeper and deeper. Help me recognize it for what it is and begin the process of removing it from my life. You can't use me as You wish if I'm surrounded by piles of squalor. So I ask You to help me, Holy Spirit, as I start the cleanup process so I can function freely and clearly when You have a job for me to do! I pray this prayer in Jesus' name!

My Confession for Today

I confess that I've been a spiritual hoarder—letting things build up in my life that hindered my effectiveness. I repent before the Lord for letting this buildup of spiritual refuse take hold in my life. If I'm going to be used mightily of Him, I have to keep my heart and soul clean, so today I commit to making this a serious endeavor in my life. I declare this by faith in Jesus' name!

Before the Year Ends

My Prayer for Today

Father, the race for this year is almost over, but it's not too late for me to come out a winner by faith in every area of my life. I surrender every obstacle that has hindered me as a result of my own thoughts and actions. I ask You to supernaturally quicken me so I can achieve the goals You desire to perform in me. I am absolutely convinced that You will perform this work in me and that You'll keep doing it until the day of Jesus Christ! I pray this in Jesus' name!

Being confident of this very thing, that he which hath begun a good work in you will perform it until the day of Jesus Christ.

Philippians 1:6

My Confession for Today

I confess that God's power is working inside me—and He will quickly do those things He has wanted to accomplish in my life this past year. My wrong choices may have hindered them from being done earlier. But right now, I choose to cooperate with the will and the power of God to see His plan for me accelerated and accomplished because of my obedience. According to Philippians 1:6, I am absolutely sure and completely persuaded that God is doing His work in me! I declare this by faith in Jesus' name!

One Year Ends and a New Year Begins

...forgetting those things which are behind, and reaching forth unto those things which are before.

Philippians 3:13

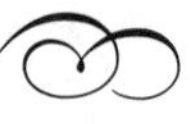

My Prayer for Today

Heavenly Father, this has been an awesome year in which You have taught me so much. My heart is overflowing with thankfulness for every challenge You've helped me overcome and for every lesson You've taught me that has helped mold me more to the image of Jesus Christ. I am simply filled with gratitude that You have done so much in my heart during this year—and I believe that the next year will be even richer and fuller than the one I am presently completing. As I reach the finish line of this year, I forget what is behind me, and I reach for what is ahead. For all of this, I give You thanks! I pray this in Jesus' name!

My Confession for Today

I boldly declare that the year before me will be the best year I've ever known in my life thus far. The Holy Spirit is energizing me—and He will help me run my race better than I've ever run it before. I say no distractions or obstacles will stop me—and that I will run until I reach the finish line! Jesus has already laid out the race before me—I only need to jump up, give it my best shot with the Spirit's power, and finish everything God wants me to achieve in this new year! I declare this by faith in Jesus' name!

Prayer of Salvation

GOD loves you—no matter who you are, no matter what your past. God loves you so much that He gave His one and only begotten Son for you. The Bible tells us that *"...whoever believes in him shall not perish but have eternal life"* (John 3:16 NIV). Jesus laid down His life and rose again so that we could spend eternity with Him in heaven and experience His absolute best on earth. If you would like to receive Jesus into your life, say the following prayer out loud and mean it from your heart.

> *Heavenly Father, I come to You now, admitting that I am a sinner. Right now I choose to turn away from sin, and I ask You to cleanse me of all unrighteousness. I believe that Your Son, Jesus, died on the cross to take away my sins. I also believe that He rose again from the dead so that I might be forgiven of my sins and made righteous through faith in Him. I call upon the name of Jesus Christ to be the Savior and Lord of my life. Jesus, I choose to follow You and ask that You fill me with the power of the Holy Spirit. I declare that right now, I am a child of God. I am free from sin and full of the righteousness of God. I am saved in Jesus' name. Amen.*

About the Author

RICK RENNER is a highly respected leader and teacher within the global Christian community. He ministered widely throughout the United States for many years before answering God's call in 1991 to move his family to the former Soviet Union and plunge into the heart of its newly emerging Church. Following an apostolic call on his life, Rick works alongside his wife Denise to see the Gospel preached, leadership trained, and the Church established throughout the world. Today Rick's broadcast "Good News With Rick Renner" can be seen across the entire former USSR, reaching a potential audience of more than 100 million viewers.

He has distributed hundreds of thousands of teaching audio and videotapes, and his best-selling books have been translated into five major languages—Spanish, Portuguese, French, Russian, and German—as well as multiple other languages that are spoken throughout the former Soviet Union.

Rick is the founder of the Good News Association of Churches and Ministries, through which he assists and strengthens almost 700 churches in the territory of the former Soviet Union. He also pastors the fast-growing Moscow Good News Church, located in the very heart of Moscow, Russia.

Rick Renner Ministries has offices in England, Latvia, Russia, Ukraine, and the United States. Rick, Denise, and their family live in Moscow, Russia.

Contact Renner Ministries

For further information about RENNER Ministries, please contact the office nearest you, or visit the ministry website at:

www.renner.org

ALL USA CORRESPONDENCE:

RENNER Ministries
P. O. Box 702040
Tulsa, OK 74170-2040
(918) 496-3213
Or 1-800-RICK-593
Email: renner@renner.org | Website: www.renner.org

MOSCOW OFFICE:

RENNER Ministries
P. O. Box 789
101000, Moscow, Russia
+7 (495) 727-1470
Email: blagayavestonline@ignc.org | Website: www.ignc.org

RIGA OFFICE:

RENNER Ministries
Unijas 99
Riga LV-1084, Latvia
+371 67802150
Email: info@goodnews.lv

KIEV OFFICE:

RENNER Ministries
P. O. Box 300
01001, Kiev, Ukraine
+38 (044) 451-8315
Email: blagayavestonline@ignc.org

OXFORD OFFICE:

RENNER Ministries
Box 7, 266 Banbury Road
Oxford OX2 7DL, England
+44 1865 521024
Email: europe@renner.org

Other Books by Rick Renner

*Build Your Foundation**

*Chosen by God**

*Dream Thieves**

*Dressed To Kill**

*The Holy Spirit and You**

*How To Keep Your Head on Straight in a World Gone Crazy**

*How To Receive Answers From Heaven!**

*Insights to Successful Leadership**

Last-Days Survival Guide

*Life in the Combat Zone**

*A Life Ablaze**

A Light in Darkness, Volume One,
Seven Messages to the Seven Churches series

*The Love Test**

No Room for Compromise, Volume Two,
Seven Messages to the Seven Churches series

*Paid in Full**

*The Point of No Return**

*Repentance**

*Signs You'll See Just Before Jesus Comes**

*Sparkling Gems From the Greek Daily Devotional 1**

*Sparkling Gems From the Greek Daily Devotional 2**

*Spiritual Weapons To Defeat the Enemy**

Ten Guidelines To Help You Achieve
*Your Long-Awaited Promotion!**

Testing the Supernatural

*Turn Your God-Given Dreams Into Reality**

*Why We Need the Gifts of the Spirit**

*The Will of God – The Key to Your Success**

*You Can Get Over It**

*Digital version available for Kindle, Nook, and iBook.

Note: Books by Rick Renner are available for purchase at: **www.renner.org**

SPARKLING GEMS FROM THE GREEK 1

1,048 pages
(Hardback)

In 2003, Rick Renner's ***Sparkling Gems From the Greek 1*** quickly gained widespread recognition for its unique illumination of the New Testament through more than 1,000 Greek word studies in a 365-day devotional format. Today *Sparkling Gems 1* remains a beloved resource that has spiritually strengthened believers worldwide. As many have testified, the wealth of truths within its pages never grows old. Year after year, *Sparkling Gems 1* continues to deepen readers' understanding of the Bible.

To order, visit us online at: **www.renner.org**

Book Resellers: Contact Harrison House at 800-722-6774
or visit **www.HarrisonHouse.com** for quantity discounts.

SPARKLING GEMS FROM THE GREEK 2

1,280 pages
(Hardback)

Rick infuses into ***Sparkling Gems From the Greek 2*** the added strength and richness of many more years of his own personal study and growth in God — expanding this devotional series to impact the reader's heart on a deeper level than ever before. This remarkable study tool helps unlock new hidden treasures from God's Word that will draw readers into an ever more passionate pursuit of Him.

To order, visit us online at: **www.renner.org**

Book Resellers: Contact Harrison House at 800-722-6774
or visit **www.HarrisonHouse.com** for quantity discounts.

DRESSED TO KILL

A Biblical Approach to Spiritual Warfare and Armor

Rick Renner's book ***Dressed To Kill*** is considered by many to be a true classic on the subject of spiritual warfare. The original version, which sold more than 400,000 copies, is a curriculum staple in Bible schools worldwide. In this beautiful volume, you will find:

- 504 pages of reedited text in paperback
- 16 pages of full-color illustrations
- Questions at the end of each chapter to guide you into deeper study

In ***Dressed To Kill***, Rick explains with exacting detail the purpose and function of each piece of Roman armor. In the process, he describes the significance of our *spiritual* armor not only to withstand the onslaughts of the enemy, but also to overturn the tendencies of the carnal mind. Furthermore, Rick delivers a clear, scriptural presentation on the biblical definition of spiritual warfare — what it is and what it is not.

When you walk with God in deliberate, continual fellowship, He will enrobe you with Himself. Armed with the knowledge of who you are in Him, you will be dressed and dangerous to the works of darkness, unflinching in the face of conflict, and fully equipped to take the offensive and gain mastery over any opposition from your spiritual foe. You don't have to accept defeat anymore once you are *dressed to kill*!

To order, visit us online at: **www.renner.org**

Book Resellers: Contact Harrison House at 800-722-6774 or visit **www.HarrisonHouse.com** for quantity discounts.

HOW TO KEEP YOUR HEAD ON STRAIGHT IN A WORLD GONE CRAZY

DEVELOPING DISCERNMENT FOR THESE LAST DAYS

400 pages
(Paperback)

The world is changing. In fact, it's more than changing — it has *gone crazy*.

We are living in a world where faith is questioned and sin is welcomed — where people seem to have lost their minds about what is right and wrong. It seems truth has been turned *upside down*.

In Rick Renner's book ***How To Keep Your Head on Straight in a World Gone Crazy***, he reveals the disastrous consequences of a society in spiritual and moral collapse. In this book, you'll discover what Christians need to be doing to stay out of the chaos and remain anchored to truth. You'll learn how to stay sensitive to the Holy Spirit, how to discern right and wrong teaching, how to be grounded in prayer, and how to be spiritually prepared for living in victory in these last days.

Leading ministers from around the world are calling this book essential for every believer. Topics include:

- Contending for the faith in the last days
- How to pray for leaders who are in error
- How to judge if a teaching is good or bad
- Seducing spirits and doctrines of demons
- How to be a good minister of Jesus Christ

To order, visit us online at: **www.renner.org**

Book Resellers: Contact Harrison House at 800-722-6774 or visit **www.HarrisonHouse.com** for quantity discounts.

The Harrison House Vision

Proclaiming the truth and the power
of the Gospel of Jesus Christ with excellence.
Challenging Christians
to live victoriously,
grow spiritually,
know God intimately.

Connect with us on

Facebook @ **HarrisonHousePublishers**

and Instagram @ **HarrisonHousePublishing**

so you can stay up to date with news

about our books and our authors.

Visit us at **www.harrisonhouse.com**

for a complete product listing as well as

monthly specials for wholesale distribution.